Experiences with Financial Liberalization

RECENT ECONOMIC THOUGHT SERIES

Editors:

Warren J. Samuels
Michigan State University
East Lansing, Michigan, USA

William Darity, Jr.
University of North Carolina
Chapel Hill, North Carolina, USA

Other books in the series:

Magnusson, Lars: MERCANTILIST ECONOMICS
Garston, Neil: BUREAUCRACY: THREE PARADIGMS
Friedman, James W.: PROBLEMS OF COORDINATION IN ECONOMIC ACTIVITY
Magnusson, Lars: EVOLUTIONARY AND NEO-SCHUMPETERIAN APPROACHES TO ECONOMICS
Reisman, D.: ECONOMIC THOUGHT AND POLITICAL THEORY
Burley, P. and Foster, J.: ECONOMICS AND THERMODYNAMICS: NEW PERSPECTIVES ON ECONOMIC ANALYSIS
Brennan, H.G. and Waterman, A.C.: ECONOMICS AND RELIGION: ARE THEY DISTINCT?
Klein, Philip A.: THE ROLE OF ECONOMIC THEORY
Semmler, Willi: BUSINESS CYCLES: THEORY AND EMPIRICS
Little, Daniel: ON THE RELIABILITY OF ECOONOMIC MODELS: ESSAYS IN THE PHILOSOPHY OF ECONOMICS
Weimer, David L.: INSTITUTIONAL DESIGN
Davis, John B.: THE STATE OF THE INTERPRETATION OF KEYNES
Wells, Paul: POST-KEYNESIAN ECONOMIC THEORY
Hoover, Kevin D.: MACROECONOMETRICS: DEVELOPMENTS, TENSIONS AND PROSPECTS
Kendrick, John W.: THE NEW SYSTEMS OF NATURAL ACCOUNTS
Groenewegen, John: TRANSACTION COST ECONOMICS AND BEYOND
King, J.E.: AN ALTERNATIVE MACROECONOMIC THEORY
Schofield, Norman: COLLECTIVE DECISION-MAKING: SOCIAL CHOICE AND POLITICAL ECONOMY
Menchik, Paul L.: HOUSEHOLD AND FAMILY ECONOMICS

Experiences with Financial Liberalization

edited by
Kanhaya L. Gupta
Professor of Economics
University of Alberta

Springer Science+Business Media, LLC

Library of Congress Cataloging-in-Publication Data
Experiences with financial liberalization/edited by Kanhaya L. Gupta.
p. cm.—(Recent economic thought series)
Includes index.
ISBN 978-94-010-6257-2 ISBN 978-94-011-5370-6 (eBook)
DOI 10.1007/978-94-011-5370-6
1. Finance—Developing countries. 2. Monetary policy—Developing countries. I. Gupta, Kanhaya K. (Kanhaya Lal), 1935– .
II. Series.
HG195.E96 1997
332'.09172'6—dc21 96-48563
CIP

Originally published by Kluwer Academic Publishers, New York in 1997
Softcover reprint of the hardcover 1st edition 1997

Printed on acid-free paper.

For J. John Lang

Contents

Contributing Authors

Ebenezer Asem is a graduate student in economics at the University of Alberta, Edmonton, Canada.

Jean-Claude Berthélemy is Professor of Economics at the University of Paris 1 (Sorbonne) and is currently Head of Research at the OECD Development Centre in Paris. Expert on African economies, he has written extensively on development issues such as debt, finance, macroeconomic policies, and agriculture. His recent contributions include a monograph on financial development policy and growth published by the OECD Development Centre.

Patrick Conway is Professor of Economics at the University of North Carolina in Chapel Hill. He centers his research efforts on the issues of developing and transitional economies facing the world market and has published widely in the academic press. He has written two monographs, entitled *Economic Shocks and Structural Adjustment: Turkey After 1973* and *Currency Proliferation: The Monetary Legacy of the Soviet Union.* He has also worked with the Peace Corps and the U.S. Department of State and has been a visiting scholar with the World Bank and the International Monetary Fund.

Peter J. Drake has been Vice-Chancellor of Australian Catholic University since its foundation in 1991. He was previously Deputy Vice-Chancellor at the University of New England, Armidale, where he was also Professor of Economics from 1972 to 1990. He has held positions in economics at the University of Melbourne and was Hallsworth Research Fellow at the University of Manchester and Nuffield Fellow at the University of London. Professor Drake is the author of *Money Finance and Development,*

Economic Growth for Australia, *Financial Development in Malaya and Singapore* and many published articles in the fields of money, trade, and economic development.

Nazim Kadri Ekinci teaches at the Middle East Technical University, Ankara, Turkey.

Maxwell J. Fry is the Tokai Bank Professor of International Finance at the University of Birmingham. He has published widely on monetary and financial aspects of economic development, both in academic journals and as books. Among his many books are *Money, Interest and Banking in Economic Development* (Johns Hopkins University Press, 1988, 2nd ed. 1995), *Central Banking in Developing Countries: Objectives, Activities and Independence* (with C.A.E. Goodhart and Alvanro Almeida, Routledge, 1996), and *Emancipating the Banking System and Developing Markets for Government Debt* (to be published by Routledge in 1997). He also has had assignments with various countries and organizations including the ADB, the International Monetary Fund, the World Bank, and the OECD.

Irena Grosfeld is Professor at the Centre National de la Recherche Scientifique, Département et Laboratoire d'Economie Théorique et Appliquée (DELTA) in Paris. She has published articles on privatization, enterprise restructuring, and financial reforms in Central and East European economies. Her publications include "Modelling Planners' Investment Behavior: Poland 1956–1980" (1986), "Reform Economics and Western Economic Theory: Unexploited Opportunities" (1990), "Comparing Financial Systems: Problems of Information and Control in Economies in Transition" (1994), "Triggering Evolution: The Case for a Breakthrough in Privatization" (1995), "Defensive and Strategic Restructuring in Central European Enterprises" (with G. Roland, 1995).

Kanhaya L. Gupta is a Professor of Economics at the University of Alberta, Edmonton, Canada. His recent related publications include *Financial Liberalization and Investment* (with Robert Lensink, 1996) and *Interest Rates and Budget Deficits: A Study of the Advanced Economies* (with B. Moazzami, 1996).

Robert Lensink is Associate Professor in Macro Economics at the Department of Economics, University of Groningen, the Netherlands. His areas of specialization are economic development and international macroeconomics. He has authored and coauthored four books and many articles around this subjects. His most recent books are *Financial Liberalization and Investment* (with K.L. Gupta, Routledge, 1996) and *Financial Development and Economic Growth* (edited with Hermes, Routledge, 1996).

Kate Phylaktis is Reader in International Finance and Director of the Research Centre in Financial Development at the City University Business School, London. She has published numerous research papers on foreign-exchange controls, money demand, and exchange-rate determination, especially in high-inflation economies; on the behavior of black market exchange rates; and on the financial structure of developing countries. She is the author of "Financial Data of Banks and Other Financial Institutions," "International Finance and the Less Developed Countries" (with M. Pradham), and "The Banking System of Cyprus, Past, Present and Future."

Rob Vos is a Senior Lecturer at the Institute of Social Studies at Hague. His main teaching and research areas include international finance, stabilization policies, income distribution and poverty, and general equilibrium modeling. His works in these areas have been published as books and articles. His latest publication is *The Philippine Economy: Stray Cat of East Asia* (with J. Yap, Macmillan and St. Martin's Press, 1995).

Acknowledgment

As usual, my very special thanks to Charlene Hill for her excellent secretarial help in putting together this volume.

Preface

This volume is yet another one in the series "Recent Economic Thought" published by Kluwer Academic Publishers under the general editorship of Professors William Darity, Jr. of the University of North Carolina at Chapel Hill and Warren J. Samuels of Michigan State University, East Lansing.

The nature and the scope of the current volume are relatively straightforward. It tries to provide a broad spectrum of experience with policies relating to financial liberalization around the globe over the last two to three decades. As far as I am aware, broad international coverage of this topic has not been undertaken in another single volume.

There is no denying that the most widely prevalent economic ideology today is that of free-market or deregulated economies. While there are many aspects to policies that go under the rubric of economic liberalization, my concern in this volume is with policies relating to financial liberalization, particularly its domestic aspects.

There is by now a sizeable body of theoretical and aggregative empirical literature in this area. But generally missing are works that document and analyze the experiences of individual countries or sets of countries. This kind of evidence is important in its own right but is particularly so for lessons to be drawn for the future, for there is no denying that aggregative econometric studies, which are the norm in the empirical field, cannot substitute for countrywide studies. The aim of this volume is to add to the relatively small body of this literature.

I have endeavored to include representative works from different areas of the world, particularly works relating to countries where published studies are not readily available. As far as possible I have tried to draw contributors from different parts of the world. This will have the virtue, hopefully, of allowing different perspectives to emerge.

The studies being reported in this volume are very much in the spirit of the series. Ever since the publication of McKinnon's (1973) and Shaw's (1973) seminal works, few areas of government policy have attracted more attention or been more controversial than the question of financial deregulation, particularly its domestic aspects, both in developed and in developing countries and now in transition economies as well. After two decades of extensive debate, there is as yet no consensus even on whether financial development causes real growth, growth causes development, or they cause each other! Similar disagreements exist about the sequencing of reforms. For example, what should be the order of reforms—all sectors deregulated simultaneously or in some optimal sequencing? How does financial liberalization fit in with general macroeconomic stabilization? Is all government intervention in financial markets undesirable? If so, then how do we deal with financial market failures caused by asymmetries of information? Why in some countries have policies of "financial repression" yielded positive results, whereas in other countries policies of financial liberalization have failed? The list goes on. The basic point is that this area is rife with controversies that have become even more acute since the demise of the former Soviet Union.

As the articles in this volume show, there may not be a unique answer to many of these questions. The answers may be country-specific or circumstances-specific. At the end of the day, we may find that instead of searching for some grand, universally applicable paradigm, we may have to learn to accept the uniqueness of each country and design policies to fit its needs and aspirations rather than to fit them into some predefined model. If the volume contributes to our understanding of the complexities and the uniqueness of individual experiences, I believe it will have more than served its purpose.

The chapters are divided into four parts by geographical regions. Part I deals with the African region. Its two chapters deal with very different aspects of financial liberalization. In Chapter 1, Jean-Claude Berthélemy offers a case study of Senegal, which serves as a representative case study of countries in the Franc Zone. He documents in considerable detail the historical reasons for the crisis in the banking sector and then goes on to offer an explanation for the failure of the policies of financial liberalization, particularly with respect to interest rates, to ameliorate the situation. The basic argument hinges on the role of hysteresis. The policies of financial repression that were followed from 1960 to the 1980s continued to have adverse effects well after they had been abandoned.

In Chapter 2 Ebenezer Asem and Kanhaya L. Gupta deal with an altogether different aspect of the policy of financial liberalization. The chapter examines the implications of different aspects of the policy of financial liberalization for seigniorage in Ghana. In 1988 Ghana embarked on comprehensive financial-sector reforms to complement the Economic Recovery Program initiated in 1983. The main goal of the reforms was to scrap the system of direct credit controls and replace it with an indirect monetary control in which financial institutions were free to make decisions strictly on the basis of economic criteria. The measures included interest rate deregulation, removal of direct credit ceilings, swapping of nonperforming assets of banks for Central Bank bills and withdrawal of government participation in the financial sector. We know from the analytical literature that seigniorage depends, among other things, on the mode of control and the behavior of the financial system, and therefore the reforms can be expected to influence seigniorage. Since seigniorage constitutes an important source of revenue for the government in Ghana, it is important to understand the way it is affected by the financial-sector reforms. The chapter addresses this question first theoretically and then empirically.

Part II examines the experiences of countries in Asia and Latin America. The four chapters in this section include case studies of Australia, China, the Philippines, and Chile.

Chapter 3 by Peter J. Drake looks at the situation in Australia's financial sector as it existed until the 1970s. Until then the system was highly rigid and regulated. However, thereafter and particularly since 1983 the system became greatly liberalized. A variety of forces accounted for this development. Drake examines the winners and losers of the reforms and claims that on the whole the history of financial deregulation in Australia must be considered a success story. But Drake also cautions about unbridled freedom of economic behaviour to the neglected of concerns for social justice and the environment.

Chapter 4 by Maxwell J. Fry is a plea for the early introduction of financial liberalization policies, particularly those relating to the deregulation of interest rates, which are currently set by administrative fiat, in China. He argues that the current system of monetary control—namely, the use of credit ceilings—and the development of a market-driven economy have led to various inconsistencies. After discussing the pros and cons of liberalized versus regulated interest rates, he goes on to suggest that deregulated interest rates will be beneficial for the Chinese economy because they will allow for better monetary control, lead to lower and more stable inflation, encourage higher savings rates, and lead to a more efficient allocation of resources.

In Chapter 5 Rob Vos examines the case of the Philippines, which he likens more to countries in Latin America than to the Asian tigers. His main theme is why the Philippines did not display the sustained and rapid growth of the fast-growing East Asian economies. Vos's approach is to identify factors that are a prerequisite for the success of financial liberalization policies. He then shows how these prerequisites were not met and how the financial reform policies instead had a destabilizing effect. At the same time he goes on to suggest that the experience of the Philippines is not too different from countries that suffered from banking crises following financial reforms. He discusses the measures that can be taken to avoid such outcomes.

The final chapter in this section, Chapter 6, deals with Chile. Kate Phylaktis provides a broad-based survey of the stabilization and liberalization policies in Chile since 1973 when Chile first launched an ambitious program of economic liberalization. Phylaktis takes us through different phases of the various policies and their outcomes. Her survey leads her to draw a number of conclusions, which relate to the order of reforms and stabilization policies and support the popular belief that stabilization should precede liberalization. She also suggests that liberalization of domestic financial markets should precede that of the foreign sector. In the domestic sector, before any form of deregulation is introduced, special attention should be paid to the supervision and the regulation of the banking industry. Finally, she emphasizes the importance of credibility in the pursuit of government policies. Chilean government's failure to act decisively in the face of major economic disruptions caused considerable skepticism about the sustainability of its liberalization policies. However, she concludes that without the reforms the stabilization policies of the more recent years would not have succeeded.

Part III deals with the experiences of the Central and the East European countries. Its three chapters each deal with a different aspect of the financial reform program. Chapter 7 by Patrick Conway deals with the problem of cash shortage that was experienced by the countries in the former Soviet Union immediately after independence. He discusses alternate explanations for this phenomenon but claims that the most plausible explanation lies in terms of the role played by financial repression, which is indicative of financial market distortions. This claim is demonstrated by the use of a three-sector model and some descriptive evidence. The examples of Georgia and the Ukraine are cited to show that merely treating the symptoms rather than dealing with the financial-market distortions led to more problems. On the other hand, the case of Estonia is presented as the example where the problem was solved by dealing with the cause and not the symptom. Estonia introduced successful financial-sector reforms.

In Chapter 8 Irena Grosfeld tackles a very different issue. Her chief concern is with the form of financial institutions that should be introduced in economies in transition. She suggests that these countries need information about investment opportunities. Thus, her question is whether the banks are the most appropriate form of financial institution that can generate such information. She expresses serious reservations on this account. In particular, she argues against the ability of a banking system to perform this role if it is too closely tied with the firms. She suggests that too much commitment by the banks to firms will reduce their ability to provide this sort of information. She then goes on to discuss alternate forms of financial institutions that might play this role. The Czech Republic and Poland are used as examples to support her arguments.

Chapter 9 by Kanhaya L. Gupta and Robert Lensink also deals with the commercial banking sector, but its focus is very different from that of the Grosfeld paper. They examine the portfolio behavior of commercial banks in Poland with a view to simulating the effects of financial liberalization policies on this behavior. The chapter specifies, estimates, and simulates the model. It captures special features of the Polish economy. For example, it explicitly distinguishes between domestic and foreign-currency-denominated deposits and the effects of changes in default rates on the lending behavior of banks. Simulation results seem to confirm the significance of these factors and suggest that models that assume perfect substitutability between the domestic and foreign-currency-denominated deposits may be misleading.

The last part of the volume deals with the Middle East experience. Chapter 10, by Nazim Kadri Ekinci, is a detailed description of the experience of Turkey with financial liberalization policies, which started in 1980. After the initial success of the domestic financial liberalization policies, the situation worsened. Domestic financial liberalization policies failed because of mistakes in the external financial liberalization program as well as long delays in creating an adequate regulatory and supervisory institutional framework for the banking system. The problem was exacerbated by continuing large budget deficits and large public-sector external debt, which led to what he calls the "internal transfer problem." The chapter goes on to discuss the serious consequences of this particular issue in the Turkish context.

References

McKinnon, R.I. (1973). *Money and Capital in Economic Development.* Washington, DC: Brookings Institution.

Shaw, E. (1973). *Financial Deepening in Economic Development.* New York: Oxford University Press.

Experiences with Financial Liberalization

edited by

Kanhaya L. Gupta
Professor of Economics
University of Alberta

Kluwer Academic Publishers
Boston/Dordrecht/London

I THE AFRICAN EXPERIENCE

1 FROM FINANCIAL REPRESSION TO LIBERALIZATION
The Senegalese Experience

Jean-Claude Berthélemy

Introduction

Like many other developing countries, Senegal has been through different phases in its financial policy, which have led it to implement successively a managed monetary policy characterized by repressive financial practices followed by a liberal one. What happened in Senegal, and elsewhere, would seem to suggest that reversing policies over a period of time does not necessarily lead to a corresponding reversal in the performance of the economy in question or in its financial system. A hysteresis effect occurs, which means that the bad policies initially implemented can continue to have negative effects long after they have been discontinued.

The interpretation of this statement that I propose to examine in this chapter is based on the premise that interaction between the financial sector and the real sector can give rise to multiple equilibria. Such an argument, already developed in Berthélemy and Varoudakis (forthcoming), means that a possible low equilibrium may exist, where the economy would have an inefficient financial sector and weak growth. Such an equilibrium is stable, so that in the event of an inappropriate financial policy pushing the economy in its direction, it will be difficult for that economy to break away from it later. The principal argument of this chapter is that Senegal is, and has been for a long time, in such a low-equilibrium situation.

The argument is summed up and its empirical extensions are studied in Section 1.2. I then go on to describe the failure of the financial repression policy practised by Senegal from 1960 to the end of the 1980s. This period can be broken down into two phases: the first can be qualified as passive repression, lasting from 1960 to 1973 (Section 1.3), followed by a second, active repression phase which continued up to 1988 (Section 1.4). The financial policy implemented was ineffective in both phases, and the active repression period led to the breakdown of a major part of the banking system. The reorganization, followed by liberalization of the banking system, which has since been implemented, has not had a noticeable impact either in terms of the dynamism or the efficiency of that system, as is demonstrated in Section 1.5. My concluding remarks form Section 1.6.

The Cumulative Process of Financial Underdevelopment

My starting point is that there is a reciprocal effect between financial development and economic growth. This reciprocal influence can give rise to the existence of several states of equilibria and consequently to the appearance either of a virtuous circle of development or, on the contrary, of a poverty trap.

I consider the financial system as a whole throughout, without making any distinction between banks, nonbanking financial intermediaries, and stock markets. Choosing between direct and indirect finance is as difficult to deal with in theory as in practice, and I do not look at it. Indeed, it is of no interest in this particular case, as the formal Senegalese system consists solely of a banking sector. The influence of the financial system on growth can, whatever the form it takes, impact on at least two areas. In the first instance, the financial system can reinforce growth by making capital more efficient. In the second, the volume of savings and investment can be negatively affected by the weakness of the financial system.

In the case of Africa, the argument in terms of efficiency of capital is especially important for the simple reason that capital is an extremely rare commodity. The cost of misallocations affecting the efficiency of capital must therefore be, intuitively, even higher due to the scarcity of capital, as it then includes a high opportunity cost when wasted. For this reason alone it would be a grave mistake to underestimate the place that the financial sector should be accorded in African economic policies. Senegal is no exception.

The inverse relationship between growth (or the level of economic development) and the development of the financial system can be looked at from two main angles.

First, strong growth, or simply a high standard of living, implies the availability of a greater volume of savings to be intermediated. Since some of the costs involved in the financial system are fixed, it could therefore be assumed that the growth of the real economy would enable the financial sector to become more efficient, whether in savings collection or in asset management. In the case of Senegal, the savings ratio has always been very low, varying between +12 percent and –7 percent of GDP. Such a weak savings ratio is obviously a serious obstacle to the development of the financial sector.

Second, the size of the financial sector also can effect its market structure. When fixed costs exist, the number of financial intermediaries who can make money and the degree of competition in the financial sector are greater when the savings ratio is high. This will have a positive effect on the payoff to savers for a given productivity of capital and also on the capacity of the financial system as a whole to propose attractive products to savers. A lack of competition was undoubtedly a negative factor in the case of Senegal, where fewer than ten banking establishments were in business during the major part of the period being examined.

The reciprocal influence between the financial sector and the growth of the real economy that I have described above can lead to the appearance of a vicious circle that tends to lead toward a poverty trap. The initial weakness of the financial system means that investment is both reduced and less efficient, which means that growth is low too. The backlash to this state of affairs is that the slowdown in growth makes the financial system less efficient and correspondingly reduces its activity.[1]

If dynamic reciprocal linkups exist between financial development and real growth, and if those linkups are translated through the existence of several possible states of equilibria, then the effect of the initial financial development on growth cannot be linear. It is to be expected that below a certain threshold of initial financial development, an economy will be "trapped" to a certain extent in an equilibrium of financial underdevelopment linked to weak growth, whereas above this threshold there will be a positive growth characterized by a reciprocal virtuous linkup between financial and real developments. If this is the case, growth and growth explanatory factors should be modified by the crossing of such a threshold, which must be identified. This threshold defines "convergence clubs"—those groups of countries that show a specific conditional convergence behavior pattern. Berthélemy and Varoudakis (1996) have demonstrated the pertinence of this conclusion through a test on international comparison data and have worked out a threshold for financial development below which the growth of the economy is blocked. This threshold corresponds on average[2] to an M2/GDP ratio equal to 19 percent.

Berthélemy and Varoudakis also have demonstrated that the growth of the financial activity is itself affected in turn by this threshold effect. This financial sector will converge toward a state of high equilibrium if it is initially buoyant enough. Moreover, financial repression (as measured by negative real interest rates) has a negative influence on financial development for the group of countries converging toward high equilibrium but has no significant effect on the group converging toward the low equilibrium. In other words, financial repression is not good as it can bring about an underdevelopment of the financial sector, but it has no visible impact on the financial situation when this sector is effectively caught in a poverty trap situation. This is only natural: financial repression can break the buoyancy of the financial sector only if that sector is in fact buoyant, which is not the case for an economy in the low equilibrium of financial underdevelopment and weak growth situation.

Which means that there is a form of hysteresis in policies of financial repression: as soon as the financial sector and the economy as a whole are dragged down toward the low equilibrium, it then becomes extremely difficult for that economy to break away again. Senegal has lived through such a situation on two separate occasions.

Passive Financial Repression[3]

In the ranking of countries based on the econometric exercise presented above, Senegal, at independence, was among the countries with relatively high initial financial development, which should have made possible a conditional convergence toward a high equilibrium. However, it remained in this category for only a few years. In fact, Senegal had a financial deepening ratio in the region of 21 percent at the beginning of the 1960s, but that ratio was artificially inflated at that time, due to the large number of expatriates who still provided a large chunk of the financial savings. After independence in 1960, the ratio of financial deepening plummeted rapidly to reach 13 percent in 1966, putting Senegal in the category of weakly developed countries in financial terms (Figure 1.1).

Expatriate departures can explain such a movement to a certain extent, but it was also probably a result of the policy of financial repression implemented at the time, which led to the fixing of real interest rates (on

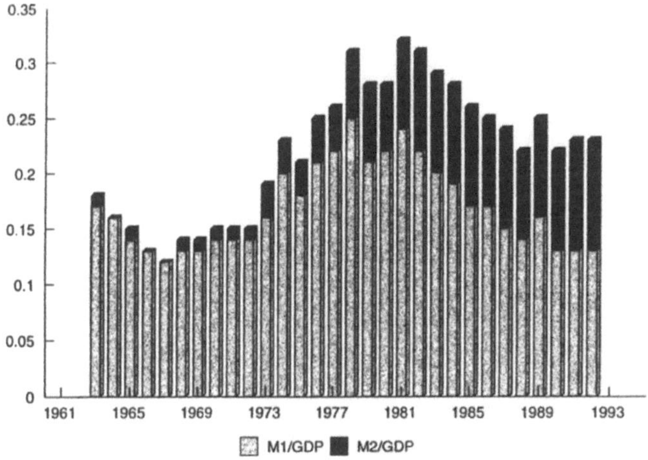

Figure 1.1. Financial deepening ratio

deposits) that were almost systematically negative. This policy continued until the mid-1980s (Figure 1.2). It is very likely that non-interest-bearing rates had a negative impact on local collection of financial resources, either because they discouraged people from saving or because the available money left the country to find more profitable rates elsewhere, which was easy thanks to the complete mobility of capital with France. It is less sure that, at a later stage, real interest rates had a determining effect: as I show later, the lowest real interest-rate period, which occurred during the 1970s, coincided with the least bad performance in terms of financial savings collection. Moreover, this is in line with the cross-section econometric equations that I referred to in the preceding section. Indeed, the impact of real interest rates on the development of financial activity would not appear to be demonstrated in the cases of countries that, like Senegal from the mid-1960s onwards, were clearly below the initial financial development threshold.

At the beginning of the 1960s, Senegal had a very rudimentary financial infrastructure. Between 1961 and 1973, there were only five banks, four of which were affiliates of foreign commercial banks. The fifth was a local development bank that was set up after independence. Very few branches existed outside Dakar. The postal service was also incapable of organizing an efficient collection system for savings, as postbook savings operations were centralized at Dakar until recently, which made for long delays for even the simplest financial operations. In all, when post offices are included,

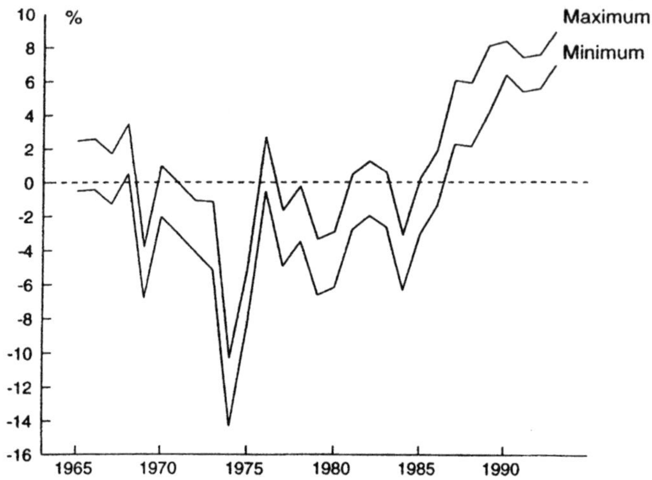

Figure 1.2. Creditor real interest rates

the density of the network for savings collection in Senegal was somewhere in the region of one branch for every 50,000 people, which is extremely low. Given the fact that no new banks were created until the 1970s, despite the rapid demographic expansion during the same period, the inadequacy of the banking system could only get worse in the 1960s.

To make matters worse, the banking system was initially very uncompetitive, because of its small size but also because of the restraints imposed by the lending policy, which were such that the sharing of the market was less the result of competition between banks than one of an administrative allocation of ceilings on rediscounting and by the credit squeeze. The monitoring by the BCEAO (Banque Centrale des Etats de l'Afrique de l'Ouest)[4] of both creditor and debtor interest rates, and consequently of the intermediation margins, made any competition on prices impossible.

In such a context, it is easy to understand the total lack of buoyancy in the banking system, linked to both supply and demand factors.

At the outset, the savings ratio in Senegal was weak, standing at less than 10 percent of GDP on average up to the mid-1970s. It became even weaker after that time. In addition, the financial savings collected by banks, as measured by quasi-money (M2–M1), represented a tiny fraction of the total savings amount (an average of only 4 percent until the mid-1970s)

(Figure 1.3). This weak level of financial saving was undoubtedly further accentuated by the nondevelopment of the banking system, due to a cumulative process in line with the analysis set out in the preceding section, but it was also an outcome of the low level of income and of the interest-rate policy, which maintained real creditor rates at negative values for virtually all of the period up to the end of the 1980s.

Second, intermediation margins for the banks monitored by the BCEAO were very tight, which meant that they had little incentive to look for new customers, whether for loans or for deposits. The gross margins for low-interest loans, granted to priority sectors and companies, stood at only 1 percent. The fact that banks were obliged to set aside almost 70 percent of their credit for these priority sectors, even though such loans were not profitable, is another reason for the general morosity of the banking credit market in Senegal at that time. Finally, the application of a 17 percent tax (Taxe sur les Prestations de Services, or TPS) to both borrowing and lending interests was yet another reason to explain the lack of buoyancy in the banking intermediation sector. This tax clearly had a negative effect on banking intermediation.

The credit policy implemented between 1960 and 1973 was relatively conservative, which is why this period can be described as a period of passive financial repression. It was based on the refinancing of a part of the bank loans by the BCEAO, with the goal of orienting credit toward priority sectors. The refinancings granted to the banks were subject to a ceiling,

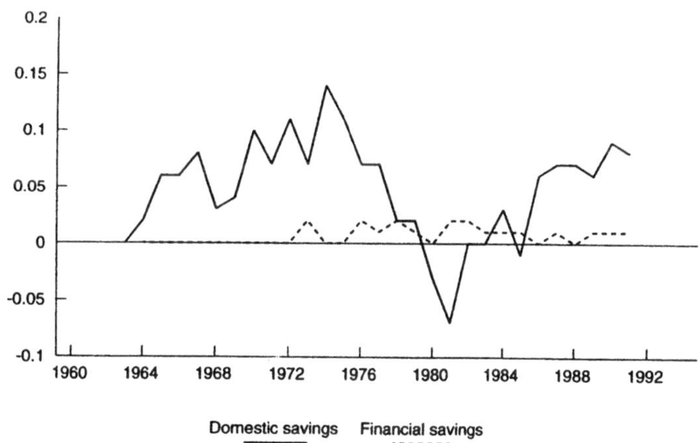

Figure 1.3. Savings/GDP Ratio

which was used as a monetary policy tool, along with the obligation imposed on the banks to respect a liquidity ratio. In addition, loans to the state had a ceiling based on tax revenue[5] to avoid the risk of a monetary financing of the deficit, which would have meant unmanageable inflationary consequences in the framework of a fixed parity system with France.

Between 1963 and 1967, fewer loans were granted by banks to the economy. They then increased, with a marked acceleration at the beginning of the 1970s, due to imported inflation along with the implementation of a more hands-on approach to economic policy by the government, which led to the setting up of extensive credit lines to parastatals. However, there is no evidence that the monetary policy and the monitoring of credit had a direct effect on these evolutions. It could be said that the monetary policy was not particularly restrictive either before or after the 1973 changes. The banks generally did not reach the ceilings set up for rediscounts by the BCEAO. The period was marked by a lack of dynamism on the part of the banks, which remained resolutely turned toward the established way of funding a traditional trade economy, in a context that was characterized by the absence of any real competition and the absence of initiative—both causes and consequences of the weakness of the volume of savings in the banking system.

Active Financial Repression

From 1973 onward, there was a marked evolution in monetary aggregates and in the structure of the financial sector. These trends can be linked, to a certain extent, to the handing over of greater monetary autonomy to the West African Monetary Union (WAMU) in 1974. This led to less vigilance in the loan-granting policy and to a more hands-on financial policy, which could be described as actively repressive in contrast to the preceding period, when financial repression went hand in hand with a passive response from both the monetary authorities and the government. Besides the greater freedom of action granted to the BCEAO, this watershed came about essentially as a result of new approaches adopted by the Senegalese government, which tried to stimulate the economy in different ways.

The Senegalese government rightly considered the lack of buoyancy in the banking sector to be an obstacle to development. In an attempt to overcome this handicap, the authorities encouraged the creation of a number of new banking establishments, wholly or partially funded by public funds for the most part. It was also made easier for foreign banks to open offices. By 1981, the number of banks had doubled (from five to ten, and

1986, there were fifteen). In addition, the statutory difference between commercial banks and development banks was eliminated, in line with the same objective of stimulating the contribution of the banking sector to development. Finally, an initial overhaul of the monetary policy led to the creation of a so-called money market, centralized at the BCEAO. This, however, was not a real money market, since the interest rate for the market was fixed by the BCEAO, based on the French money market rate and the internal situation of WAMU and not on a balancing out of the supply and demand of liquidities. The BCEAO bought up all the liquid assets on offer from the banks at this preestablished rate. While it was certainly needed, the introduction of such a "market" did not play a determining role in the development of the banking system as a result.

It remains to be seen if these moves would have created a new buoyancy in the banking sector in the long term, along with increased competition within the banking sector itself. The M2/GDP ratio did improve, but only slowly, and it remained modest. It reached 20 percent at the beginning of the 1980s, and financial savings represented on average 25 percent of total domestic savings between 1973 and 1989.

Nevertheless, this evolution did not represent a real progression in the financial development of the country as it was not accompanied by a learning process that would have made the banking intermediation sector more efficient. On the contrary, in fact the movement was accompanied by a progressive falloff in the solvency of the banks, which led in turn to an inefficient allocation of the available funds, leading notably to a major crisis period in the banking sector at the end of the 1980s. This crisis episode culminated in the bankruptcy of many outlets in the sector, which meant that an important part of what had been built up during the 1970s had proved to be nonviable. In the long run, the advances made were only superficial, and an analysis of this failure provides a number of useful lessons about our understanding of the financial problems facing countries such as Senegal.

First, we cannot be sure that the inflation of quasi-money, which was very marked in the 1970s, corresponded in fact to a modification in the propensity to save for private agents. It is true that, on average, the ratio between the variation in the stock of quasi-money and domestic savings increased significantly. However, the extreme variations in this ratio from one year to the next indicates that there is no stable link between domestic and financial savings, either before or after 1973. As demonstrated in Figure 1.3, financial savings rose in proportion to GDP at the start of the 1970s, while domestic savings plummeted over the same period and real interest rates were still very discouraging (Figure 1.2). Moreover, the recovery in domestic savings from 1981 onward, a result of the adjustment policy, was concomitant with an inverse stagnation of financial savings, despite positive real interest rates from 1985 onward.

To explain this phenomenon, we must look to the evolution in savings structure and in funding needs, which sheds a new light on the 1970s: the growth in the quantity of quasi-money should not be taken to be a result of a financial savings behavior pattern among private agents, but rather as the quasi-money funding of a public sector needing more and more funds. To really understand what happened, we must distinguish between the effect of private savings and that of public savings in the evolution of quasi-money. In practice, it tends to be mostly private agents who display financial savings behavior patterns. However, in Senegal's case, the public sector has a greater need for funding than a capacity to fund. A rise in public-sector savings does not therefore necessarily mean a rise in financial savings. In fact, such a rise will, all things being equal, bring about a falloff in the need for funding in the public sector, which also implies a falloff in the demand for funding from the public sector to the financial system. If the financial savings recorded are the result of an equilibrium between the various funding offers (from private agents) and the demand for funding means (especially by the public sector), the effect of public savings on financial savings could be negative instead of positive.

This hypothesis has been verified in econometric terms. While private savings (SP) always have a positive effect on financial savings, public savings (SG) have, on the contrary, a negative effect. The best estimation of a descriptive equation for financial savings (as measured by the variation in the stock of quasi-money) is as follows:

$$\Delta(M2 - M1) = -2.45 + \underset{(2.8)}{0.06}\,SP(-1) - \underset{(2.3)}{0.03}\,SG(-1) + \underset{(7.5)}{0.02}\,GDP(-1) \quad (11.0)$$

$$R^2 = 0.72 \quad AR(1) = -0.48$$

It was impossible to introduce a real interest-rate variable into this equation. In spite of its rudimentary character, it highlights an important driving force behind growth in the M2/GDP ratio during the 1970s: the growth in demand for funding for the public sector, which in turn fed the growth of monetary aggregates. As will be seen later, this evolution came about as a result of a major policy shift in terms of the funding of public development expenditure in the 1970s. Needless to say, this equation, with its mixture of supply and demand, has only a descriptive value and can in no way be interpreted as a reflection of financial savings *behavior*. Nevertheless, the parameter linked to private savings can be read as the reflection of financial savings for the private sector. According to the estimation given for this parameter, the marginal rate for transformation of domestic savings into financial savings, somewhere in the region of 6 percent, is very low. There would therefore seem, according to this equation, to have been no modifications in behavior patterns underlying the poor results in terms of financial savings collection, but rather an inflation of the financial aggregates linked to the beefing up of funding needs for the public sector.[6]

Second, the increase in the number of banks, the majority of which were public, was implemented despite the lack of real banking skills, either at bank level or in terms of the monitoring skills of the BCEAO. The Senegalese example, although not the only one, proves that the development of a banking sector cannot be decided on paper. As a result of the lack of expertise, numerous loans were granted without any real analysis or any real followup of the beneficiaries and without the necessary supervisory backup from the BCEAO. It very quickly became clear at the beginning of the 1980s that the number of bad loans had significantly increased, which initially meant that some banks were strapped for cash and eventually that most were pushed toward insolvency.

Third, the banks were under considerable pressure—and sometimes obliged—to grant many loans to semipublic bodies, which soon proved incapable of honoring their commitments. Evidence of the expansion of the funding needs of the public sector can be seen at this stage. Such a deliberately implemented policy of parastatal indebtedness corresponds to a context where there was a managed and state-driven orientation of the economic policy. Many public companies were created in the 1970s in Senegal to compensate for weaknesses in the private sector, and some private companies were even nationalized. Moreover, the debt load of companies with regard to banks was an indirect way of getting round the rule on the control of monetary financing of the deficit imposed by the franc zone (see note 5). The state was able to pass on a certain number of functions or expenditures to state companies, which guaranteed the funding necessary thanks to the advances supplied by the banks.

The classic example of inept financial management of the public sector in the 1970s was the Office National de Commercialisation et d'Assistance au Dévelopment (ONCAD), a funding and backup organization for the peanut-growing industry, which became insolvent at the beginning of the 1980s. It went to the wall in 1982, leaving more than 60 billion CFA francs' worth of unpaid debts, which represented the equivalent of almost 20 percent of the bank loans to the economy at the time, to which had to be added around 30 billion francs in unpaid interest. When ONCAD failed, the main banks were obliged by the authorities to take on a share of the outstanding amounts, which were supposed to be reimbursed at a later date by the state.

In other words, a part of the additional deposits recorded at that time in the banking system stemmed from an inflation of credits granted to the public and semipublic sectors and did not in any way represent a financial development. The bank statistics declared to the central risk bank give some idea of the extent of the movement, even if they contradict the consolidated accounts for the banks published by the BCEAO, and should therefore be treated with caution. The private-sector risks declared between 1970 and 1972 were 2.5 times higher than those declared for state-owned companies, but this ratio fell to 1.2 in 1974 and stayed between 1.2 and 1.4 for the next ten years (until 1983).

Overall, there was a virtually unmonitored distribution of credit under the pretense of satisfying development policy goals. The BCEAO had neither the means nor the clout needed to impose even the most basic monitoring on the banks in terms of their credit management. It had very limited means of verifying whether the banks were respecting basic rules of precaution. To make matters worse, the final responsibility was split between the BCEAO and the Senegalese government, so neither assumed it fully. The investigative powers the BCEAO did have were extremely limited. Finally, in spite of its theoretically independent status, the BCEAO had always been subject to the wishes of the governments of its members countries.

The data published by the BCEAO are also revealing in that it classified only 5 percent of loans as bad up to 1988, while an examination of the accounts of bankrupt banks (which represented two-thirds of the total sum distributed by the banking system as a whole at the end of 1987) shows that their results contained 56 percent nonperforming loans. The data published by the BCEAO clearly underestimated the gravity of the problems faced by the banks. Even if it had been capable of a thorough followup of banking credit policies, which was not always the case, the BCEAO was never capable of drawing the appropriate conclusions in terms of its own monitoring role. Many of these loans had been given for political reasons, either to companies or private individuals, and the BCEAO was powerless to do anything about it. The end result was that it allowed an increasingly critical state of affairs to develop, with eight of the fifteen banks in the marketplace finally going to the wall.

The BCEAO had signaled mismanagement in the credit system by the end of the 1970s. It had reacted by reining in the growth of the monetary aggregates by means of credit controls, fixed individually for each bank and allocated by the National Credit Committee, without, however, suppressing the ceiling imposed on rediscounting. These controls did introduce some sort of control into the working of the banking system but were not enough to prevent the collapse of that system. In reality, the credit containment was managed in such a way that those banks that were already in difficulty received preferential treatment in terms of its application. As a result, the discretionary powers accorded to the National Credit Committee left the program wide open to massive interference by the government, which gave preferential treatment to the struggling banks by allowing them to refinance their loan deadlines in order to prevent them from going to the wall. These banks benefited from such preferential treatment both in terms of their credit ceilings and rediscounting by the BCEAO to such an extent that by the mid-1980s the growth rate of their loans was two to three times higher than that of healthy banks. Consequently, the introduction of credit controls and the way they were managed accentuated the fragility of the banking sector in the early 1980s rather than putting the situation right.

Restructuring and Financial Liberalization

By 1985, the banking system was obviously in serious trouble. The authorities had data that revealed the existence of large sums of nonperforming loans in bank accounts. Nevertheless, they waited until 1987 before finally asking for an audit, under pressure from the World Bank. The results of this audit showed that nine public and private banks or financial establishments were indeed in serious financial difficulties, bordering on insolvency. Partial measures, such as the consolidation and refinancing at preferential rates of outstanding debitor amounts owed to the BCEAO, were not enough to salvage the situation, which had gone too far by this stage. After numerous consultations, the government drew up a reorganization and liberalization plan for the banking sector that was adopted at the end of 1988.

According to the policy declaration on the banking sector made by the Ministry of Economics and Finance in November 1989, six establishments were to be split, with their healthy sections used to form new entities, while the frozen debts were to be regrouped in a liquidatory structure. Unfortunately, this reorganization plan was slow to be implemented and did not go as far as the promises made by the government in 1989. The structure of the banking sector was also reviewed as part of the reorganization plan, with the goal of introducing more competition and stricter management standards, along with more operational monetary policy tools. Most of these measures were adopted at WAMU level, as all the member countries were experiencing the same difficulties as Senegal, to a greater or lesser degree.

First and foremost, bank monitoring was reinforced, with the BCEAO setting up a (supranational) banking commission to be responsible for supervision. Second, the BCEAO introduced measures aimed at making it more difficult to avail of its refinancing facilities, which were made more expensive and harder to obtain. Reserves on deposits were also made mandatory in December 1992. Third, the sectorial credit policy was dropped. Fourth, credit containment was eliminated in January 1994 and replaced by a more standard mode of monetary regulation through mandatory reserves. Finally, the structure and level of interest rates were partially freed, with notably a total freeing of debtor rates, on condition of respecting the ceiling that corresponded to the usury lending rate. These changes were intended to improve the payback for banking intermediation activities and therefore act as a positive incentive to avail of them. The elimination of the TPS on creditor interest was also intended as a spur to banking intermediation activities.

What were the results of this policy? The banking sector became healthier to a certain extent, but it still remained shaky and, more important, incapable of being a driving force for development. After the restructuring process, only eight banks remained, in more or less working order. With the exception of one successfully privatized bank, there is no evidence for the time being that these banks are up to playing a dynamic role in financing growth, despite the liberalization of the monetary policy with regard to the fixing of interest rates and banking margins.

The banking system as a whole did not acquire, during the credit inflation phase, the financial skills it needs to be more effective. The surviving banks have recovered in terms of their liquid assets, but they are still not lending. Up to October 1993, they opted instead to pile up portfolio holdings remunerated by the BCEAO through the so-called money market, rather than take risks. From that date onward, changes in the functioning of the money market prevented them from doing so, as the BCEAO no longer absorbs excess liquidity offered by banks. As a result, the excess liquidity of these banks is such that some have even decided to refuse deposits. Only a few have tried to get out of this impasse by diversifying their financial products, with the creation of activities such as leasing and venture capital.

In terms of credit, 70 percent of loan operations are now short term, and the share of industrial loans has been reduced from 21 percent of the total credit in 1986 to 15 percent in 1990, with a new emphasis being given to commercial activities. Small and medium-sized Senegalese outlets still find it as difficult to obtain funding for long-term projects. Banks refuse to even open accounts for private individuals unless they can guarantee a minimum deposit level (200,000 CFA francs, equivalent to U.S. $400), which effectively means that the vast majority of the population has no access to banking facilities. Following the closure of some banking establishments, the number of branches has fallen from sixty-five in 1986 to forty-six in 1990 (compared with forty in 1976). It would therefore seem extremely premature to draw any positive conclusions on the effect of the financial liberalization process at this time (1996).

Conclusion

At independence, Senegal had a very basic financial system, but one that nevertheless functioned, mainly to feed the needs of the colonial economy. In the 1960s, the system deteriorated, especially following the departure of some of the expatriate population and under pressure from a monetary and credit policy that worked against the development of banking intermediation activities. Senegal has since made two attempts to break out of this stalemate situation.

Initially, in the mid-1970s, an attempt was made to set up a fully functional financial system. However, the financial repression then in operation, which was characterized by extremely negative real interest rates, the absence of a local savings capacity, and state interference in the allocation of credits by banks very quickly made this policy inoperative. As a result, Senegal found itself, by the mid-1980s, in a worse state than it had been ten years earlier, with a banking system on the verge of collapse and in need of drastic reorganization measures.

Between 1985 and 1995, these restructuring measures were half-heartedly implemented, and a more liberal credit policy was worked out. The accounts of the surviving banks were made healthier as a result—to the extent that they now find themselves with excess liquid assets—and interest rates were raised to very high positive levels, with the exception of 1994, when inflation was affected by the mechanical effects of the 50 percent devaluation of the CFA franc. This trend can only contribute even more to the excess liquidity of the banks.

While the steps taken were necessary, it is still difficult to see their positive effects as yet. The fundamental problem that still remains to be solved is the incapacity of the banks to identify and select investment opportunities and to take appropriate risks once they have done so. This is the outcome of thirty years of policies that were totally unadapted to the stimulation of financial services. It is obvious that the more liberal monetary policy put into operation at the beginning of the 1990s, especially the freeing of interest rates, cannot compensate for a learning process that did not take place. It will therefore not be enough to remedy the situation.

Acknowledgments

The author was greatly helped by the input from Abdoulaye Seck, Aristomene Varoudakis, and Ann Vourc'h. The opinions expressed are his alone and do not in any way implicate the OECD.

Notes

1. This argument is developed in full in Berthélemy and Varoudakis (1996).
2. This 19 percent threshold is an average, as there is also a threshold effect related to educative development, which means that there are four and not only two clubs of convergence. See Berthélemy and Varoudakis (1996) for further details.
3. This section and the two following sections draw extensively on Berthélemy, Seck, and Vourc'h (1996). The data used are the result of calculations made by these authors based on official figures (central bank and Ministry of Finance).
4. The BCEAO is a common central bank for all the countries in the West African Monetary Union (WAMU). Until 1974, the head office of the BCEAO was in Paris, and its monetary policy was strictly monitored by France as part of the franc zone system.
5. The ceiling still exists and is currently 20 percent of the tax yield for the preceding year.
6. It should also be noted that a Chow test did not reveal any structural instability in the parameters, especially at the beginning of the 1970s.

References

Berthélemy, J.C., A. Seck, and A. Vourc'h. (1996). *Growth in Senegal: A Lost Opportunity?* OECD, Development Centre Study.

Berthélemy, Jean-Claude, and Aristomene Varoudakis. (1996). "Economic Growth, Convergence Clubs, and the Role of Financial Development." *Oxford Economic Papers*, vol. 48, p. 300–328.

2 FINANCIAL REPRESSION AND SEIGNIORAGE IN GHANA

Ebenezer Asem and Kanhaya L. Gupta

Introduction

Seigniorage has been an important source of revenue for many developing countries and particularly for Ghana.[1] The ability to raise seigniorage is associated with government's sovereign monopoly in issuing fiat money. Following the definition of seigniorage by many economists—for example, Blanchard and Fischer (1990)—the total seigniorage revenue is defined to consist of inflation tax, which is the rate of inflation multiplied by the real money stock, and the growth in real money balances.

Various reasons account for why seigniorage is an important source of revenue for many developing countries. It is well documented that the financing of government deficits is a major reason for governments' need to raise seigniorage (Dornbusch and Fischer, 1986; van Wijnbergen, 1989; Buiter, 1990). This is particularly true in many developing economies for a number of reasons. First, governments' revenues in many developing countries are constrained by low income and trade taxes, and the avenues for borrowing are limited by underdeveloped financial sectors,[2] resulting in persistent deficits on governments' budgets. Second, seigniorage is an easy source of revenue for many governments in developing countries because the monetary authorities in many of these countries are subordinates to the fiscal authorities (see Espinosa-Vega, 1995). Thus, the monetary authorities are "compelled" to finance any size of the fiscal deficit that the fiscal authorities decide on. A third feature that makes extraction of seigniorage attractive in developing countries is that institutional factors constrain the portfolios of domestic financial assets available to the private sector (see Adam, Ndulu, and Sowa, 1996). The menu of financial assets is very limited, and this constrains the substitution opportunities out from domestic currency and hence imposes a high cost of portfolio adjustment on the private sector, which the governments can exploit. These peculiar features make seigniorage extraction attractive in many developing countries and hence in part explain why revenue from seigniorage are often higher in developing countries.

The effect of financial-sector adjustment on this traditional source of government revenue is not very clear in the literature. It is easy to find models that demonstrate that seigniorage will increase with financial liberalization (see Kapur, 1992), and it is also easy to find models that suggest that seigniorage will fall with liberalization (see Adam, Ndulu, and Sowa, 1996). One reason for this apparent lack of consistency in the results is that the various models analyze different aspects of a financial liberalization program. For example, Kapur (1992) examined the effect of interest-rate deregulation on seigniorage. He argued that an upward adjustment of controlled interest rate will induce a switch of deposits from the informal to the formal financial sector where reserves are required. This will increase the money demand and hence increase seigniorage. On the other hand, Adam, Ndulu, and Sowa (1996) explored the effects of liberalization measures such as relaxation of exchange controls, creation of *bureaus de change*, development of domestic financial asset markets, and development in financial technology. They argued that these will lower the seigniorage capacity of the economy by increasing the elasticity of substitution between the base money and other financial assets. Even if the same aspect of financial liberalization is analyzed, different results can be obtained depending on the modeling approach. For example, Kapur (1992) argued that liberalization will lead to an increase in seigniorage. Asem (1996) demonstrated that this result can be reversed if one takes account of household demand for money, which was ignored in Kupur's model. Thus, one of the main objectives of this chapter is to contribute to this area of literature and throw some light on the complex interaction between financial liberalization and seigniorage. Specifically, we analytically examine the effects of interest-rate deregulation and the removal of preferential loans allocations. Second, we apply the model to the Ghanian economy and empirically examine these effects on seigniorage.

In 1988 Ghana embarked on comprehensive financial sector reforms to complement the Economic Recovery Program initiated in 1983. The goal of the reform was to scrap the system of direct credit controls and replace it with an indirect monetary control in which financial institutions were free to make decisions on purely economic criteria. The measures taken involved interest-rate deregulation, removal of direct credit ceilings as well as preferential loans, swapping of nonperforming assets of commercial banks for Central Bank bills, lifting of restrictions on foreign currency holdings, and gradual withdrawal of the government's participation in the financial sector. These financial-sector reforms became necessary when it became apparent that the real sector was finding a lot of difficulties in maintaining the modest improvements it recorded at the initial stages of the Economic Recovery Program. Thus, the financial adjustment was expected to make the financial sector more efficient in its financial intermediary role and provide a vehicle for the real sector to sustain its gains.

Even though it is clear in the literature on seigniorage that the behavior of the financial sector has various implications for seigniorage, these implications have received little, if any, attention in assessing the effects of financial liberalization on the economy. The various aspects of the financial reform have specific implications for seigniorage. Of course, it is a difficult task to try to capture all aspects of financial liberalization in one model, and hence most models deal with one or another aspect of financial liberalization. In this chapter, therefore, we focus on the effects of interest-rate deregulation and the abolition or gradual removal of preferential loans. Interest-rate deregulation will increase the returns on deposits with the formal-sector financial institutions at the expense of other forms of assets such as informal-sector deposits and cash. Since the informal sector holds minimal or no reserves, a shift of deposits from the informal sector will tend to increase the economy's demand for money, while a shift from cash to formal-sector deposits will reduce the economy's demand for money. Thus, even if the rate of inflation and economic growth are unaffected by interest-rate deregulation, the change in money demand will provide a source of change for seigniorage. Removal of preferential loans and preferential interest rates will increase the profitability of creating loans, and this will induce banks to create more loans. The demand for bank cash holdings will thus be affected in the sense that the creation of more loans will reduce banks' demand for excess reserves while increasing their holdings of required reserves. This will tend to reduce the demand for cash by the banks and hence will adversely affect seigniorage.

Measurement of Seigniorage

The relevant tax base for inflationary finance is all nonindexed financial assets including notes and coins in circulation as well as cash reserve holdings of the commercial banks. The importance of both bank and nonbank holdings of cash for seigniorage in Ghana is shown in Table 2.1. The table shows that banks' holdings of high-powered money is high relative to the holdings of the nonbank sector. It accounted for more than half of the nonbank holdings in the periods after the reforms. The evidence suggests that over 34 percent of the seigniorage extracted during the period was from cash holding by the banking sector. This suggests that the importance of the banking sector as in the analysis of seigniorage in Ghana should not be overlooked.[3] Apart from this, the banking sector is closely connected to the money-creation process and therefore the real seigniorage that the government can exact. It would thus be appropriate to examine the government's revenue from seigniorage using both the private non-bank and the banking sector's holdings of cash as the base. The tax effects of inflation on inside money is redistributive in the sense that the tax burden on deposit holders is offset by the gain to the holders of liabilities to the banking sector. The government, therefore, does not directly benefit from the inflationary effect on inside money.

Even though the concept of seigniorage is straightforward, its measure is not. This has resulted in the proposal of various measures, including the rate of inflation multiplied by the real value of outside money (Friedman, 1953; Bailey, 1956), the rate of monetary growth multiplied by real outside money (Cagan, 1956; Marty, 1967), and nominal interest rate multiplied by real outside money (Phelps, 1971). Drazen (1985) argues that in general

Table 2.1. Nonbank sector and bank sector cash holding, 1986 to 1992 (Figures in millions of cedis).

Year	*Nonbank Sector*	*Bank Cash Reserves*
1986	25,053.5	8,678.5
1987	36,881.2	16,370.7
1989	62,226.8	35,688.4
1990	78,410.3	47,818.4
1991	80,585	52,924.2
1992	101,854.2	59,359.6

Source: *Bank of Ghana Quarterly Economic Bulletin* (January–March 1991 to 1994).

seigniorage per capita is given by $S = \theta m + (r - n)a$, where S is seigniorage, θ is the rate of growth of money supply, m is the real money stock, r is the real interest rate, n is the population growth rate, and a is net assets acquired by printing money. Thus θm is the current flow of revenue, and the second term is the revenue from assets purchased due to issuance of money, netting out that part of revenue used to keep a constant. He derives the previous measures of seigniorage as special cases of his general formulation.[4]

The methods suggested by Friedman and Bailey (method 1) and that by Cagan and Marty (method 2) were used to measure seigniorage in Ghana for the period 1970 to 1993. The method suggested by Phelps was not used

Table 2.2. Seigniorage as a percentage of government revenue[a] for Ghana from 1970 to 1993.[b]

Year	*Method 1*	*Method 3*
1970	5.9%	1.8%
1971	17.4	1.8
1972	34.2	14.8
1973	7.8	11.6
1974	17.2	16.6
1975	14.4	22.8
1976	29.5	43.7
1977	40.0	67.0
1978	54.9	66.0
1979	21.1	47.9
1980	31.3	49.3
1981	49.5	76.2
1982	21.0	32.1
1983	30.3	63.8
1984	24.8	28.4
1985	16.6	7.3
1986	20.2	14.2
1987	15.7	20.2
1988	20.2	18.4
1989	10.8	14.1
1990	1.3	16.7
1991	0.2	6.2
1992	25.6	6.9
1993	1.8	8.9

a The government's revenue includes seigniorage.
b The data are from *International Financial Statistics*.

because of the problems involved in using it to assess seigniorage in Ghana. As pointed out by Drazen (1985), Phelp's method is relevant when printed monies are used to acquire assets on which interest are earned. In Ghana, it is difficult to determine government assets that were purchased by printing money, and the official interest rates did not reflect the market rates most of the time.

Following Cukierman, Edwards, and Tabellini (1992), we measured seigniorage by using reserve money. The results, given in Table 2.2, indicate that the average revenue for seigniorage as percentage of government revenue was higher in the period before the financial liberalization (1970 to 1987) using both methods. The average seigniorage revenue as percentage of government revenue is 26.4 percent, and it is 33 percent for the prereform period using methods 1 and 2, respectively. The same averages are 10 percent and 11.8 percent for the postreform period using method 1 and 2, respectively. This indicates unambiguously that the relative contribution of seigniorage to government revenue fell after the liberalization measures were adopted.

Seigniorage Maximizing Rate of Inflation

In measuring seigniorage we adopt Cagan-Marty measure of seigniorage—that is, the growth rate of money supply multiplied by the stock of real money balances. This provides a more general measure of seigniorage and has been used by many economists including Friedman (1971) and Siegel (1981).

The demand for high-powered money in the nonbank and banking sectors of an economy can be defined as

$$M^d = f(Y, \pi, r, P) + kD(\pi, r, P(L), P) + ER(\pi, r, P(L), P), \quad (2.1)$$

where M^d is the demand for nominal cash balance by both the banking and the nonbanking sectors. The first term on the right-hand-size is the nonbank sector demand for cash, and it is a function of income (y), inflation (π), the domestic real interest rate (r), and the price level (P). Theory suggests that $f_P, f_y > 0$, and $f_\pi, f_r < 0$.

The last two terms represent banks demand for cash, which is given by required cash (kD) and excess cash (ER) holdings. Required cash holding is made up of the reserve ratio (k) multiplied by deposits. Deposits depend not only on the demand for deposits by the nonbank sector, but also on the banks' willingness to create deposits, which depends largely on profits the banks make on loans. This is rather important in financially repressed economies where interest rates offered on deposits are set well below "equilibrium" rates (see, for example, Fry, 1988) and credit ceiling and preferential loans are well in place.

When the interest rate is set below its equilibrium rate, commercial bank deposit demand by households falls. In the absence of any further regulation, the demand for deposits can be appropriately captured by its demand determinants. However, where further regulation (for example, credit ceilings and preferential credit allocations) exists, the demand for deposits cannot be appropriately captured solely by households demand. To see this we can decompose the demand for deposits into nonbank-sector and bank-sector demands. The nonbank-sector demand is the demand by the households sector, which is usually what is described by the standard deposit demand functions. The bank-sector deposit demand, on the other hand, is derived from the deposits that banks create and that they in turn demand. This is basically influenced by the profitability of creating loans. Thus, even though the initial deposits are made by the households, the banks increase demand deposits in the economy by creating deposits (an activity that takes place between the banks and the firms). Thus, for an economy where there is no credit ceiling or preferential loan allocation, the deposit creation by banks will be more than where bank credit operations are inhibited by credit ceilings and preferential allocations. This means that in financially repressed economies the demand for deposits can increase if governments, for example, lift restrictions on preferential loans allocations or credit ceilings. This will increase profits on loans, and hence, banks will expand deposit creation. This will shift banks' demand of cash from excess reserves to required reserves. In this sense, it will be appropriate to model the demand for deposits to be a function of banks' willingness to create deposits, which is basically influenced by the profitability of granting loans. It should be mentioned that bank loans in these economies are basically supply determined since interest on loans is also set below loan equilibrium rates.

In economies where interest rates are controlled and preferential loans are imposed, banks' profits will depend on the amount of loans allocated to preferential sectors (L_p) and the amount of loans allocated to the other sectors (L_o). Preferential sectors are sectors that the government sees as vital to the economy (these sectors typically include the agricultural sector). Two typical features of preferential lending affect banks' profits. First, default rates are usually higher in these sectors than in the other sectors, and so banks will voluntarily lend to these sectors only if they can charge higher lending rates to compensate for the higher risk they face in lending to these sectors. Thus, if lending rates are the same for the preferential and other sectors, banks will not in general lend to these preferential sectors. A second factor that affects banks' profits in preferential lending is that they are often required to charge preferential rates on these loans, which are usually set below the general controlled lending rates. These characteristics of the preferential sectors discourage lending to these sectors, and the government "forces" the banks to grant such loans by specifying that a certain proportion of the total loans should be given to the preferential sectors. Assuming that banks engage in lending activities only to generate income, then the profit of a bank can be defined as

$$Z(L) = i_p(1-\theta_1)L_p + i_o(1-\theta_2)L_o - C, \tag{2.2}$$

where C is the bank's operational cost, θ_1 is the probability of defaulting on preferential loans, θ_2 is the probability of defaulting on the other loans, i_1 is the net interest rate on preferential lending, and i_o is the net interest on other loans. The bank's revenue is thus made up of interest earned on preferential loans, $i_p(1 - \theta_1)L_p$, and that earned on other loans, $i_o(1 - \theta_2)L_o$.

Since the default rate is assumed higher in the preferential sectors than in the other sectors, θ_2 is less than θ_1. It will also be assumed, as is common in many LDCs, that the government determines the interest rate that should be charged on all loans (i_o) as well as the rates that should be charged on preferential loans (i_p), and typically $i_p \leq i_o$. Preferential interest rates can thus be written in terms of the other rates as $i_p = \tau_o$, where $\tau \leq 1$. In this case, repression through the offering of preferential interest rate will, of course, mean that $\tau < 1$.

As mentioned earlier, the government also sets the percentage of loans that should be granted the preferential sectors, and hence preferential loans can be written as some proportion of total loans—that is, $L_p = \sigma L$, where $\sigma < 1$. In this scenario the government can repress the financial sector in three ways—that is, it can repress by the use of i_o, σ, and τ. Given the above relationships, equation (2.2) can be rewritten as (2.3):

$$Z(L) = i_o\left[(1-\theta_2)L + \left(\tau(1-\theta_1) - (1-\theta_2)\right)\sigma L\right] - C. \tag{2.3}$$

From equation (2.3), the effects of changes in the government's repressive instruments on banks' profits can be examined by taking the partial derivative of the banks' profits with respect to the various repressive instruments. These give

$$\frac{\partial Z(L)}{\partial \sigma} = i_o\left[\tau(1-\theta_1) - (1-\theta_2)\right]L < 0, \quad \text{since } \tau(1-\theta_1) < (1-\theta_2) \tag{2.4}$$

$$\frac{\partial Z(L)}{\partial \tau} = i_o(1-\theta_1)\sigma L > 0 \tag{2.5}$$

$$\frac{\partial Z(l)}{\partial i_o} = (1-\theta_2)L + [\tau(1-\theta_1)-(1-\theta_2)]\sigma L < 0. \tag{2.6}$$

From (2.4), financial liberalization, which takes the form of decreasing the proportion of preferential loans, will increase banks' profits. It should be mentioned that even if $\tau = 1$—that is, there is no repression through preferential interest rates—σ will still be an effective policy instrument, provided $\theta_1 < \theta_2$ (albeit less repressive). From equation (2.5) an increase in the preferential interest rates will increase banks' profits. However, in this case if the government sets $\sigma = 0$—that is, it does not require that a certain proportion of loans should be made to the preferential sectors—then the use of τ will not be effective as an instrument of repression. This is because the banks will not lend to the preferential sectors, and hence their profits will not be affected by controlling the lending rates to these sectors. From (2.6) an increase in the interest rate to the other sectors will also increase banks' profits, but the presence of both σ and τ weakens i_o as a repressive instrument. Thus, as expected, the effect of repressing the financial sector through controlling the lending rates or setting preferential interest rates or determining the proportion of loans that should be allocated to the preferential sectors is to reduce banking profits and discourage deposit creation. Lower deposits creation will mean that the demand for required reserves will be lower and that the demand for excess reserves will be higher for any given deposits by households.

During financial liberalization, some of the major policy changes are relaxation of control on i_o, gradual removal of the sectorial allocation of credits, and an increase in preferential lending rates at rates faster than that on the other loans to narrow the gap between the two lending rates. The effect of liberalizing the financial sector, as captured by equations (2.4), (2.5), and (2.6), is an increase in banks profits, which will encourage deposit creation. Increased profits from lending activities will lead to an increase in loans by the commercial banks (since loans are basically supply determined in financially repressed economies) and a counterpart increase in deposits. This results in an increase in the demand for required reserves and a decrease in excess reserves (as the opportunity cost of excess reserves increases). The money demand by the nonbanking sector will also be influenced by changes in the interest rate. Typically, increases in the interest rate[5] will reduce the demand for money, all things being equal. Both the effect of a reduction in money demand and in excess reserves in favor of an increase in deposits will reduce real balance and hence have adverse consequences for seigniorage.

Given that default rates are assumed fixed,[6] the profits of the banks can be written as a function of i_o, σ, and τ—that is, $Z(L) = P(i_o, \sigma, \tau)$. Substitution of this into (2.1) gives

$$M^d = H(Y, \pi, r, p) + KD'(\pi, r, i_o, \tau, \sigma, P) + ER(\pi, r, i_o, \tau, \sigma, P). \tag{2.7}$$

From equation (2.7) one can specifically analyze the effect of changes in the various repressive instruments on the money demand. A given amount of cash deposit by the households (C^*) will be held by banks as required reserve or excess reserve and hence

$$C^* = KD'(\pi, r, i_o, \tau, \sigma, P) + ER(\pi, r, i_o, \tau, \sigma, P).$$

If the government relaxes financial repression through an increase in τ or i_o or a decrease in σ or any combination of these, C^* will be affected by these policy instruments, *ceteris paribus*. Any of these forms of liberalization will increase banks' profits on loans and will result in banks' reducing excess reserves in favor of creating more loans (deposits). Since only a fraction of the fall in excess reserves will be held by the banks in the form of required reserves, the cash holding of the banks will fall. This has adverse consequences for seigniorage. In addition to this, if the increase in banks' profits permit them to increase the deposit rate or if the government increases the deposit rates as well, as is often the case where deposit rates are also controlled, the demand for money by household will fall in favor of more deposits. Again, only a fraction of the fall in money demand by the households will be held by the banks as required reserves, and the money demand in the economy will fall further. Thus, banks' portfolio adjustment and the portfolio adjustment by the household will reinforce each other as far as the seigniorage implications are concerned. Thus, one can argue that ignoring the banking sector in analyzing the effect of liberalization on seigniorage may not have any qualitative effects but it may have quantitative implications.

Using equation (2.1) the growth rate of the economy's demand for money, g_m, can be written as

$$g_m = g_H\lambda_H + kg_D\lambda_D + g_E\lambda_E, \quad \text{and } \lambda_H + k\lambda_D + \lambda_E = 1, \tag{2.8}$$

where g_H, g_D, and g_E are the growth rates of the nonbank-sector money demand, reserve requirement, and excess reserve, respectively. λ_H, $k\lambda_D$, and

λ_E are the proportions of the nonbank cash holding, reserve requirement, and excess reserve to total cash balance, respectively.

Assuming that in the long run the rate of inflation is constant, we can write the growth rate of the nonbank-sector demand for money (g_H), reserve requirement (g_R), and excess reserve (g_E) as follows:

$$g_H = \eta_{Hp} g_p + \eta_{Hr} g_r + \eta_{Hy} g_y \tag{2.9}$$

$$g_D = \eta_{Dr} g_r + \eta_{Di_o} g_{i_o} + \eta_{D\tau} g_\tau + \eta_{D\sigma} g_\sigma + \eta_{DP} g_P \tag{2.10}$$

$$g_E = \eta_{Er} g_r + \eta_{Ei_o} g_{i_o} + \eta_{E\tau} g_\tau + \eta_{E\sigma} g_\sigma + \eta_{EP} g_P, \tag{2.11}$$

where g_i is the growth rate of the ith variable or the proportional change in the policy instrument, and η_{ij} is the elasticity of demand of i with respect to j. Seigniorage S can be written as

$$\begin{aligned} S &= \frac{M^d}{P} g_m = \frac{M^d}{P}\left(g_H \lambda_H + k g_D \lambda_D + g_E \lambda_E\right) \\ &= g_H \frac{H}{P} + k g_D \frac{D}{P} + g_E \frac{E}{P}. \end{aligned} \tag{2.12}$$

Taking the derivatives of (2.12) with respect to inflation and the various repressive instruments gives

$$\begin{aligned} \frac{\partial S}{\partial \pi} &= \frac{H}{P}\left[\eta_{Hp} + g_r \frac{\partial \eta_{Hr}}{\partial \pi} + g_y \frac{\partial \eta_{Hy}}{\partial \pi}\right] + g_H \frac{\partial \overline{H}}{\partial \pi} \\ &+ \frac{E}{P}\left[g_r \frac{\partial \eta_{Er}}{\partial \pi} + g_{i_o} \frac{\partial \eta_{Ei_o}}{\partial \pi} + g_\tau \frac{\partial \eta_{E\tau}}{\partial \pi} + g_\sigma \frac{\partial \eta_{E\sigma}}{\partial \sigma}\right] + g_E \frac{\partial \overline{E}}{\partial \pi} \\ &+ k \frac{D}{P}\left[g_r \frac{\partial \eta_{Dr}}{\partial \pi} + g_{i_o} \frac{\partial \eta_{Di_o}}{\partial \pi} + g_\tau \frac{\partial \eta_{D\tau}}{\partial \pi} + g_\sigma \frac{\partial \eta_{D\sigma}}{\partial \pi}\right] + k g_D \frac{\partial \overline{D}}{\partial \pi} \end{aligned} \tag{2.13}$$

$$\begin{aligned} \frac{\partial S}{\partial i_o} &= \frac{H}{P}\left[\eta_{Hp} + g_r \frac{\partial \eta_{Hr}}{\partial i_o} + g_y \frac{\partial \eta_{Hy}}{\partial i_o}\right] + g_H \frac{\partial \overline{H}}{\partial i_o} \\ &+ \frac{E}{P}\left[g_r \frac{\partial \eta_{Er}}{\partial i_o} + g_{i_o} \frac{\partial \eta_{Ei_o}}{\partial i_o} + g_\tau \frac{\partial \eta_{E\tau}}{\partial i_o} + g_\sigma \frac{\partial \eta_{E\sigma}}{\partial \sigma}\right] + g_E \frac{\partial \overline{E}}{\partial i_o} \\ &+ k \frac{D}{P}\left[g_r \frac{\partial \eta_{Dr}}{\partial i_o} + g_{i_o} \frac{\partial \eta_{Di_o}}{\partial i_o} + g_\tau \frac{\partial \eta_{D\tau}}{\partial i_o} + g_\sigma \frac{\partial \eta_{D\sigma}}{\partial i_o}\right] + k g_D \frac{\partial \overline{D}}{\partial i_o} \end{aligned} \tag{2.14}$$

$$\frac{\partial S}{\partial \tau}=\frac{H}{P}\left[\eta_{Hp}+g_r\frac{\partial \eta_{Hr}}{\partial \tau}+g_y\frac{\partial \eta_{Hy}}{\partial \tau}\right]+g_H\frac{\partial \overline{H}}{\partial \tau}$$
$$+\frac{E}{P}\left[g_r\frac{\partial \eta_{Er}}{\partial \tau}+g_{i_o}\frac{\partial \eta_{Ei_o}}{\partial \tau}+g_\tau\frac{\partial \eta_{E\tau}}{\partial \tau}+g_\sigma\frac{\partial \eta_{E\sigma}}{\partial \sigma}\right]+g_E\frac{\partial \overline{E}}{\partial \tau}$$
$$+k\frac{D}{P}\left[g_r\frac{\partial \eta_{Dr}}{\partial \tau}+g_{i_o}\frac{\partial \eta_{Di_o}}{\partial \tau}+g_\tau\frac{\partial \eta_{D\tau}}{\partial \tau}+g_\sigma\frac{\partial \eta_{D\sigma}}{\partial \tau}\right]+kg_D\frac{\partial \overline{D}}{\partial \tau} \quad (2.15)$$

$$\frac{\partial S}{\partial \sigma}=\frac{H}{P}\left[\eta_{Hp}+g_r\frac{\partial \eta_{Hr}}{\partial \sigma}+g_y\frac{\partial \eta_{Hy}}{\partial \sigma}\right]+g_H\frac{\partial \overline{H}}{\partial \sigma}$$
$$+\frac{E}{P}\left[g_r\frac{\partial \eta_{Er}}{\partial \sigma}+g_{i_o}\frac{\partial \eta_{Ei_o}}{\partial \sigma}+g_\tau\frac{\partial \eta_{E\tau}}{\partial \sigma}+g_\sigma\frac{\partial \eta_{E\sigma}}{\partial \sigma}\right]+g_E\frac{\partial \overline{E}}{\partial \sigma}$$
$$+k\frac{D}{P}\left[g_r\frac{\partial \eta_{Dr}}{\partial \sigma}+g_{i_o}\frac{\partial \eta_{Di_o}}{\partial \sigma}+g_\tau\frac{\partial \eta_{D\tau}}{\partial \sigma}+g_\sigma\frac{\partial \eta_{D\sigma}}{\partial \sigma}\right]+kg_D\frac{\partial \overline{D}}{\partial \sigma}. \quad (2.16)$$

The bars on the variables indicate the real value of the variables. Equations (2.14), (2.15), and (2.16) can be simplified to a large extent if we assume that the elasticities of households' money demand, banks' required demands, and excess reserves demands are not sensitive to changes in the repressive instruments. Following Adam, Ndulu, and Sowa (1996), this implies that the elasticities are weakly exogenous to the long-run demand for money function, which is a necessary condition for a valid estimation of the function. This restriction reduces equation (2.14), (2.15), and (2.16) to

$$\frac{\partial S}{\partial i_o}=g_H\frac{\partial \overline{H}}{\partial i_o}+g_E\frac{\partial \overline{E}}{\partial i_o}+kg_D\frac{\partial \overline{D}}{\partial i_o} \quad (2.14')$$

$$\frac{\partial S}{\partial \tau}=g_H\frac{\partial \overline{H}}{\partial \tau}+g_E\frac{\partial \overline{E}}{\partial \tau}+kg_D\frac{\partial \overline{D}}{\partial \tau} \quad (2.15')$$

$$\frac{\partial S}{\partial \sigma}=g_H\frac{\partial \overline{H}}{\partial \sigma}+g_E\frac{\partial \overline{E}}{\partial \sigma}+kg_D\frac{\partial \overline{D}}{\partial \sigma}. \quad (2.16')$$

Since households demand for real balances is not a function of these repressive instruments, $\frac{\partial \overline{H}}{\partial j}=0$, *for* $j = i_o, \sigma, \tau$. Thus, changes in the repressive instruments basically affect banks' intermediation activities and hence their demand for required and excess reserves. Financial liberalization, which involves changes in the three repressive instruments, will increase banks' profits and encourage loan creation, as discussed earlier. This implies an increase in required reserve at the expense of excess reserves, and hence $\frac{\partial \overline{D}}{\partial j} = -\frac{\partial \overline{E}}{\partial j}$, *for* $j = i_o$, τ, σ. Given this, equations (2.14′), (2.15′), and (2.16′) can be rewritten as

$$\frac{\partial S}{\partial j} = \left(kg_D - g_E\right)\frac{\partial \overline{D}}{\partial \sigma} \quad for \quad j = i_o,\ \sigma,\ \tau. \tag{2.17}$$

This equation suggests that seigniorage will increase when the government liberalizes the financial sector if $g_E < kg_D$ (this, of course, ignores any effect from the household sector). Intuitively, seigniorage has both a flow and a stock component, and hence changes in seigniorage can be achieved through changes in the flow or the stock component or both. Since we assume that the long-run growth rates g_E and g_D are not changed by liberalization, the changes in seigniorage can arise only from changes in the stock component. This, of course, does not mean that the growth rates of deposit and excess reserve are unimportant. A reduction in the level of real excess reserves will reduce seigniorage by the reduction in real excess reserves times g_E, and an increase in the level of real deposits will increase seigniorage by the increase times kg_D. This implies that the higher the reserve requirement and the growth rate of deposits, the more likely it is that seigniorage will increase. Whether g_D is higher than g_E for any economy is an empirical question. If they are roughly the same, then seigniorage will fall when banks reduce their excess reserves portfolio in favor of loan portfolios. This reflects the fact that real cash demand by the banks falls.

As mentioned earlier, if liberalization increases banks' profits and banks increase deposit rates as a result, or if deposit rates are increased by the government during liberalization, which is typically the case where governments control the deposit rates as well, as is the case in Ghana, then there will be additional effects. Thus, the demand for money by the economy will reduce further, and provided the growth rate of real household money demand is roughly the same as the growth rate of deposits, the seigniorage consequences will be adverse.

To solve for the seigniorage maximizing rate of inflation, we set equation (2.13) equal to zero and solve for the inflation rate under the assumption that the demand functions are homogenous of degree one in prices and that the long-run elasticities are constant. This gives (2.18):

$$\pi^* = \frac{-1}{\frac{\partial \log \overline{M}}{\partial \pi}} - \frac{1}{\frac{\partial \overline{M}}{\pi}}\Bigg[\left(\eta_{Hr}g_r + \eta_{Hy}g_y\right)\frac{\partial \overline{H}}{\partial \pi}$$

$$+ k\left(\eta_{Dr}g_r + \eta_{D\sigma}g_\sigma + \eta_{D\tau}g_\tau + \eta_{Di_o}g_{i_o}\right)\frac{\partial \overline{D}}{\partial \pi}$$

$$+ \left(\eta_{Er}g_r + \eta_{E\sigma}g_\sigma + \eta_{E\tau}g_\tau + \eta_{Ei_o}g_{i_o}\right)\frac{\partial \overline{E}}{\partial \pi}\Bigg]. \tag{2.18}$$

Equation (2.18) thus gives the inflation rate that maximizes government seigniorage. If we ignore the banking sector, then (2.18) is reduced to (2.19):

$$\pi^* = -\frac{1}{\partial \log H/\partial \pi} - \left[\eta_{Hr}g_r + \eta_{Hy}g_y\right]. \tag{2.19}$$

This result was also obtained by Adam, Ndulu, and Sowa (1996, eq. (7)) if we incorporate the black-market exchange rate as an argument in the households' demand for money function. Under these restrictions, as in their case, the Cagan unit-elasticity result can be obtained by setting $g_y = g_r = 0$. Thus, in this case the revenue-maximizing rate of inflation is the inverse of the mode of inflation elasticity of demand.

The effects of the proportion of preferential loans and preferential interest rates on the seigniorge maximizing rate of inflation can be examined by studying equation (2.20), which ignores all other influences on the seigniorage maximizing rate of inflation:

$$\pi^* = \frac{-1}{\frac{\partial \overline{M}}{\partial \pi}}\left[k\left(\eta_{D\sigma}g_\sigma + \eta_{D\tau}g_\tau\right)\frac{\partial \overline{D}}{\partial \pi} + \left(\eta_{E\sigma}g_\sigma + \eta_{E\tau}g_\tau\right)\frac{\partial \overline{E}}{\partial \pi}\right]. \tag{2.20}$$

Since changes in these repressive instruments have no implications for nonbanks' demand for cash, the result will be a change in the banks' cash-reserve portfolios. In particular, relaxation of these instruments will increase profits of intermediation, and this will lead banks to reduce their excess reserves in favor of required reserves. That is, it is reasonable to assume that the elasticities of demand for deposits and excess reserves with respect to these repressive instruments are equal in absolute terms. Under this assumption equation (2.20) can be written as (2.21):

$$\pi^* = \frac{-1}{\frac{\partial \overline{M}}{\partial \pi}}\left[\left(\eta_{D\sigma}g_\sigma + \eta_{D\tau}g_\tau\right)\left(k\frac{\partial \overline{D}}{\partial \pi} - \frac{\partial \overline{E}}{\partial \pi}\right)\right]. \tag{2.21}$$

Equation (2.21) suggests that the effect of deregulating the financial sector on the seigniorage maximizing inflation rate depends on the sensitivities of real deposit and real excess reserve to changes in the rate of inflation as well as the required reserve ratio. If the sensitivities are equal, then the seigniorage maximizing rate of inflation will increase with relaxation in financial repression. This is in tune with the effect of changes that reduce the money demand in the economy.[7]

Since data on preferential interest rates and preferential loans are difficult to obtain, it will be interesting to examine the seigniorage maximizing rate of inflation without the effects of these instruments. Ignoring these instruments gives (2.22):

$$\pi^* = \frac{-1}{\frac{\partial \log \overline{M}}{\partial \pi}} - \frac{-1}{\frac{\partial \overline{M}}{\partial \pi}}\left[\left(\eta_{Hr}g_r + \eta_{Hy}g_y\right)\frac{\partial \overline{H}}{\partial \pi} + k\eta_{Dr}g_r\frac{\partial \overline{D}}{\partial \pi} + \eta_{Er}g_r\frac{\partial \overline{E}}{\partial \pi}\right]. \tag{2.22}$$

In this case, one can consider the effect of liberalization, which involves deregulation of the interest rate on the seigniorage maximizing inflation rate. Interest-rate deregulation can be captured by an increase in the growth rate of interest (g_r). This will describe liberalization processes in which interest rates are adjusted upward gradually. In analyses where the banking sector is ignored (for example, Friedman, 1971; Adam, Ndulu, and Sowa, 1996), this will have the effect of reducing the base of seigniorage by reducing households' demand for money. Where only the banking-sector demand for required reserves is considered (for example, Siegel, 1981), the reduction in money demand is mitigated by an increase in reserve requirement. The higher the reserve ratio, the lesser will be the reduction in money demand due to increases in the interest rate. In our model, excess reserves will also fall when interest rates are increased, and like the reduction in money demand only part of the reduction will be held as required reserve. This will result in a reduction in the base money demand compared with where only household money demand and required reserves are considered. It is, however, not certain whether the base money demand will fall more than where only household money demand is modeled. This is because one has to weigh the fall in excess reserves against the increase in required reserves due to both banks' portfolio adjustment and households' portfolio adjustment.

Estimation

Although we are not interested in the short-run demand for money function, we employ a cointegration technique to determine the statistical validity of the long-run demand for money function. This technique specifies lag structures that are consistent with the long-run properties of the data, and it also reduces the problems associated with dynamic models where the variables involved are integrated of degrees greater than zero. These variables, besides the multicollinearity problems they may present, can result in an apparently satisfactory demand function owing to the trending behavior of the arguments when in reality there may be little economic relationship between them. To use this technique it is necessary to test the order of integration of our variables, for if the order of integration of the variables is different, then a linear combination of them cannot produce a stationary error series. Given that most economic applications actually involved cases where the variables are integrated of order one 1(1), it will be useful to investigate the first order of our variables. We do this by examining the cointegrating regression Durbin Watson (CIDW)[8] and the Dickey-Fuller (DF)[9] statistics for the relevant variables which are reported in Table 2.3. Y is real income measured in 1970 prices, R is the Central Bank interest rate, and π is the rate of inflation.

Sargan and Bhargara (1983) suggest the use of 95 percent critical level values of 0.386 and –3.37 for CIWD and DF statistics, respectively. The results show that we cannot reject *Ho*: that the variables are integrated of order one. Adopting the Engle and Granger's (1987) two-stage procedure, we first estimate the static OLS regression to obtain a consistent estimate of the cointegrating vector:

$$\begin{aligned} H_t &= -7.5709 + 1.2975Y_t - 0.1578\pi_t - 0.0395R_t \\ &\quad (-2.518) \quad (1.964) \quad (-0.8644) \quad (-3.171) \\ R^2 &= 0.3805 \quad DW = 1.1227 \quad DF = -3.13 \quad ADF = -2.756 \end{aligned} \tag{2.23}$$

(t-values in parenthesis).

Before we comment on the statistics from (2.23) for the estimation technique, we would first discuss it as the estimate of the long-run demand for cash by the nonbank sector. The equation shows that the income elasticity is correctly signed and is significant at a 5 percent level of test. The long-run estimate of the income elasticity at 1.295 indicates diseconomies of

Table 2.3. Unit root test for relevant variables.

Variables	ΔY	ΔR	$\Delta\pi$	ΔH	ΔD	ΔER
CIDW	1.454	2.9564	3.0986	1.0939	2.0964	2.7385
DF	–3.973	–8.928	–9.779	–3.008	–5.636	–8.274

scale in money demand by the nonbank sector. However, the situation is not that clear-cut if one considers the low degree of monetization of the country at the initial periods of the study. Money demand can increase simply by people substituting away from other forms of money assets (such as cowries) into cash as a medium of exchange, and as barter trading gives way to cash transactions. As noted by Bordes and Jonung (1981), ignoring the widening of the proportion of national income going through the market sector is likely to result in permanent income elasticity greater that unity.

The inflation coefficient is negative but is insignificant at 10 percent. This is probably a reflection of the fact that there are very few substitutes to money due to the underdeveloped nature of the financial sector. In view of this, households are unable to change their money holdings to a large degree in response to inflation. It is, in fact, this inability of households to adjust their cash holdings to changes in inflation that the governments of many developing countries exploit to extract seigniorage.

The interest elasticity is negative and significant, but its magnitude is rather small. This small elasticity of .035 could be due to the peculiar characteristics of the Ghanian economy. Interest rates have been tightly controlled most of the time, and this discourages the acceptance of deposits by banks. According to Chhibber and Shafik (1990), even with the more liberal regime at that time (financial liberalization was well underway) there was still evidence that the financial system was unwilling to accept deposits. Thus an increase in interest rates may not lead to a reduction in money demand by much because financial institutions are unwilling to accept deposits. Second, the Ghanian financial sector is characterized by a large informal sector. For example, Aryeetey and Gockel (1989) contended that the proportion of urban informal saving is more than 60 percent. Since interest rates in this informal market are substantially above the formal rates, the formal rates are redundant in the saving decision of many of the economic agents.

ADF is the augmented Dickey-Fuller statistic with a critical value of –2.84 at a 90 percent level of test. The DF critical value at 10 percent is 3.03. The CIDW statistic shows that a linear combination of the variables are integrated of order one. However, the DF statistic fails to support this suggestion at 5 percent level of test but not at 10 percent (10 percent critical value is 3.03). The ADF statistic fails at 10 percent. The failure of the ADF test is not strong enough to make the estimation technique inappropriate. This is particular true since there is no optimal theory for these tests and they are to be used as rough guides in applied work (see Engle and Granger, 1987). Given the fairly satisfactory performance of the tests, Engle and

Granger (1987) argued that the resulting cointegrating regression is a valid long-run solution where the coefficient estimates are superconsistent estimates of the long-run multipliers. Thus the use of equation (2.23) as a long-run solution is econometrically valid and implies the existence of an error correction[10] reparameterization.

The estimated long-run demand for money has various implications for the revenue-maximizing rate of inflation. If we assume a unit price elasticity of money demand, growth of real income will lower the revenue maximizing inflation rate (Friedman, 1971). He argued that this is true because seigniorage that accrues due to increases in incomes reduces monotonically as inflation increases. On the other hand, an increase in the rate of interest will decrease real money demand and increase the revenue-maximizing inflation rate. The implications of these for the seigniorage-maximizing rate of inflation is, therefore, unclear during financial reforms which result in an increase the real growth rate and the interest rate. Table 2.4 shows the estimates of the seigniorage-maximizing rate of inflation for the case of Ghana for the period before and after the reforms using equation (2.19) (that is, ignoring the banking sector).

The estimate of the seigniorage-maximizing rate of inflation is higher for the postreform period than for the prereform period. Both the real growth rate of GDP and the growth rate of interest went up during the reform period. Thus, while increases in the growth rate of real GDP increased the seigniorage-maximizing rate of inflation, it was decreased by the increase in the growth rate of interest. The increase in the seigniorage-maximizing rate of inflation due to the increase in the growth rate of interest dominated and hence the increase. This implies an overall reduction in the real money demand. In fact, the estimates suggest that real money balances increased by 5.99 percent per year due to the increase in real growth rate, while it declined by 8.3 percent per annum due to the increase in the interest rate. Following the argument that factors that increase or decrease real money demand will decrease or increase the seigniorage-maximizing rate of inflation but increase or decrease seigniorage, these estimates imply that the

Table 2.4. Comparison of actual and seigniorage maximizing inflation rate (SMIR).

Period	g_y	g_r	*RMIR*	*Actual*	*Deviation*
1970–1982	0.2%	7.1%	31.2%	49%	(17.8%)
1983–1993	4.5%	9.2%	34.3%	26%	8.3%

maximum seigniorage has declined during the reforms. The channel through which seigniorage declines here is different from the one identified by Adam, Ndulu, and Sowa (1996). They argued that short-run seigniorage will decline during liberalization due to decreased cost of adjustment. Here, the decrease in seigniorage is due to the increase in interest rate, which reduced money demand more than it was increased by the increase in growth rate.

It turns out that the estimates of the seigniorage-maximizing rate of inflation for Ghana, using equation (2.20), which incorporates the banking sector, produced implausible results (estimated equations not reported here). The estimate for the period before the reform was 268 percent and after the reforms was 302 percent. Even though these estimates are implausible, one important result from them is that the seigniorage-maximizing rate of inflation increased during the reform period. This result is consistent with the results of the estimates without the banking sector. Thus, the inclusion of the banking sector does not seem to change the basic result that liberalization has reduced the maximum seigniorage that the government can extract.

Another lesson from the estimates with the banking sector is that the seigniorage-maximizing rate of inflation is higher than without the banking sector. This implies that the reduction in the money demand is more than without the banking sector and hence that the maximum seigniorage is lower than without the banking sector. One can, therefore, argue that although the inclusion of the banking sector does not change the qualitative impact of liberalization on seigniorage, it does increase the seigniorage-maximizing rate of inflation both for the pre- and postreform periods. It probably also changes the quantitative impact of liberalization on seigniorage.

It is difficult to pinpoint the reasons for the implausible estimates. We, however, suspect that this has to do with the estimates of the sensitivities of real household money demand and real deposits to the rate of inflation.[11] In view of these implausible estimates, it is difficult to analyze the effect of the inclusion of the banking sector. There are various reasons one can advance for the implausible estimates of the sensitivities of deposit to its arguments. One reason is that the government is the major owner of most of the banks and hence that most bank managers are bureaucrats responding to political pressures rather than focusing on proper banking business with the view to maximizing profits.[12] In addition, the financial-sector regulation—that is, the imposition of credit ceilings and credit floors for the agriculture sector as well as interest-rate controls—resulted in little incentive for bank managers to compete for borrowers or depositors, which limits financial intermediation. These characteristics of the financial sector are likely to make deposits not respond to factors that determine it in the way theory suggests. Another reason, from the statistical point of view, is that there could be variable omission biases in the estimates. As mentioned earlier, various instruments were used to control the financial sector, and to the extent that these instruments influence the banking sector in a significant way, their omission can introduce serious biases in the estimates.

Conclusion

This chapter demonstrates that the banking-sector cash demand, in terms of reserve holdings, can be very important in the studies of seigniorage, especially in developing countries where cash-reserve holdings are relatively high. In particular, we argued that cash-reserve holdings of the banking sector are an important base on which seigniorage is extracted and hence must be included in analyzing the effect of financial deregulation on seigniorage. Analytically, we showed that not only do the banking-sector cash-reserve holdings matter but also that the type of reserves considered in the modeling matters. If only required reserves are considered, then interest-rate deregulation will reduce seigniorage by less compared to modeling only the demand for cash by households. We also pointed out that if, in addition, excess reserves are considered, then the demand for real balances in response to interest-rate liberalization will be less than in the scenario where only required reserves are considered. Whether the demand for money in this case will be less than when only household money demand is considered is, however, ambiguous.

The empirical estimates of the seigniorage consequences of financial liberalization in Ghana, without the banking sector, suggest that seigniorage decreased during the liberalization period. The estimates with the inclusion of the banking sector produced implausible results. However, they indicate that the inclusion of the banking sector does not have any qualitative implication. That is seigniorage fell during the deregulation period both with and without the banking sector. Another result was that the inclusion of the banking sector increased the seigniorage maximizing rate of inflation, which indicates a reduction in seigniorage both before and after the reforms. However, due to the implausible nature of the results, one cannot make firm conclusions on this. We suggested a number of possible reasons why these results are implausible. This will be an area of further research, particularly in analyzing whether the inclusion of the banking sector will mean stronger seigniorage implications or not. We are tempted by our results to say that there will be some quantitative implication. In particular, we believe that seigniorage will fall by more with the inclusion of the banking sector and that estimates without the banking sector will be underestimating the fall in seigniorage during the reforms in Ghana as, for example, in Adam, Ndulu, and Sowa (1996).

Notes

1. In Cukierman, Edwards, and Tabellini (1992), Ghana's average seigniorage as a percentage of the government's revenue was 28 percent for the period 1970 to 1982. This was the highest in a survey of seventy-nine countries for which data were available.

2. The domestic financial sectors are usually very thin, and hence the governments do not have the financial instruments to raise money. Since our focus is on printing money to finance deficits, we consider government deficits as government spending minus tax and net borrowings.

3. In Adam, Ndulu, and Sowa (1996) the effect of the financial-sector adjustment on the banks holdings of cash was ignored for simplicity.

4. See Drazen (1985) for the derivation of these special cases.

5. Increase in controlled lending rates will allow banks to increase the rates they offer on deposits, which will increase the demand for deposits (see Kapur, 1992). Alternatively, as in the case of Ghana, the government sets both the lending and the deposit rates, and during liberalization the government adjusts both rates upward. It should be noted that even if both rates are increased by the same proportion, the bank's profit rate per unit of loans will increase.

6. These rates can fall as bank efficiencies increase, and the problems of moral hazard and adverse selections are reduced. One of the objectives of financial liberalization is to make banking more efficient by enabling them to take decisions based purely on profit motives, and hence one will expect a fall in both rates with financial liberalization. This issue, however, is not taken up here.

7. Friedman (1971) argued that an increase in income will result in an increase in demand for money, and this lowers the seigniorage maximizing rate of inflation. The result here is just the reverse of this.

8. Unit root in the residual of a regression equation implies that the first-order autocorrelation coefficient is unity. Given this we expect the Durbin Watson statistic given as $2(1-\rho)$ to equal zero. Thus, in a regression of the first difference any variable thought to be $I(1)$, the significance of the DW statistic away from zero is a simple test for stationarity in the error series.

9. The Dickey-Fuller test for stationarity is based on the following regression:

$$\Delta u_t = \alpha + \lambda u_{t-1} + \left[\phi_i \sum \Delta u_{t-i}\right] + \varepsilon_t ,$$

where u_t denote the residuals from a linear regression of the variables thought to be cointegrated. The t-ratio of the coefficient of u_{t-1} provides the relevant statistic, and it has a pseudo t-distribution. Sargan and Bhargava (1983) have tabulated critical values where the null of stationarity is accepted if the test statistic is negative and significantly different from zero. The extended version (thus including the bracketed term) is the Augmented Dickey-Fuller statistic.

10. The error-correction mechanism was used in an extended sense in that it was proxied by the stationary residuals of the cointegrating regression. However, we will explain it by using a restricted version developed by Henry and Mizon, where an autoregressive relation such as

$$\Delta M_t = \alpha + \phi M_{t-1} + \delta Y_t + \sigma Y_{t-1} + \varepsilon_t$$

can be written under the assumption of a long-run proportionality between money and income as

$$\Delta M_t = \alpha + \delta \Delta Y_t + \varphi\left(M_{t-1} - Y_{t-1}\right) + \varepsilon_t.$$

The underlying assumption of this last equation that $\ln M_t = \ln K + \ln Y_t$ implies the term $(M_{t-1} - Y_{t-1})$ is an error-correction mechanism that captures the effect on ΔM_t of discrepancies between one-period lagged money balances and $k + Y_{t+1}$. Such discrepancies can arise from errors in individuals past decisions and the ECM reflects attempts to correct it. This provides a rough economic interpretation of the error-correction term used in the text.

11. In theory, $\overline{M} = \overline{H} + k\overline{D} + \overline{E}$, and hence $\frac{\partial \overline{M}}{\partial \pi} = \frac{\partial \overline{H}}{\partial \pi} + k\frac{\partial \overline{D}}{\partial \pi} + \frac{\partial \overline{E}}{\partial \pi}$. However, the estimates of these produced $-1.211 < -1.112 - 2.54 - 0.262$.

12. The Ghana government owned 100 percent of the shares of the seven of the eleven primary and secondary banks in Ghana in 1987. Of the remaining four it owned about 37 percent of the shares (Younger, 1991, Table 1).

References

Adam, C., B. Ndulu, and N. Sowa. (1996). "Efficiency Gains Versus Revenue Losses Liberalization and Seigniorage Revenue in Kenya, Ghana, and Tanzania." *Journal Development Studies*, Vol. 32(4): 531–533.

Aryeetey, E., and F.A. Gockel. (1989). *Mobilizing Domestic Resources for Capital Formation: Role of Informal Financial Markets in Ghana.* African Economic Research Consortium Working Paper.

Asem, E. (1996). "Financial Liberalization and Seigniorage." Ph.D. thesis in progress, University of Alberta.

Bailey, M.J. (1956). "The Welfare Cost of Inflationary Finance." *Journal of Political Economy* 64: 93–110.

Blanchard, O.J., and S. Fischer. (1990). *Lectures on Macroeconomics*. Cambridge, MA: MIT Press.

Bordes, M.J., and L. Jonung. (1987). *The Long-Run Behaviour of the Velocity of Circulation: The International Evidence.* Cambridge: Cambridge University Press.

Buiter, W. (1990). *Principles of Financial and Budgetary Policy*. Cambridge, MA: MIT Press.

Cagan, P. (1956). "The Monetary Dynamics of Hyperinflation." In Milton Friedman (ed.), *Studies in Quantity Theory of Money*. Chicago: University of Chicago.

Chhibber, A., and N. Shafik. (1990). *Exchange Reform, Parallel Markets, and Inflation in Africa: The Case of Ghana.* Policy, Research, and External Affairs Working Paper 427. Washington, DC: World Bank.

Cukierman, A., S. Edwards, and G. Tabellini. (1992). "Seigniorage and Political Instability." *American Economic Review* 82(3): 537–555.

Dornbusch, R., and S. Fischer. (1986). "Stopping Hyperinflation Past and Present." *Weltwirtschaftliches Archiv* 122: 1–47.

Drazen, A. (1985). "A General Measure of Inflation Tax Revenues." *Economics Letters* 17: 327–330.

Engle, R.F., and W.J. Granger. (1987). "Co-integration and Error Correction: Representation, Estimation, and Testing." *Econometrica* 55(2); 251–276.

Espinosa-Vega, M.A. (1995). "Multiple Reserve Requirements." *Journal of Money, Credit, and Banking* 27(3): 762–776.

Friedman, M. (1971). "Discussion of the Inflationary Gap." In Milton Friedman (ed.), *Essays in Positive Economics*. Chicago: University of Chicago.

Fry, M.J. (1988). *Money, Interest, and Banking in Economic Development*. Baltimore, MD: John Hopkins University Press.

Kapur, B.K. (1992). "Formal and Informal Financial Markets, and the Neo-Structuralist Critique of the Financial Liberalization Strategy in Less Developed Countries." *Journal of Development Economics* 38: 63–77.

Marty, A. (1967). "Growth and the Welfare Cost of Inflationary Finance." *Journal of Political Economy* 75: 71–76.

Phelps, E.S. (1971). "Inflation in a Theory of Public Finance." *Swedish Economic Journal* 75: 67–82.

Sargan, J.D., and A. Bhargava. (1983). "Testing Residuals from Least Squares Regression for Being Generated by the Guassian Random Walk." *Econometrica* 51: 153–174.

Siegel, J. (1981). "Inflation, Bank Profits, and Government Seigniorage." *American Economic Review* 71: 352–355.

van Wijnberger, S. (1989). "External Debt, Inflation, and the Public Sector: Towards Fiscal Policy for Sustainable Growth." *World Bank Economic Review* 3: 297–320.

Younger, S. (1991). *Monetary Management in Ghana*. Cornell Food and Nutrition Policy Program Working Paper No. 8.

II THE ASIAN AND LATIN AMERICAN EXPERIENCE

3 FINANCIAL DEREGULATION IN AUSTRALIA

A Success Story?

Peter J. Drake

The Regulated Finance Market

Australia emerged from World War II with a very narrow, rigid, and highly regulated financial market. It consisted institutionally of small numbers of banks, life insurance firms, housing finance organizations, and companies devoted to pastoral/agricultural finance, marketing, and management. Direct equity finance was available to public corporations, and liquidity to their shareholders, via the stock exchanges located in the various state capital cities and some provincial towns. Among, and indeed within, these several compartments of the finance market, competition was restrained by government regulation or private monopolistic practices. In external financial relations, Australia was subject to an officially determined exchange rate (fixed with occasional adjustment until the late 1970s; thereafter a "managed" variable until 1983) and to restrictions on the movement of foreign capital, and its earnings, to and from this country. The banking sector was the largest and dominant component of the finance market. It monopolized intermediation, domestic payments, and foreign-exchange transactions.

While the dominance of the banking sector and the rigidity with which bank business was conducted had prominent roots in wartime financial controls and postwar banking legislation, Australia had from much earlier times been susceptible to social thinking that government should manage the financial system in the interests of the nation. This thinking goes back to the early twentieth century and found expression in the formation of the Commonwealth Bank as "a people's bank" in 1911 and later in the 1936 Royal Commission on Banking. The interventionist view, of course, was quite compatible with intellectual opinion immediately after the war and particularly with belief in the duty of government to attempt macroeconomic management via monetary and fiscal policies. Australia was one of the earliest countries to embrace Keynes's ideas and translate them into practice.

Given the dominance of the banks, monetary controls were applied, by the government's central bank, to the deposit and loan interest rates offered and charged by the banks; to the terms for which banks could offer deposit interest (notably *not* on current accounts); to the range and proportions of assets that the banks could hold; and to the growth rate of banks' assets and liabilities. In return, the existing banks were protected by very high entry walls, which specifically excluded foreign competitors. This, of course, created the conditions for cartel behavior. In retail banking, restrictive trade practices prevailed, with uniform conditions and terms of trade. There was little variety in customer offerings, with the borrowing rates identical across all forms of deposits. No interest was offered on current (checking) accounts, account-keeping charges were uniform, and so forth. Most banks were represented throughout Australia in an extensive branch system, with many branches presumably operating unprofitably. Banks engaged in "full line forcing" to obtain and retain custom (for example, the granting of a mortgage loan would be conditional on the borrower's willingness to shift all the family banking business to the lending bank).

A more or less stable equilibrium prevailed in this system so long as the existing banks retained monopoly of the check payment mechanism, were not threatened as financial intermediaries and, of course, were secure from new banks. The first line has held fast, but the second was breached in the 1950s and eroded subsequently while the third, as we shall see, gave way in the 1980s.

Altogether, Australia exhibited symptoms of financial repression with a stagnant banking sector, a low—and at times even declining—ratio of financial assets to GDP, and a significant volume of finance flowing directly from lenders to borrowers (particularly government borrowers) rather than being intermediated. At the end of World War II, Australia's government debt was greater than the current value of GDP. The substantial volume of government securities not only inhibited the issue of private paper but limited the scope for interest-rate flexibility because of a desire to "keep faith" with the holders of government debt: any rise in interest rates would, of course, have diminished the capital value of outstanding government securities. Moreover, in the early postwar years the authorities believed in the virtue of low interest rates for economic development and wished to be able to sell further government securities to fund public infrastructure. Grenville (1991, p. 7), in a good account of these conditions, observes that "an important theme in the deregulatory story is the gradual removal of this constraint which government funding placed on the financial sector."

The Impetus for Change

As the Australian economy grew and diversified in the postwar period, and nonbank financial intermediaries emerged, the central bank's leverage on the economy—exercised through direct controls on the banks—began to weaken. As uncontrolled alternatives to bank finance became more available, prominent, and popular, the central bank had to press harder and more often on the controlled banks in order to run an anti-inflation monetary policy. "But the more [the banking sector] was squeezed, the smaller it would become, and the narrower would be the transmission channels of monetary policy. Secondly, there was an 'internal dynamic' to the deregulatory process. As one control on the banks was lifted, this put more pressure on the remaining controls" (Grenville, 1991, p. 31).

There was a need to open up general transmission channels for monetary policy. Fortunately, the time was ripe from the 1970s to do this. The intellectual pendulum had swung away from state ownership and intrusion in economic activity, from controls, and even from Keynesian thought and toward the free-market philosophy. Central banks around the world, and Australia was no exception, retreated from bank activity controls in favor of more generalized influences on money supply aggregates and market interest rates.

In the Australian case, by the late 1960s the central bank was employing open-market operations as its primary tool but still using bank controls in a supplementary way. The general level of interest rates became the main focus of monetary policy. Acceptance of variability of interest rates, and capital values, was assisted by the fact that outstanding government debt had by 1970 fallen to around 30 percent of GDP: the sensitivities of bond holders were no longer so important. During the 1970s, qualitative and quantitative lending controls were eased, the Statutory Reserve Deposit ratio was reduced, banks were permitted to offer market interest rates on several forms of deposits, and banks were given a greater measure of freedom to conduct foreign-exchange transactions. In the early 1980s bank constraints were eased further.

At the end of 1983, the Australian dollar was floated in a free market for foreign exchange. During 1985 and 1986, foreign banks were permitted to undertake general banking business in Australia, and restrictions on bank assets, liabilities, and interest rates were largely eliminated. In the securities markets, the hitherto closed-shop and uniform fixed commissions of the stockbrokers were swept away between 1983 and 1986. The former compartmental divisions in the Australian finance market have since disappeared or shrunk, and a diversity of financial enterprises compete ruthlessly for retail, wholesale, and international business. A far greater variety of services and conditions is offered to clients by the banks and their numerous competitors.

It is best to proceed with a few words about the foreign-exchange market, since the floating of the dollar and the opening up of Australia to international capital movements, which impinge substantially on the banks, other intermediaries, and the securities markets, have been major influences in the rapid and extensive transformation of the whole Australian finance market.

The Foreign Exchanges

Prior to deregulation, not only were spot rates of exchange governed by the monetary authorities, but forward exchange cover was very restricted. The official forward cover market was confined to forward delivery of foreign currency to cover exposures arising from trade in goods and services. Capital account transactions could not be covered officially, trade cover had to be taken within seven days of the exposure being incurred and could not normally be reversed, and forward margins in the official cover market were set by the Reserve Bank. These inflexibilities, which especially inhibited international investment flows, gave rise to a hedge market, pioneered by merchant banks ("money-market corporations," in official jargon). The merchant banks began as brokers between clients requiring forward-exchange facilities that the official market could not provide and soon moved into dealing forward as principals. The merchant banks were restricted to hedge operations; they were precluded from providing deliverable forward, let alone spot, currency, which were preserves of banks authorized by the Reserve Bank to deal in foreign exchange. The total forward-exchange book of the trading and merchant banks rose from $16 billion in 1981 to $39 billion by the end of 1983, with the share taken by the merchant bank hedge market rising from 50 percent to 75 percent (Hopkinson, 1984, p. 8).

The market is now larger and stronger in several respects, and the number of participants has grown substantially. Whereas in 1981 there were only about ten dealers, at the end of 1986 there were eighty-three financial institutions authorized by the Reserve Bank to undertake a full range of foreign-exchange dealing transactions; by April 1996, the number had declined to seventy-two. The list not only obviously includes all banks (old and new, local and foreign) but also money-market corporations (merchant banks) of both Australian and overseas origin (Reserve Bank of Australia, 1987, p. 27). Foreign buyers and sellers have also been attracted to the Australian market, to take advantage of competitive prices (compared with other international currency markets) and of the eastern Australian (Sydney and Melbourne) time zone (which provides business hours when Singapore, Hong Kong, and Tokyo are closed). Bank dealings in foreign currency, formerly conducted in overseas centers, have to a great extent returned home.

The virtually complete freedom to move money into or out of Australia, through some eighty authorized dealers in foreign exchange, at rates of exchange determined by market supply and demand, has led, not surprisingly, to ebbs and flows of foreign-exchange transactions and a fluctuating exchange rate. The Reserve Bank may still seek to influence the exchange rate by altering the volume of funds flowing across exchanges, but in practice the Bank's participation in the market declined steadily during the 1980s and dramatically in the early 1990s, such that by 1993 its transactions were infrequent and in 1994 it made none. The Bank no longer regulates the exchanges.

The growth of the foreign-exchange market, as indicated by turnover, has been dramatic: between March 1985 and September 1986 the turnover (all currencies) in spot exchange leapt from a daily average of less than $5 billion to well over $15 billion; daily turnover in currency swaps went from about $2.5 billion to over $10 billion; and the volume of forward exchange deals about trebled to approach $4 billion daily. In 1994 to 1995, these magnitudes were $21.463 billion, $26.527 billion and $1.882 billion, respectively. There is further a market in foreign-exchange options with an average daily turnover of $50,665 billion in 1994 to 1995 (Reserve Bank of Australia, various issues).

All told, competition in foreign-exchange markets has raised volumes, reduced margins between buying and selling prices, and generated a rapid expansion of employment and improvement in skills. The growth in size and complexity of the foreign-exchange markets has been greatly propelled by rapid and cheap improvements in international communication and electronic data processing. Without these technological advances, the current volume and intricacy of foreign-exchange transactions could not be carried out within the constraints of time and profitability. Moreover, the wide and cheap availability of computerized data processing enables many more participants to monitor and analyze transactions in the markets. "As communications, analysis and data processing technologies converge, markets will inevitably reflect underlying flows more closely, and they are likely to price risks more accurately. This will lead to deeper and more stable markets" (Hopkinson, 1984, p. 11).

Banks and Near-Banks

This is not the place for a comprehensive review of the many developments that have occurred among banks and near-banks in Australia. A vast literature already exists, springing largely from the deliberations of the Campbell Committee of Inquiry (Australian Financial System Inquiry, 1982) and the subsequent deregulatory measures initiated by government. Here we seek merely to pinpoint the major observable consequences of the dismantling of controls in the banking sector.

Throughout the first forty postwar years, the licensed banks in Australia were local enterprises, limited in number. For most of the period, there were six or seven "major trading banks" and a like number of savings banks (some of which were under the same roof with a trading bank), together with a handful of local or regional banks that had no network of branch offices. All labored under various central bank controls on asset structure, volume and direction of new lending, deposit categories, and the interest rates paid to depositors and charged to borrowers.

Trading banks in Australia were subjected to the dual reserve requirements of a statutory reserve deposit ratio (SRD) and a liquid assets and government securities ratio (LGS), both calculated in relation to deposit liabilities and determined by the Reserve Bank of Australia (the central bank). The former ratio was a legal imposition; the latter, a convention that the banks had agreed to observe. Both ratios were variable at the discretion of the Reserve Bank. The statutory reserve deposit ratio was varied considerably (in the range 3.0 to 9.4 percent of deposit liabilities) during the 1970s, but the LGS ratio had remained at 18 percent of deposit liabilities since 1962, except for the period February 1976 to March 1977 when it was 23 percent. Since the rate of interest payable to the banks on their statutory reserve deposits in the Reserve Bank was always very low and the rate of return of LGS assets "tight" in relation to the interest and administrative costs of collecting deposits, the reserve requirement controls handicapped the profitability and competitiveness of the banks. (It may be argued, however, that the prudential aspects of these requirements in underpinning the safety of bank deposits as a component of the money supply was socially desirable and that the banks enjoyed a corresponding advantage in the marketplace for funds by appearing to have an official guarantee of their deposits.)

The banks were also substantially restricted by interest controls on both sides of their ledgers: ceilings on the rates of interest they could offer on fixed deposits (as well as limitations on the maturity terms of such fixed deposits), proscription from paying interest on current accounts, and ceilings on the rates of interest chargeable on various categories of loans and advances to customers. Special controls were applied to the savings banks (most of which functioned as distinct divisions of the major banks). the chief constraint being official regulation of the maximum interest rate chargeable on housing loans.

The banks were further subjected to central bank direction from time to time in the form of quantitative ceilings on the volumes of certain categories of lending, qualitative controls on the directions of bank lending, and general moral suasion. Finally, the banking sector was restricted in size and degree of competition by the legal device of the licensing of banks. With hindsight, it is surprising how tamely, and for so long, heavy central bank direction was accepted by the banks. Presumably the climate of the times in the aftermath of the 1930s Depression and World War II disposed society generally to be compliant with official regulation that was consistent with the "cheap money" policy, stemming from Keynesian ideas, which prevailed in Australia until the 1970s. In that climate, too, the banks may have perceived the countervailing benefit of protection from foreign competition in the Australian market.

The containment of the licensed banks had led first to the development of a substantial group of finance companies, largely subsidiary enterprises of the banks, that concentrated on providing the consumer credit from which banks were debarred. Later merchant banks—predominantly of foreign origin—sprang up to compete against the banks in the lucrative field of large-scale corporate lending, especially to finance international trade and investment. Finally, permanent building societies and, to a lesser extent, credit unions took advantage of the restraints imposed especially on the savings bank departments of the major banks and moved, aggressively and successfully, into the business of deposit repository of so-called small savings from wages and salaries. In turn, the merchant banks promoted cash management trusts, which also took deposits away from the savings banks.

The regulatory pattern that restrained the major banks also conferred a degree of economic rent by protecting them from competition within their designated activities. As deregulation, and so overt competition, became imminent, the banks' strategic perception was that they would have to regroup as stronger units to withstand the expected competition from the entry of large international banks—hence the 1981 mergers of the Bank of New South Wales with the Commercial Bank of Australia to form Westpac Banking Corporation, and of the National Bank of Australia with the Commercial Banking Company of Sydney to form the National Australia Bank. The effect of these mergers was to reduce to four the number of major Australian banks: Westpac Banking Corporation, National Australia Bank, Australia and New Zealand Banking Group, and the Commonwealth Bank of Australia. In addition, there were the newer local commercial banking enterprises (Macquarie Bank, Australian Bank), the various state government banks, and the remnants of the regional banks and the building societies. But the big four were overwhelmingly predominant and remain so.

The 1980s saw rapid and extensive dismantling of the official restrictions on banks. Prudential controls were rationalized by the gradual replacement of the LGS ratio convention by a prime assets ratio, set at 12 percent of each trading bank's total nonshareholder liabilities, which are invested in Australian dollar assets within Australia. The prime assets consist of notes and coin, balances with the Reserve Bank, treasury notes and other Commonwealth government securities, and loans to authorized money-market dealers secured against Commonwealth government securities. The SRD ratio was later replaced by a requirement for banks to keep with the Reserve Bank noncallable deposits (NCD) equivalent to 1 percent of their noncapital liabilities in Australia. Interest at a below-market rate is paid on these deposits. In addition, consistent with the 1988 Basle Accord among world central banks, banks in Australia are also expected to maintain a ratio of shareholder capital to risk-weighted assets of at least 8 percent. In 1995 this ratio, averaged for all banks, exceeded 12 percent (Reserve Bank of Australia, 1995, p. 40).

In December 1980 the interest-rate ceilings on fixed deposits were removed, and in March 1982 the minimum term for interest-bearing fixed deposits was reduced to fourteen days. Since August 1984 the banks have been permitted to pay interest on current accounts and, with the simultaneous removal of the fourteen-day rule, compete vigorously in the on-call wholesale market. The separate identification of savings banks and related rules were abolished. Quantitative lending guidance ceased in June 1982, and little has been heard in recent times of qualitative controls on bank lending.

Above all else, the banking sector was thrown open to vigorous competition (and prospective enlargement) by the allocation of bank licenses to foreign banks.

Table 3.1 provides a good overview of the fluctuations in market shares among banks and nonbank financial institutions in the first phase of deregulation up to 1986. Banks, which had been losing ground to the nonbank financial intermediaries since the 1960s, raised their share of assets; state banks and new banks encroached on the assets share of the major banks (although, as we shall see shortly, the major banks have lately been doing very well). The nonbank financial institutions lost their share, as the elimination of constraints on bank lending eroded the hitherto protected positions of specialist institutions. Within the nonbank sector, the declining relative shares of the finance companies and building societies were counterbalanced by the growth of money-market corporations (merchant banks).

Table 3.1. Assets of financial intermediaries June 1980 to 1986 (percentage of total).

	1980	*1983*	*1986*
Banks:			
Major	47.2%	45.3%	43.7%
State	9.2	9.5	10.0
Other	1.4	1.8	1.9
New[a]	—	—	4.5
Total	57.8%	56.6%	60.1%
Nonbanks:			
Finance companies	17.8%	16.5%	11.4%
Building societies	10.9	10.0	7.8
Money-market corporations	6.5	8.7	12.0
Other[b]	7.0	8.2	8.7
Total	42.2%	43.4%	39.9%

Source: Reserve Bank of Australia (1986), *Bulletin* (October): 15.

a Banks established since March 1985 (twenty-one).

b Includes general financiers, authorized money-market dealers, pastoral finance companies, cash management trusts, and credit cooperatives.

Large transfers of assets from merchant banks, finance companies, and other nonbanks occurred during 1985 and 1986 in the formation of the first wave of foreign banks, many of which had hitherto been operating in Australia in nonbank form. These transfers of assets from nonbanks to banks during 1985 and 1986 were reflected in the diminished market share of finance companies, but they also highlight the remarkable performance of the money-market corporations, which grew dramatically as a group, notwithstanding a big shift of assets into the bank sector by a subgroup of foreign bank affiliates.

It is not necessary to deal at length here with the complex composition and history of the institutions enveloped by the term *money-market corporations* (Reserve Bank of Australia, 1987, pp. 1–8). This group must, however, be given prominent recognition, for it would be difficult to overstate their historical importance in shaking up, from the 1960s, the hitherto compartmentalized and cosy Australian financial sector. As merchant banks, money-market dealers, bill brokers, cash management and securities trusts, and foreign-exchange dealers, their influence has been profound and the activities that they pioneered have been eagerly adopted by the major banks. Close links exist between money-market corporations and banks, and deregulation has permitted rationalization of activities between each bank and its money-market corporation subsidiary or affiliate. The figures in Table 3.1 even understate the importance of the latter insofar as assets and activities have been transferred to parent banks since 1984.

In 1985, fifteen new foreign banks were granted banking authority to operate in Australia. By 1995 Australia had thirty foreign-owned banks—fifteen as locally incorporated subsidiaries and fifteen as branches of overseas firms. These thirty banks accounted in 1995 for 12 percent of total bank assets in Australia (Reserve Bank of Australia, 1995, p. 44). The conjunction of these new entrants into the licensed banking business and the undoing of restraints hitherto binding the preexisting banks has released huge competitive energies into the banking industry in Australia.

Australian domestic banks in 1995 numbered nineteen, including the four dominant banking groups already mentioned, newer local commercial banking enterprises, various state government banks, several former building societies, and the remnants of the old regional and local banks. All told therefore, Australia had forty-nine authorized banks, domestic and foreign, by 1995.

The foreign banks admitted in 1985 began with total capital of $1.575 billion and staff of 4,000, including those in preexisting merchant banks and finance company subsidiaries. A survey of these banks conducted in late

1985 indicated that they expected to employ 8,645 people and operate 246 branches within five years, by which time they expected to have about 20 percent of the banking market (*Asian Business*, 1985, p. 3). Performance has been rather less rosy than the new banks might have expected individually. Retail banking has been profitable for only a few of the new entrants; wholesale lending to the corporate sector is the engine of profit, with eleven of the new banks drawing 40 percent or more of their profits from that source. The very keen competition has benefited customers through diversified and improved services and significant cuts in spreads (margins between borrowing and lending rates of interest). The pressure on margins was so acute as to push some banks into riskier lending and to seek a greater proportion of revenue from fees for services.

The effects of competitive spurs as seen by the new foreign banks is confirmed by the experience of the old major bank groups. Table 3.2 reveals that, during the first two years in the deregulated and competitive environment (1984 to 1986), the big four as a whole increased their assets by some 50 percent but suffered declining average annual returns on shareholders' funds in the order of 3.5 and 4.5 percentage points. Spreads contracted, causing the major banks also to seek to enlarge the fees-for-service stream of revenue (Hohne, 1984, p. 78). Nine years later (1995) three of the four major banks had largely restored the rate of return on shareholders' funds, but Westpac was still pulling out of its collapse of market share in the early 1990s.

Personal loans, including consumer lending by way of credit cards, constitute a growing proportion of bank lending; this trend has been fostered by aggressive marketing and the ready extension of credit card borrowing limits. New styles of housing loans, featuring easier terms and wider eligibility, have been introduced. Competition in this field has been intensified by the advent of new, nonbank financiers specializing in home loans.

Corporate lending and international banking, often intertwined, are areas of intense competition from the foreign banks and the money-market corporations. Corporations have become increasingly aware of their market power and glad to be wooed by bankers who, in the process, have adopted several innovative forms of assistance including off-balance-sheet items such as endorsements of corporate paper. In the hectic competition for business enterprise banking, the four major banks have done remarkably well, for two main reasons. First, the representational strength of their vast branch networks has given them a big advantage within Australia over new competitors. Second, deregulation has allowed them to expand greatly their overseas operations where, unlike many international banks, they

Table 3.2. Major banks, assets, returns employment, and productivity, 1984, 1986, and 1995.

	Group Assets ($ billion)			Average Return on Shareholders' Funds (percent)			Employment Group Total (full-time equivalent)			Productivity Indicator[a] Group Group Assets ÷ Employment		
Bank	*1984*	*1986*	*1995*[b]	*1984*	*1986*	*1995*	*1984*	*1986*	*1995*[b]	*1984*	*1986*	*1995*[b]
Westpac	40.428	60.715	105.835	19.3%	15.7%	13.4%	41,008	45,323	31,416	0.98	1.34	3.37
ANZ	35.854	56.630	112.587	17.7	13.1	17.6	36,789	39,018	39,240	0.97	1.45	2.87
NAB	27.505	42.397	147.077	17.7	14.2	17.8	22,474	23,711	45,585	1.22	1.79	3.23
Commonwealth	30.497	39.646	99.595	18.3	14.5	16.1	35,043	38,451	35,822	0.87	1.03	2.78

Source: Annual Reports. Figures refer to years ending September 30 for Westpac, ANZ, and National Australia Bank and to years ending June 30 for Commonwealth.

a Group assets (a stock variable) are here used as proxy for the immeasurable flow variable of group output or value added.

b The levels of group assets and employment in 1995 reflect not only growth but also the contributions of overseas subsidiaries, especially in the case of the National and the ANZ where, respectively, 42 percent and 40 percent of group assets were overseas.

have not been unduly handicapped by prior burdens of doubtful debts in less developed countries.

Employment fluctuations are an interesting feature of the major banks since deregulation. Table 3.2 reveals an overall rise in personnel of 11,000 between 1984 and 1986, notwithstanding a remarkable surge in worker productivity. Employment growth occurred despite conscious attempts by the major banks to take advantage of technological change by substituting cheap capital for expensive labor. Although electronic banking led to a proportionate, but probably not an absolute, reduction in paper transactions (which require human processing), the desired fall in employment levels did not occur initially because of very rapid growth of total business. Subsequently, however, all four majors have achieved significant increases in labor productivity. This is clearly evident with the Commonwealth and Westpac, which achieved staff reductions *pari passu* with asset increases, but is masked for ANZ and NAB because of their acquisitions of assets and staff overseas.

Deregulated competition has weakened the relative position of the near-banks. Building societies grew very rapidly during the 1970s (they had only 4.5 percent of total assets of financial intermediaries in 1970) but lost market share in the 1980s due to renewed competition from banks, as they began to enjoy diminished regulation, and from the new high-interest, easy-access cash management trusts that were promoted vigorously by the merchant banks.

The building societies also suffered from the general rise in interest rates and restraints on housing loan interest rates that also buffeted the old savings banks. However, the principal reason for the deceleration of building society growth seems to have been heightened competition for small savings from banks, cash management trusts, and credit unions, all aided by technological improvements that have permitted very refined funds management and the provision of finely tuned rates of interest to depositors.

Finance companies have also fallen victim to hot competition for householder deposits and, on the other side of the balance sheet, for so called retail lending to final consumers. The finance companies have responded in part by moving into wholesale intermediation for business and commerce. As already mentioned, the initiative for the development of finance companies in the early postwar years came from the then heavily regulated banks. Most finance company assets are now under the control of the major banks, with about one-quarter controlled by the foreign-owned banks.

Table 3.3, which spans a period of fifteen years, displays the long-term decline of market share of the near-banks (nonbank financial

Table 3.3. Financial system assets (percent of system).

	At June 1980	*At June 1995*
Banks	42%	47%
Nonbank financial intermediaries	32	15
Total intermediaries	74	61
Funds managers and insurers	26	39

Source: *Reserve Bank of Australia Bulletin* (1996), (April): 38.

intermediaries) and a corresponding strengthening of the position of the banks. This reflects, in part, the important feature that many former building societies, finance companies, and merchant banks have been converted into, absorbed by, or taken over by banks over the years.

The near-banks, however, are by no means finished and have time and again shown the ability to appropriate segments of an open and dynamic finance market. For example, in 1995 and 1996 the big four banks were slow to transmit falling interest rates to housing loans. The smaller banks and the near banks then competed so aggressively and successfully for home loan borrowers that the big banks were obliged to cut their home loan rates significantly in response.

Episodes such as this inevitably give rise to attempts at market reorganization. At the time of writing, there is a good deal of bid and counterbid that seems likely to result in either the amalgamation of some smaller banks or takeover of them by one of the big four.

Table 3.3 also shows a striking shift of asset share in the whole financial system from intermediaries to funds managers and insurers. While traditional life insurance business has been rather stagnant, there has in recent years been very substantial growth of private pensions and superannuation plans written by the life offices. To a substantial extent this arises from generous income tax concessions extended toward contributions to such plans by a government that is anxious to boost private savings for retirement in order to alleviate the social pensions burden. However, and perhaps inconsistently, current government policy forbids unions between any of the big four banks and the three largest insurance companies (National Mutual Life, Australian Mutual Provident, Colonial Mutual Life) in order to maintain the so-called seven separate pillars of finance. Generally, the life insurance and superannuation companies in Australia offer a range of deposit and trust investments, and also loans, in competition with the banks, but they are denied participation in the check payments system. Repeated attempts by one major life office to unite with a major bank have been overruled, and the life office has since pursued a strategy of demutualization, incorporation, and sale of 51 percent of equity to an international insurance group.

In another case, a 1995 merger between the State Bank of New South Wales and the Colonial Mutual Life Assurance Company created nominally Australia's first bank assurance institution, although the components of the consolidated group have thus far continued to function as related organizations rather than as one integrated financial institution.

It now seems a distinct possibility that, in the not-too-distant future, the wall that presently separates banks from the life insurance and superannuation sector will be completely dismantled.

Institutional change and development, the blurring of former sectional boundaries, and ebbs and flows of activity within the wide markets for money and finance that have followed the deregulation of the 1980s have in turn and—not surprisingly—led to official interventions that some describe as reregulation but are better regarded as financial supervision. To some extent the new requirements focus on consumer protection and the provision of a sufficiency of information, which one central banker styles "product regulation" (Thompson, 1996), but the main thrust of official concern has been with the stability of the financial system and the various categories of institution within it—in other words, prudential supervision. So far as banks are concerned, the relevant supervisory agency is the Reserve Bank, which pursues its prudential responsibilities through the licensing, supervision, and inspection of individual banks, through management and control of the payments system and interbank settlements, and by the *noncallable deposits* (*NCD*) mechanism described above.

Since 1992, nonbank financial intermediaries, such as building societies and credit unions, have been subject to the oversight of the Australian Financial Institutions Commission. Insurance companies and superannuation and pension funds fall under the prudential supervision of the Insurance and Superannuation Commission. No financial institution is subject to supervision by more than one authority, but coherence has been sought by the creation in 1992 of the Council of Financial Supervisors, whose member authorities are the Reserve Bank, the Australian Financial Institutions Commission, the Insurance and Superannuation Commission, and the Australian Securities Commission, whose responsibilities lie in the securities markets and stock exchange to which we now turn.

The Stock Exchange

Deregulation in the stock exchanges has been substantial and recent, owing largely to two influential official reports: the Campbell Report and the

Trade Practices Commission's (TPC) consideration of the rules of the stock exchanges (Australian Financial System Inquiry, 1982; Trade Practices Commission, 1982). Both reports extolled the prospective benefits of deregulation if applied to the restrictive *internal* rules of the stock exchanges about admission to the stockbroking industry and the fixed rates of commission charged by brokers. For many years the stockbrokers resisted such changes and fought fiercely to retain control of what they perceived to be their industry exclusively.

In seeking to retain their own restrictions on entry into stockbroking and their fixed commissions, the stock exchanges argued that

- Restricting the practice of stockbroking to natural persons was necessary in order to ensure that brokers bore unlimited personal liability for their actions, and to avoid any conflict of interest that might arise by pursuing stockbroking simultaneously with other financial functions such as banking; and
- Negotiated brokerage rates would cause, as a result of pressure from big institutional clients, diminished services and higher brokerage charges for small investors, a reduction in the number of brokering firms, and a concentration of business in Sydney and Melbourne, possibly leading to the eventual demise of the Perth, Hobart, Adelaide, and Brisbane exchanges.

The TPC was not sympathetic to these arguments and disallowed the stock-exchange rules both about participation, partnership, and broker activities and about uniform scales of brokerage incorporating a minimum base transaction fee. A short transitional period was allowed for the exchanges to implement the TPC decision, but, by late April, 1984, participation in stockbroking had been opened to financial institutions and brokerage rates had become negotiable between broker and client.

Restructuring of the ownership of broking firms quickly occurred, and lower rates of commission have been negotiated by the big institutions (superannuation and pension funds, investment trusts, and so on), which account for such a large share of stockbroker business. Each of the major banks then took a substantial share in a stockbroking firm.

Apparently paradoxically, the stock exchanges in recent years have been subjected also to rigorous *external* regulation and surveillance flowing from a series of uniform and nationwide companies and securities industry laws enacted by the Commonwealth and the states between 1979 and 1991. The origins of all this legislation, which proceeded through several stages, can be traced to parlous excesses of unregulated stock-market behavior during the mining-based share boom of the late 1960s. The self-regulatory code of the stock exchanges was then seen to be inadequate, in design and enforcement, to provide even basic protection to investors. A cautious and even distrustful public turned noticeably away from the stock market and thus diminished the availability of equity finance for Australian companies.

This led—after much publicity and inquiry—to a phase of hybrid or dual supervision and regulation of the several stock exchanges located in the capital cities of the various states. The framework of control was national, but the administration was local. There was a set of federal and state acts and related codes entrusted, in a supervisory and coordinating sense, to a National Companies and Securities Commission (NCSC). However, the registration of companies (which generated revenue) and the day-to-day administration of the acts and codes was in the hands of the several Corporate Affairs Commissions (CAC) of the individual states. The states were unwilling to yield complete control to the federal government, not merely because of the inevitable loss of administrative revenues from registration and so on but also because of differences in constitutional philosophy, commercial law, and a genuine and strong sense of local (state) community and identity (not entirely frivolously has Australia been described as six states in search of a nation). However, there came in the late 1980s a further wave of sharemarket instability and a corresponding decline in public trust such as to drive the states, willy nilly, to embrace a new national system of corporate and stock-exchange supervision.

The mineral-based share boom of the 1960s has been mentioned above. The Australian stock market has always had a significant, and above-average, component of resource stocks, which are inherently more volatile than industrial shares. This is because of worldwide fluctuations of commodity prices as the business cycle makes its swings and of random discoveries of new deposits of rare minerals. These considerations make the Australian stock markets more susceptible than most to booms and busts.

In the 1980s a worldwide boom occurred in equity shares. This is not the place to discuss the reason for the world share boom (and bust) of the 1980s, but it is helpful to remember that parts were played by lax central banks (permitting excessive growth of money supplies), the OPEC oil price crisis of the early 1980s, and volatile international capital movements (undermining national monetary autonomies). The vicissitudes of the Australian stock exchange need to be seen in this context. In the United States the boom ran from August 1982 (Dow Jones index at 900) to August 1987 (Dow Jones at 2,722). Over roughly the same period, the Australian "all-ordinaries" share price index increased fourfold, despite the experience in 1986 of drops in commodity prices and the floating Australian dollar and a corresponding rise in interest rates. The share boom remained well fueled as a consequence of the earlier deregulation of the banks, which were only too willing to finance leveraged takeovers, share trading, and straight-out punting in the share market.

The inevitable bust loomed, and it arrived with great force in late 1987. When Black Friday hit the New York Stock Exchange on October 19, 1987, the response in Australia was swift and sharp: a day later the Australian index had dropped 25 percent, and by the end of the year it had fallen by 40 percent. This market collapse revealed not only loose lending by banks but also market irregularities, inadequate trading rules, ineffective legal controls, and the inefficiencies of multiple administrations. The collapse also precipitated a substantial shakeout of the corporate sector: corporate mismanagement and crime on a grand scale came to light, and major losses were inflicted not only on shareholders (who lost an estimated $10 billion of shareholders' funds) but also on Australian and overseas banks and other lenders to the corporate sector. These events provided the necessary impetus to introduce the next, nationally integrated phase of corporate and sharemarket controls. Fortuitously, 1987 had also seen the integration of the six state stock exchanges (which since 1937 had operated under the umbrella of the Australian Associated Stock Exchanges) into a truly national organization, the Australian Stock Exchange (ASX). The existence of the ASX was greatly conducive and complementary to the establishment in 1991 of a single national regulatory body, the Australian Securities Commission (ASC), which displaced the hybrid control of the NCSC and the state CACs.

The ASC is well aware of the costs, and the potential inefficiency and inflexibility burdens, of regulations on sharetraders and companies seeking to operate honestly according to their perceived best interests. But the ASC is obliged to balance the efficiency of the securities markets against the maintenance of investor confidence in the honesty of those markets. In this respect, the role of the ASC is analogous to that of the Reserve Bank in its imposition of prudential controls on the banks so as to protect the public good of money.

In providing integrated, national regulation and supervision of all corporations and the stock exchange, the new legislation introduced tougher control of prospectuses, insider trading rules, and rigorous responsibilities for the directors and senior executives of corporations (especially in relation to loans and benefits obtained by them from their companies). There is legislative focus on disclosure, not merely of directors' interests in company transactions but also in respect of continuous disclosure to the public of all material information of importance to shareholders, lenders, and creditors of companies.

Simultaneously, the continuing and rapid advance of computer-based information and communications technology has facilitated great improvements in the dissemination of information to all participants in the world of corporations and stock markets, and in the conduct, processing, and recording of market transactions.

All told, the contribution of technological advance, the emergence and streamlining of the ASX and the achievement of a national ASC to govern corporations and markets have brought the sharemarket in Australia to the strongest and most trustworthy stage of its history. It is impossible to isolate the effects of deregulation from all other influences, but it seems reasonable to conclude that the restructuring of the stockbroking industry and the greater competition within it have contributed greatly to the growth of trade and asset values in the stock market (see Davies and Drake, 1996).

Winner and Losers

Above all else, deregulation has fostered innovation and diversity in the banking sector. Real returns to bank depositors have improved since deregulation; bank borrowers are probably better off too. Product innovation and variation among the major banks has been dramatic, clearly in response to competition in conjunction with rapid technological change in payments processing. There are more banks offering longer and more varied product menus than there were fifteen years ago. A long list of product innovations includes automatic teller machines, interest-bearing checking accounts, card savings accounts, PIN for credit and debit cards, automatic sweep facilities, Master card and Visa card for domestic and overseas use, electronic funds transfer at point of sale (EFTPOS), fixed-rate mortgages, variable-repayment home loans, equity mortgage loans, telephone banking, mobile and home banking, retirement services, business credit cards, payroll systems, mortgage offset accounts, investment home loans, cash management accounts, and varied terms, balances, and interest-crediting forms of term deposits.

It is important to notice that this is a list of available new products. No customer is forced to use any of them or to abandon the old standard products that remain available (though sometimes within a different price structure). As Harper puts it so nicely, "Elderly folk who cannot operate an ATM or commit a PIN to memory can continue to operate a standard passbook account, depositing and withdrawing cash via a flesh-and-blood teller during normal banking hours. Even such customers as these, however, have benefited from longer banking hours, shorter teller queues and, at least in some cases, higher rates of interest since deregulation" (Harper, 1991, p. 75).

The public at large has been the main beneficiaries of financial deregulation. For nonbusiness customers of financial institutions as a group there is now a very great variety of remunerative stores for savings and flexible forms of borrowing within the bank and near-bank sectors. The real rewards for lending have risen, while the costs of borrowing have fallen. For industry in general, restructuring has been facilitated by financial resources flowing more easily to the productive sector. For business and firms, there have emerged vast menus of choice for acquiring financial assets and for borrowing from financial institutions, domestically and offshore in both cases. Jobs, incomes, and career opportunities in the financial sector as a whole have increased. The nature of financial work has become more interesting, responsible, and challenging. Bank clerks no longer bend to repetitious clerical work; routine recording has passed to electronic means.

These broad statements, however, should not be misread to suggest that a general widening of financial opportunities has brought benefits to every individual or group of Australians. Most have had some share in the indirect benefits flowing from more effective monetary policy, from less volatility and uncertainty in short-term interest rates and foreign-exchange rates, and from increased competition and productivity in the financial sector. Many, but by no means all, have had direct benefits—or at least the opportunity for access to them—from deregulation. But there have also been direct and identifiable losers. It is salutary, therefore, to identify the main direct gainers and losers from the deregulation process.

Most of the direct gains flowed from the elimination of bank credit rationing and the diminution (rather than full elimination) of bank cross-subsidies between products.[1] The sufferers from credit rationing had included not only high-risk borrowers but also those without a prior credit position with the individual bank, those without collateral security to pledge in support of a loan, and women. Deregulation has favored all these groups in terms of prospective availability of bank credit.

The cross-subsidy picture is more complex. The major cross-subsidy under the old regime arose from the prohibition of payment of deposit interest on current accounts. It could be argued that if current-account (check) deposits are as liquid as currency, there is no need to pay interest on them, just as currency holders receive no interest from the issuers of currency; but that view disregards the benefit to the banks and the cross-subsidies that accrue among bank customers. The nonpayment of interest on current accounts provided the banks with interest-free funds, inflicted major penalties on current account depositors, and subsidized all other bank activities, most notably the free provision of payments transfer facilities to all persons who issued or received checks. Possibly the largest and fairest result of deregulation has been to reward current account depositors for the use of their monies (no longer lent entirely interest-free to the banks) and to impose on rather reluctant users some of the costs of maintaining the check payment system. The old pattern of cross-subsidization also particularly penalized less well-to-do depositors and borrowers, those who made few bank transactions (including check writing), and (indirectly) the urban clients of banks. Correspondingly, the old practices particularly favored well-to-do depositors and borrowers, those who made many transactions, and rural customers. Deregulation has removed the hidden subsidies formerly enjoyed by the latter groups and improved the availability of services, increased returns, and lowered costs for the former groups.

Some significant losers have been farmers and small businesspeople who no longer enjoy low-rate overdrafts, well-to-do persons who had preferred access to subsidized housing loans, and those who had made much use of ancillary services such as safety-deposit boxes and travel administration formerly provided free by banks. Not only farmers but rural populations, in general, have suffered significant inconvenience by the wholesale closure of bank branches in country areas. Many towns and villages now lack any branch of any bank, whereas in the past there were commonly two or three rival banks. This development is the cause of much current contention, not merely because of the reductions in banking services but also because of the loss of population and society as bank staff are moved out of the country areas.

Consumer benefits beyond the banking sector per se have accrued to Australians traveling abroad, through freedom of exchange and the greater safety, convenience, and economy of making overseas payments via international credit cards. Integration and linkage of financial institutions have make credit cards and check-writing facilities available also through nonbank institutions such as credit unions. On the stock exchange, most buyers and sellers have gained from negotiable commissions; but the big players have gained most, while some small investors have been deterred by transactions costs and brokers generally have experienced falls in income or loss of employment.

The increased financial intermediation and the integration and connection of financial institutions nationally and internationally have benefited the banks at the expense of nonbank financial institutions and direct (nonintermediary) lenders and borrowers. Integration with international financial markets has brought the prices of Australian securities and property closer to parity with equivalent foreign assets. Curiously, the foreign banks whose entry did so much to catalyze competition with and among the Australian banks have won little domestic business in Australia presumably because they have largely eschewed retail bank competition. If this is the case, the implication must be that the Australian banks enjoy a significant measure of protection behind the walls of their extensive and expensive branch networks.

So far as economic growth is concerned, deregulated competition in the financial sector has, first, enlarged output and employment in the sector itself; finance sector employment rose from 8 percent of total Australian employment in 1980 to 11.5 percent in 1990 (Phelps, 1991, pp. 88–89). Second, it has generally increased the supply of finance to industry and commerce and eased access to it, thus encouraging investment generally. While some producers, notably in agriculture, may have suffered the loss of priority access to bank credit on privileged terms, the freer financial markets have reduced cross-subsidies and other imperfections and so lessened earlier distortions in the relationships between relative risks and borrower rates of interest. Insofar as the prospective profitability of investment proposals and the creditworthiness of borrowers are now more keenly calculated, society is spared the misallocation of resources to low-grade investment uses. This too is a favorable development for economic growth.

Some concluding comments seem appropriate on the paradox of deregulation and reregulation. As has been described above, the stock exchange has experienced structural and operational deregulation within the market more or less simultaneously with external regulation of the conduct of the industry. Similarly, the banking industry has been greatly freed of anticompetitive controls but new prudential regulations have been imposed. On a broader canvas, the long-standing Australian institutional forms of wage determination and tariffs have been watered down while at the same time legislation and authorities concerned with protecting the environment and consumers have been established. It is salutary to remember that freedom of economic behavior must be exercised with a sense of responsibility and justice, otherwise society will inevitably curtail the economic freedoms, perhaps in ways and to degrees that may be inimical to economic growth and development.

A success story? On balance, clearly the answer is yes—so far. But now Australia's financial system is moving rapidly into the next phase of its evolution, driven by internationalization, competition and competition policy, and communications technology. The forms and degree of any future regulation will be an important element in the story.

Postscript

In June 1996 the Commonwealth Treasurer initiated an Inquiry into the Australian Financial System to "undertake a stocktake of the results of financial deregulation of the Australian financial system since the early 1980s, seek to establish a common regulatory framework for overlapping financial products, and propose ways of dealing constructively with further financial innovation. It will make recommendations on the nature of future regulatory arrangements that will best ensure an efficient, responsive, competitive and flexible financial system to underpin stronger economic performance, consistent with financial stability, prudence, integrity and fairness" (public advertisement). The Inquiry is to report by March 31, 1997.

Acknowledgments

This chapter includes revision of material first prepared by the author for Drake and Nieuwenhuysen (1988). I have also found particularly valuable the volume produced by Macfarlane (1991), especially the contributions therein by Grenville, Valentine, Harper, and Phelps. I am grateful, too, for helpful comments made by H.W. Arndt.

Note

1. The next few paragraphs draw on Harper (1991).

References

Asian Business. (1985). 72 (November): 3.

Australian Financial System Inquiry. (1982). *Final Report*. Canberra: AGPS.

Davies, P.H., and P.J. Drake. (1996). "The Stock Exchange." In Lewis and Wallace (1996).

Drake, P.J., and J.P. Nieuwenhuysen. (1988). *Economic Growth for Australia*. Melbourne: OUP.

Grenville, S. (1991). "The Evolution of Financial Deregulation." In Macfarlane (1991).

Harper, I. (1991). "Competition: Choice and Diversity, Gainers and Losers" In Macfarlane (1991).

Hohne, A. (1984). "Technical Innovation in Financial Services." In Weston (1984).

Hopkinson, M. (1984). "Innovation in Australian Foreign Exchange Markets." In Weston (1984).

Lewis, M.K., and R.H. Wallace (eds.). (1996). *The Australian Financial System*. Melbourne: Longman.

Macfarlane, Ian (ed.). (1991). *The Deregulation of Financial Intermediaries*. Sydney: Reserve Bank of Australia.

Phelps, L. (1991). "Competition: Profitability and Margins." In Macfarlane (1991).

Reserve Bank of Australia. (1987). *Bulletin* (January): 27.

Reserve Bank of Australia. (Various issues). *Bulletin*.

Reserve Bank of Australia. (1995). *Report and Financial Statements 1995*. Sydney: Reserve Bank of Australia.

Thompson, G.J. (1996). "Prudential Supervision and the Changing Financial System." Reserve Bank of Australia. *Bulletin* (April): 30–37.

Trade Practices Commission. (1982). *Draft Determination and Summary of Reasons: Application for Authorisation by the Australian Associated Stock Exchanges*. Canberra: AGPS.

Weston, R. (ed.). (1984). *Innovation in the Australian Financial System*. Melbourne: La Trobe University.

4 INTEREST-RATE LIBERALIZATION AND MONETARY CONTROL IN CHINA

Maxwell J. Fry

Introduction

The end of China's Cultural Revolution in December 1978 heralded a gradual process of economic liberalization and reform. In the financial sector, the monobank system was abandoned in favor of a two-tier banking system in which the People's Bank of China (PBC) became the central bank and its commercial lending activities were transferred to four specialized banks. While China's financial sector has changed since 1978, the credit plan remains the key instrument of monetary policy. Credit ceilings are set for each specialized bank, and subceilings are also imposed for specific types of loans, such as working capital and fixed investment loans. Although banks have some discretion in varying interest rates, China's interest rates are basically determined by administrative fiat (Tseng et al., 1994, pp. 13–18).

Inconsistencies between the development of a market-based economy and the use of credit ceilings as the main instrument of monetary policy have become increasingly apparent. Since 1993, therefore, the Chinese authorities have accelerated the pace of financial sector reforms. Part of these reforms include greater flexibility in, and eventually market determination of, interest rates (Tseng et al., 1994, pp. 18–19). This chapter addresses some issues raised by prospective interest-rate liberalization in China.

Prerequisites for Successful Interest-Rate Liberalization

International experience over the past twenty years indicates that there are five prerequisites for successful interest-rate liberalization (Fry, 1995, pp. 454–460):

- Adequate prudential regulation and supervision of deposit money banks (DMBs), implying minimal levels of accounting and legal infrastructure;
- A reasonable degree of price stability;
- Fiscal discipline taking the form of a sustainable government borrowing requirement that avoids inflationary expansion of reserve money by the central bank either through (1) direct domestic government borrowing or (2) the indirect effect of government borrowing producing surges of capital inflows that require large purchases by the central bank if exchange-rate appreciation is to be avoided;
- Profit-maximizing, competitive behavior by the DMBs;
- A tax system that does not impose discriminatory explicit or implicit taxes on financial intermediation.

In the Chinese context, the first prerequisite implies that insolvent borrowers with perverse credit demands must be removed from the pool of potential bank borrowers.[1] Firms whose liabilities exceed their assets and whose managements are not affected positively by improved economic performance of their firms should be excluded from the process of credit allocation through the market mechanism. A similar condition applies to banks and bank managements. They too must start in a state of solvency with accumulated bad debts removed from their balance sheets and management given financial incentives to improve performance. Both bank performance and the exclusion of insolvent borrowers are the tasks of improved prudential supervision and regulation of the Chinese commercial banks.[2] In the Chinese context, better information, accounting, auditing, and disclosure requirements are urgently needed to enable banks to improve both screening and monitoring of borrowers.

Assuming that these five conditions are met or that efforts are underway to ensure that they are met within a few years, China should benefit from interest-rate liberalization in three ways:

- Better monetary control and hence lower and more stable inflation,
- Improved allocation of scarce investible funds, and
- Higher levels of saving, which, in turn, permit more investment without accelerating inflation.

Alternative Modes of Monetary Control

To achieve low and stable market-determined interest rates in China requires the PBC to pursue active and precisely executed monetary control with indirect market-based techniques. At present, the ability of the PBC to pursue active monetary policy aimed at containing inflation is severely limited by the political process by which credit allocation is determined. Two changes are imperative:

- The volume of credit allocated outside a market environment must be held well below the total volume of credit that the PBC decides is consistent with the objective of achieving a given price level target.
- The PBC must no longer automatically fund the DMBs' lending plans. In other words, the DMBs must compete for deposits and other sources of funds to extend loans that they believe to be profitable rather than obtain automatic recourse from the PBC.

Once the PBC has the authority to influence the total volume of credit in the economy, it can choose between three basic alternative methods of monetary control. Since the money supply M is the liability side of a simplified consolidated balance sheet of the banking system (the monetary survey) in which net foreign assets NFA and domestic credit DC are the assets ($M = NFA + DC$), any change in DC is necessarily accompanied by the same change in M, provided NFA remains unchanged. All three methods of monetary control involve affecting the money supply by influencing the volume of credit.

The first method of influencing the volume of credit, which is used by virtually all the central banks in the OECD countries, is for the central bank to set the price (that is, the interest rate) of its advances to the DMBs and to supply whatever demand is forthcoming at that price as illustrated in Figure 4.1. By so doing, the central bank affects all other interest rates in the economy. If the advance rate is raised and bank loan rates are initially below the new advance rate, DMBs will choose not to borrow. However, as they repay their previous advances to the central bank, their reserves will decline. Their choice is then to call in loans or to borrow from the

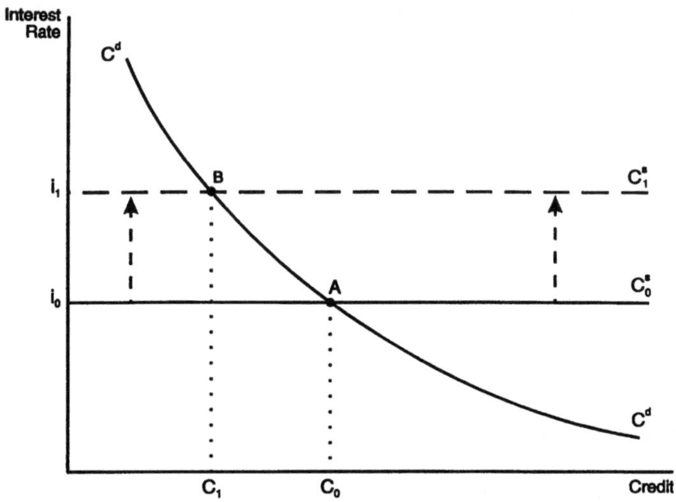

Figure 4.1. Setting interest rates to control credit volume

central bank at the higher advance rate. They will borrow rather than reduce loans only if they can pass on the higher costs of their advances from the central bank in the form of higher loan rates. Provided demand for credit is negatively related to the loan rate (that is, downward sloping), the volume of bank credit will fall in either case. The main problem here is that the actual volume of credit created is not under the direct control of the central bank and may exceed the central bank's target at the selected interest rate.

Alternatively the central bank can influence the volume of bank credit by setting the volume of advances it is prepared to offer the DMBs and allowing the price (that is, the interest rate) to be determined by the interplay of market forces as shown in Figure 4.2. Some form of auction system can be used to allocate the fixed quantity of advances to those DMBs who are willing to pay the highest rates. At one extreme, the central bank can auction the entire volume of advances it is prepared to make available to the DMBs. Alternatively, it may auction part of this facility and then provide additional access at some markup over the preceding auction rate. In such case, DMBs have a market incentive to acquire their advances through the auction, but the central bank provides a safety net for those DMBs that fail to acquire sufficient reserves through the auction. However, the safety net must always be provided at a rate higher than the auction rate for the auction process to work. The perceived problem here is that the interest rate established in the auction is not directly controlled by the central bank and may exceed the level deemed appropriate.

In an attempt to get the best of both worlds, many central banks have set both the quantity and the price of their advances as illustrated in Figure 4.3.

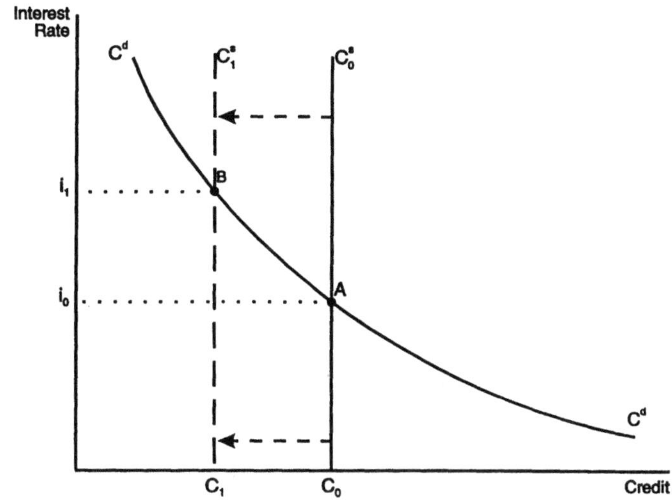

Figure 4.2. Interest rates determined by credit demand

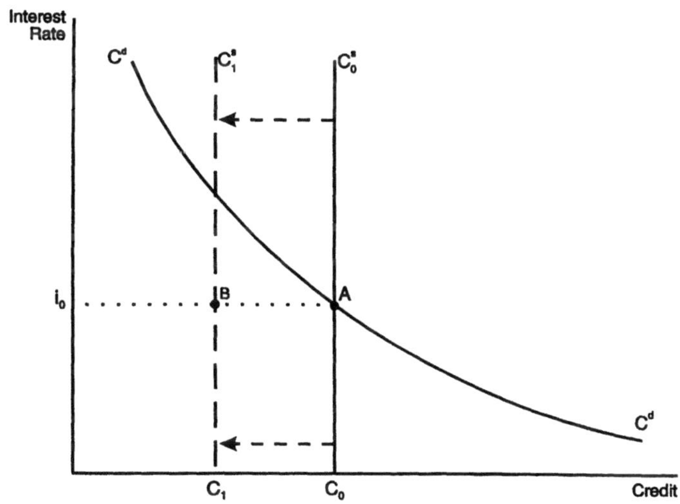

Figure 4.3. Setting both quantity and price of credit

In this way, neither the volume of credit nor the interest rate can exceed their target levels.

Disadvantages of Low Interest Rates Imposed by Administrative Fiat

Unfortunately, low interest rates achieved in this manner distort the economy in four ways. First, low interest rates produce a bias in favor of current consumption and against future consumption. Therefore, they may reduce saving below the socially optimum level. Second, potential lenders may engage in relatively low-yielding direct investment instead of lending by way of depositing money in a bank. Third, bank borrowers able to obtain all the funds they want at low loan rates will choose relatively capital-intensive projects. Fourth, the pool of potential borrowers contains entrepreneurs with low-yielding projects who would not want to borrow at the higher market-clearing interest rate. To the extent that DMBs' selection process contains an element of randomness, some investment projects that are financed will have yields below the threshold that would be self-imposed at market-clearing interest rates.

Perhaps the most critical defect of low fixed interest rates in the present Chinese context is that low controlled interest rates contribute to inflationary pressure resulting from excessive monetary expansion by reducing the real demand for money. In the simplest balance sheet of the banking system, the banks hold loans L and reserves R as their assets and deposits D as their liabilities:

Assets		Liabilities	
Reserves	R	Deposits	D
Loans	L		

The balance-sheet identity implies $R + L = D$. Naturally, this balance-sheet identity is still preserved if one divides both assets and liabilities by nominal GNP Y:

Assets		Liabilities	
Reserves	R/Y	Deposits	D/Y
Loans	L/Y		

When nominal deposit rates remain fixed, the ratio D/Y falls as inflation accelerates because households and firms choose to hold smaller money balances in relation to their expenditure levels due to the rising cost of holding money. Therefore, the ratio $(R + L)/Y$ also must fall. If the ratio R/L remains roughly constant, then both R/Y and L/Y fall as D/Y falls. Since L/Y is the ratio of bank loans to the nominal value of output, business firms find themselves facing a credit squeeze as inflation rises. Unable to obtain the necessary loans to cover the costs of their working capital, some firms may be unable to stay in business. The aggregate level of output in real terms would then fall. In this case, therefore, the deterioration of money reduces the extent to which the banking system administers the country's payments mechanism and intermediates between savers and investors; performance in both functions is related. Perhaps the former effect reduces income levels, while the latter effect reduces income growth.

The inefficiencies created through interest rates that are administratively set below their competitive free-market equilibrium level are illustrated in Figure 4.4. Here the demand for credit is equated with investment, and the supply of credit is equated with saving. Although saving: Sg_0 at a rate of economic growth g_0 is depicted as a positive function of the real rate of interest, the interest-elasticity of saving in most countries tends to be small. The line FF represents financial repression, taken here to consist of an administratively fixed nominal interest rate that holds the real rate r below

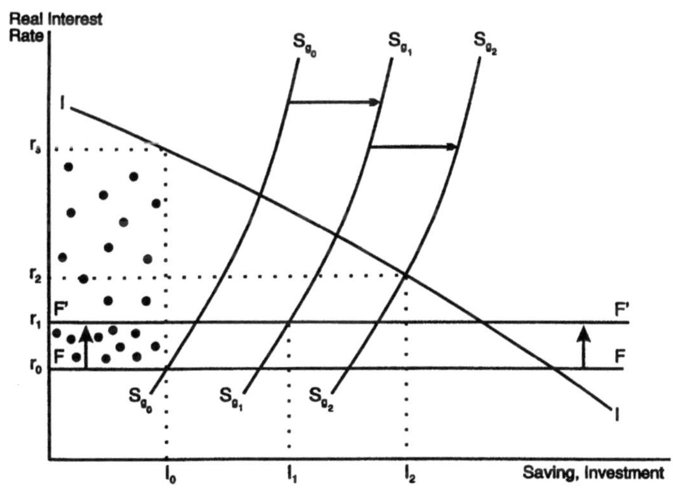

Figure 4.4. Saving and investment under interest-rate ceilings

its equilibrium level. Actual investment is limited to I_0, the amount of saving forthcoming at the real interest rate r_0.

If the interest-rate ceiling applied only to savers' interest rates (only to deposit but not to loan rates of interest), the investor-borrower would face an interest rate of r_0, the rate that clears the market with the constrained supply of saving I_0, in Figure 4.4. The spread $r_3 - r_0$ would be spent by a regulated but competitive banking system on nonprice competition (advertising and opening new bank branches). These nonprice services, however, may not be valued at par with interest payments; real money demand invariably declines with a decrease in the explicit real deposit rate of interest.

In fact, there are loan rate ceilings as well as deposit rate ceilings in China. Although private DMBs can evade loan rate ceilings through compensating balances, they seem to be observed by state-owned DMBs and for most public-sector borrowing. To the extent that DMBs do observe loan rate ceilings, nonprice rationing of loanable funds must occur. Credit is allocated not according to expected productivity of the investment projects but according to transaction costs and perceived risks of default. Quality of collateral, political pressures, "name," loan size, and covert benefits to loans officers may also influence allocation. The investments that are financed under such conditions are illustrated by the dots in Figure 4.4. Even if credit allocation is random, the average efficiency of investment is reduced as the loan rate ceiling is lowered because investments with lower returns now become profitable. Entrepreneurs who were previously deterred from requesting bank loans now enter the market. Hence, adverse selection in terms of social welfare occurs when interest rates are set too low and so produce disequilibrium credit rationing of the type described here. Adverse selection also occurs when interest rates rise too high because equilibrium credit rationing is not working properly.

Loan rate ceilings discourage financial institutions from taking any risks; risk premia cannot be charged when ceilings are binding and effective. This itself may ration out a large proportion of potentially high-yielding investments. In the financially repressed economy there is, therefore, a tendency for the investments that are financed to yield returns barely above the ceiling interest rate r_0. These are shown in Figure 4.4 by the dots lying just above *FF* but below *F′F′*. Another drawback of loan rate ceilings is that they tend to deter bank spending on loan assessments. Since even in an unrepressed situation DMBs are likely to underspend on screening, this additional deterrence may be worse for social welfare than another form of repression that affects the financial system at a margin that is initially undistorted.

Under selective or directed credit programs, DMBs are required to allocate minimum percentages of their asset portfolios for loans to priority sectors of the economy at subsidized loan rates of interest. Part of the critical problem of loan delinquency encountered in virtually all directed credit programs is due to the fact that these subsidized loan rates, which are typically negative in real terms, discourage prompt loan repayment. High delinquency and default rates reduce the flexibility (less credit available for new investment) and increase the fragility of financial systems.

Raising the interest rate ceiling from *FF* to *F′F′* (from r_0 to r_1) in Figure 4.4 increases saving and investment. Changes in the real interest rate trace out the saving function in this disequilibrium situation. Raising the interest-rate ceiling also deters entrepreneurs from undertaking all those low-yielding investments illustrated by the dots below *F′F′*. They are no longer profitable at the higher interest rate r_1. Hence, the average return to or efficiency of aggregate investment increases. The rate of economic growth rises in this process and shifts the saving function to Sg_1; the saving ratio is invariably influenced positively by the rate of economic growth.

Thus the real rate of interest as the return to savers is the key to a higher level of investment and as a rationing device to greater investment efficiency. The increased quantity and quality of investment interact in their positive effects on the rate of economic growth. The policy prescription for the financially repressed economy is to raise institutional interest rates or to reduce the rate of inflation. Abolishing interest-rate ceilings altogether produces the optimal result of maximizing investment and raising still further investment's average efficiency. This is shown in Figure 4.4 by the equilibrium r_2I_2, and the higher rate of economic growth g_2.

Disastrous Experiences with Interest-Rate Liberalization and the Emergence of Excessively High Real Interest Rates

Unfortunately, several interest-rate liberalization experiments have failed to produce the optimum results depicted at r_2, I_2, and g_2 in Figure 4.4. The basic problem lies in the perverse reaction to higher interest rates by insolvent and nonprofit-motivated firms. By definition, an insolvent firm (one whose liabilities exceed its assets) is unable to repay its loans. Hence, it is not deterred from borrowing by a higher cost. It simply continues, if it can, to borrow whatever it needs to finance its losses. These inevitably increase with an increase in the interest rate, which drives up the firm's cost of servicing its loans. Hence, such enterprises exhibit the upward-sloping demand for loans illustrated in Figure 4.5. Clearly, raising interest rates in this situation increases rather than decreases the quantity of credit and therefore does not produce the desired monetary contraction. Indeed, the increased demand for credit by those who will not be repaying their loans drives the interest up to such high levels that solvent, profit-motivated firms become insolvent when the cost of borrowing exceeds the expected return on the firm's assets by any significant margin.

Newly liberalized financial sectors subject to inadequate prudential supervision and regulation have magnified the impact of exogenous shocks by accommodating distress borrowing by insolvent firms. In this way, DMBs in these countries compound the problem of insolvency in the real sectors of the economy. Because distress borrowers push real interest rates to levels at which virtually no economic activity can be profitable, solvent businesses start to face liquidity crunches, which then force them to borrow at rates that they know are unmanageable. Hence, the accommodation of distress borrowing propagates more insolvency.

Extraordinarily high real loan rates also appear when a substantial proportion of a country's DMBs have zero net worth or bank managements believe that shareholders as well as depositors are implicitly insured by the government. Without any incentives, bank managements may simply be unconcerned about the solvency of their state-owned institution. The exceptionally high real interest rates produce an epidemic effect: the false

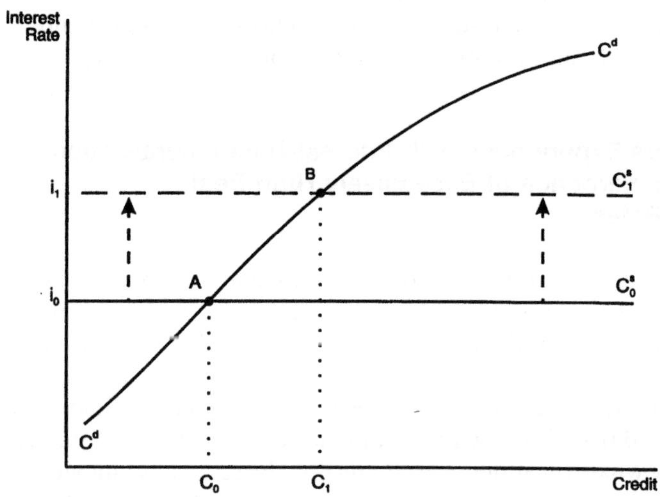

Figure 4.5. Perverse demand for credit by insolvent firms

credit demand by distress borrowers puts upward pressure on interest rates, which in turn drags down other firms. The supply of funds is made available because of explicit or implicit deposit insurance. Demand rises because of firms' expectations that the government will eventually bail out nonfinancial as well as financial enterprises. When net worth is zero, firms have every incentive to gamble on a government bailout in the future. The end result is financial and economic paralysis.

Financial distress results in reduced investment and worse resource allocation through the distressed financial sector. When nonperforming loans rise, DMBs have fewer resources for new lending. Furthermore, DMBs often extend more loans to large firms unable to repay their old loans in an attempt to conceal their own losses, a practice known as *evergreening*. In this way, loan demand rises, real interest rates increase, and investment declines. Attempts to lower interest rates by government decree in Argentina, Bolivia, and Yugoslavia made matters worse by accelerating inflation and capital flight. The ensuing disintermediation and lower demand for domestic financial assets compounded the DMBs' difficulties. An alternative solution, which is likely to accelerate bank insolvency, is to stop DMBs from continuing to lend to insolvent borrowers. Clearly, preventing bankruptcy at all costs is highly inefficient.

In general, excessively high real institutional interest rates signal unsound lending in which DMBs throw good money after bad money to enable borrowers to meet their interest payments. The solution is better regulation and supervision. Indeed, the typical response to such financial crises has been to strengthen prudential regulation and supervision, as well as to bring all financial institutions under a uniform regulatory framework. In Malaysia, for example, all financial institutions now come under the Banking and Financial Institutions Act of 1989. Experiments with two-tier financial systems have been abandoned as governments realized that it was impossible in practice to avoid bailing out insolvent financial institutions so that they could repay their depositors. Behind virtually all financial crises that have occurred in the past two decades lies the critical issue of explicit or implicit deposit insurance because it affects the behavior of both depositors and bankers.

Ronald McKinnon (1993, pp. 84–91) emphasizes the adverse selection problem that arises with deposit insurance when inflation is high and unstable. When macroeconomic instability causes positive correlation between returns on alternative bank-financed projects, banks may no longer seek to reduce adverse selection through credit rationing. If deposit insurance protects depositors, banks may choose riskier lending strategies when macroeconomic instability produces strongly correlated outcomes.

This is because favorable outcomes produce large bank profits, while unfavorable outcomes resulting in massive bank losses are borne mainly by the deposit insurance agency. Hence, instead of lowering the loan rate to reduce adverse selection when instability increases, banks may have an incentive to raise it. When banks operate under such conditions of macroeconomic instability and deposit insurance protects depositors, effective prudential regulation and supervision is imperative. A second-best solution may be to impose a ceiling on loan rates of interest.

Samuel Talley and Ignacio Mas (1992, pp. 330–331) conclude that the extent of moral hazard caused by implicit deposit protection schemes (IDPSs) or explicit deposit insurance schemes (DISs) depends on

> (1) whether protection is extended to bank management and shareholders, and (2) the feeling of safety imparted to depositors. Insofar as DISs operate through a set of established rules, they can completely eliminate the expectation of managers and shareholders that they will benefit from the insurer's actions. Because such options are not ruled out in IDPSs, these systems are likely to result in greater moral hazard on the part of bankers. It seems likely that the conversion [from IDPs to DIS] would result in less moral hazard on the part of the bankers, but more moral hazard on the part of the depositors.

However, Talley and Mas (1992, pp. 334) then suggest that there is no point in setting up explicit deposit insurance systems unless countries

> (1) have at least a fairly stable banking system, (2) have an effective prudential regulation and bank supervision system, and (3) exhibit a willingness to adequately fund a DIS and give it the necessary government backup support that may be required to get the system through a period of stress. In our judgment, there probably are relatively few developing countries that now meet these conditions.

There has been increasing recognition that prudential regulation and supervision is a key prerequisite for financial stability. In their absence, financial systems are prone to financial crises, as witnessed by Chile, which experienced high real interest rates in the 1980s: "These incredibly high interest rates on peso loans represented, in large part, the breakdown of proper financial supervision over the Chilean banking system. Neither officials in the commercial banks themselves nor government regulatory authorities adequately monitored the creditworthiness of a broad spectrum of industrial borrowers" (McKinnon, 1991, p. 383).

Deposit insurance also has ramifications on the international front. Vihang Errunza and Joseph Ghalbouni (1986, p. 229) argue that it throws more risk onto the international financial markets. McKinnon (1991) believes that deposit insurance is responsible for the entry of banks into the riskier long-term international financial markets. John Cuddington and Gordon Smith (1985, p. 8) suggest that the high proportion of net international capital flows routed through financial institutions over the past decade is due to deposit insurance and expectations of government bailouts. Heinz Arndt and Peter Drake (1985) and McKinnon (1991) advocate regulations that would get banks out of the long-term international capital market.

Like financial liberalization, deposit insurance works well when banks are regulated and supervised effectively. Deposit insurance per se does not guarantee an appropriate solution to financial crises, as witnessed by Venezuela and Colombia (Morris et al., 1990, pp. 78–79). Success necessitates complementary systems to detect and confront banking problems when liquidation is not desirable. Given the prerequisite of adequate bank supervision, however, deposit insurance has been highly effective in maintaining financial stability.

The conclusion that interest rates can rise beyond their growth-maximizing levels in certain circumstances is supported by Figure 4.6, which traces out the effect of changes in the real deposit rate of interest on economic growth. This figure is produced using the mean values of all the explanatory variables, with the exception of the real deposit rate of interest, in an estimated growth rate equation for sixteen developing countries. Initial estimates of the relationship between the rate of economic growth YG, the investment ratio IY, and the real rate of interest RD, for the period 1970 to 1988 took the form

$$YG = \beta_1(IKY) + \beta_2\left[IKY \cdot (RD + \beta_3) \cdot (RD + \beta_3)\right]. \qquad (4.1)$$

Since the parameter b_3 was not significantly different from zero, although its negative value implies that growth is maximized at some positive real interest rate, it is dropped from the estimate from which Figure 4.6 is derived.

The mean value of the real deposit rate for this country sample is zero with a standard deviation of 23 percent. Its minimum value is –83 percent and its maximum value 221 percent. The line C_n denotes two standard deviations below the mean of all negative interest rates in the control group of countries (Argentina, Brazil, Chile, Egypt, India, Mexico, Nigeria, Pakistan, Sri Lanka, Turkey, and Venezuela), E_n denotes two standard deviations below the mean of all negative interest rates in the five East Asian economies in this sample (Indonesia, Korea, Malaysia, Philippines, and Thailand), E_p denotes two standard deviations above the mean of all zero or positive interest rates in the five East Asian economies, while C_p denotes two standard deviations above the mean of all zero or positive

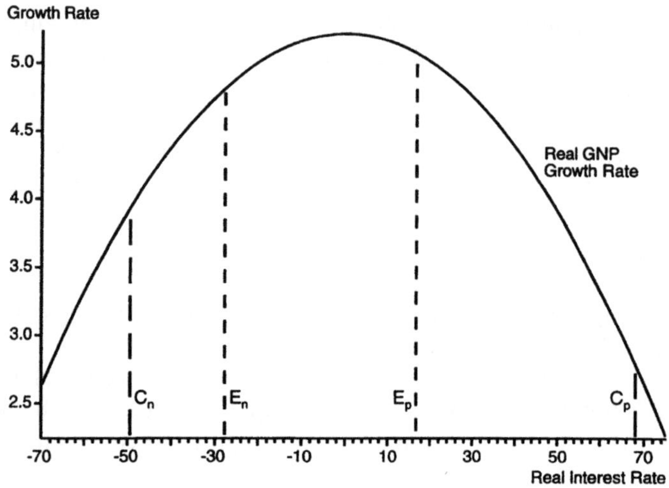

Figure 4.6. Effect of real interest rate on economic growth

interest rates in the remaining eleven countries. Evidently, real interest rates deviated from their growth-maximizing level far more in the control group countries than they did in the East Asian economies. Indeed, the range of real deposit rates observed in the East Asian economies exerted virtually no negative effect on the rate of economic growth. In fact, the continuously compounded output growth rate in the East Asian countries averaged 6.2 percent over the observation period compared with 3.9 percent in the control group. Referring to work by Guillermo Calvo and Fabrizio Coricelli (1992), José De Gregorio and Pablo Guidotti (1993, p. 11) claim that real interest rates are not a good indicator of financial repression or distortion. They suggest that the relationship between real interest rates and economic growth might resemble an inverted *U* curve:

> Very low (and negative) real interest rates tend to cause financial disintermediation and hence tend to reduce growth, as implied by the McKinnon-Shaw hypothesis. . . . On the other hand, very high real interest rates that do not reflect improved efficiency of investment, but rather a lack of credibility of economic policy or various forms of country risk, are likely to result in a lower level of investment as well as a concentration in excessively risky projects.

In other words, large negative and large positive real interest rates may well exert the same deleterious effect on economic growth. De Gregorio and Guidotti abandon real interest rates in favor of domestic credit to the private sector divided by GNP as a measure of financial development. Here, this problem is addressed by using the square of the real deposit rate. This ensures that large positive and negative values exert the same effect, presumably negative, on economic growth. I also find that the square of the black market exchange-rate premium has a marginally higher explanatory power than its level.

As indicators of financial repression, the black market exchange-rate premium averaged 6.2 percent in the East Asian countries compared with 42.6 percent in the control group, while the square of the real deposit rate was ten times greater in the control group than it was in the East Asian countries over the same period. Differences in these two measures of financial repression account for 1.7 of the 2.3 percentage point difference in the output growth rates between these two country groups. In other words, these two distortions explain approximately 75 percent of the difference in output growth rates between these two country groups (Fry, 1994, pp. 16–17).

Examining quarterly data for real interest rates in China for the period 1983 to 1993 suggests that Chinese real rates have fallen within the range exhibited by the sample East Asian economies.[3] The highest quarterly real interest rate lies very close to E_p. While the lowest quarterly real interest rate fell below E_n, it reflects an outlier for a quarter during which several price controls were lifted. However, data provided by the PBC for 1994 indicates that complacency over the present system of fixed interest rates in China is far from justified; real interest rates turned negative by a considerable margin in 1994, although they rose in 1995 and 1996.

Perverse Borrowers, Wildebeest Bankers, and Prudential Supervision

Before interest-rate liberalization in China can produce the beneficial allocative and anti-inflationary effects discussed above, pathological borrowers with perverse credit demands must be removed from the pool of potential borrowers and DMBs put on a sound footing. These are tasks for improved prudential supervision and regulation of DMBs. Essentially, those firms whose liabilities exceed their assets and whose management is not affected positively in some form by better economic performance of their firms should be excluded from the process of credit allocation through the market mechanism. Their behavior in a market environment is inappropriate.

The same criteria—solvency and profit motivation of management—also apply to the DMBs themselves. The present structure of interest rates suggests that the monetary authorities regard banking as a zero-cost activity: average lending rates are set at virtually the same level as average deposit and rediscount rates. Hence, aggressive competitive behavior is not rewarded by higher profits. Nonetheless, over the past decade the Chinese banking system has grown at a staggering rate, whether measured in nominal or real terms. This rapid growth creates yet another potential problem in the form of a knowledge bottleneck. Even a short visit makes one immediately aware of the considerable investment in human capital now being undertaken to achieve the objective of establishing Bangkok as a regional financial center for Indochina. Obviously, financial expertise and experience cannot be acquired overnight. This suggests that prudential regulation and supervision is all the more important in rapidly growing financial sectors, such as China's, than in those growing less dramatically.

In several countries, rapid expansion of lending by newly liberalized banks has resulted in just as high levels of nonperforming assets as did directed credit policies under financial repression. Most banking systems simply lack the expertise needed to make good commercial judgments. In any case, they cannot acquire more of such expertise at the moment financial liberalization occurs. Hence, prudential regulation and supervision are doubly imperative at the outset of financial liberalization to curtail the worst excesses of inexperienced and untrained bankers (Villanueva and Mirakhor, 1990; Vittas, 1992).

A new and simplified, if not immediately liberalized, interest-rate structure must ensure that DMBs can increase their profits by aggressively competing for deposits and lending these funds at their own discretion and at their own risk to sound borrowers. In this situation, good bank management would ensure the soundness of the bank. However, the burden of previous directed and unprofitable lending must be also be removed. Once DMBs have been restructured so that nonperforming policy loans are removed from their balance sheets, prudential supervision and regulation must ensure that DMBs are prevented and protected from returning to a state of insolvency. In other words, DMBs must be effectively deterred from lending to insolvent borrowers. Clearly, this necessitates the abolition of any policy-imposed requirements on the DMBs to extend loans to particular borrowers. The DMBs must be responsible for their loan lending decisions. Prudential regulation and supervision can also be applied to assist DMBs in their task of establishing safe and sound banking practices.

Experience indicates that interest-rate liberalization typically raises at least two major questions. The first is how to curb or counter an explosion in consumer lending after financial liberalization, particularly when it takes the form of the abolition of credit ceilings. The second is how to confront the herd instinct possessed by bankers throughout the world.

International evidence suggests that easier access to consumer credit lowers private saving ratios in the medium term (Jappelli and Pagano, 1994; Liu and Woo, 1994; Patrick, 1994). A burst of consumer lending following financial liberalization may also jeopardize monetary control or squeeze out investment lending. Perhaps the pragmatic answer lies in imposing high downpayment requirements for mortgages and loans for durable consumer goods at the outset of the liberalization program. Subsequently such requirements can be gradually reduced, particularly when the economy is in no danger of overheating.

Many newly liberalized banking systems have become overly enthusiastic about property development, credit card lending, and housing only to find that expected returns failed to materialize. Loan officers have an incentive to follow the herd when it comes to sectoral lending decisions. To be wrong in the company of most other loan officers is excusable. To be wrong in isolation may not be forgiven so readily.

Loan officers can be compared to a herd of wildebeest moving from one watering hole to another. As one hole runs dry and the surrounding grass is overgrazed, the herd moves on to a new source of water and pastures. The first to arrive at the new watering hole do well; the laggards struggle to survive. Competition conditions the behavior of members of the herd.[4] This herd instinct among bankers takes the form of bank lending surging into particular sectors or activities only to withdraw again after delinquency and default rates rise.

Occasionally this herd instinct degenerates into lemming-like behavior when bankers all rush into a new activity with virtually no consideration of the risks involved. The macroeconomic problem is that such credit surges produce bubbles in which prices are increased solely as a result of the credit injections. When the bubbles burst, DMBs are left with collateral worth considerably less than the loans that are now nonperforming. The end result is financial crisis.

An Extension of the Risk-Weighted Capital-Adequacy Standard

One specific way of containing systemic risk inherent in overexuberant financial sector growth, the herd instinct, and herd or lemming-like lending behavior involves deterring excessive lending concentration to (1) a single sector of the economy, such as construction or real estate, (2) a single region of the country, such as the coastal areas, or (3) a single borrower through the application of risk-weighted capital-adequacy requirements. These would be aimed at gradually raising the marginal cost of excessive growth in loans of all particular types. Thus, a bank that increased risk through rapid expansion of any loan category by either changing the composition of its portfolio or increasing its total portfolio size would incur increased risk weighting on all loans in its high-growth categories.

Such a system could start with an increased risk weighting on all loans in any category whose growth exceeded, say, 25 percent in real terms by the actual percentage growth of this loan category. For example, a 30 percent growth of loans in any specific category would involve an increase in risk weighting of 30 percentage points on each loan.

In this way the price mechanism can be used, for example, to increase the financial institutions' marginal cost of property lending, so raising interest rates on such loans and deterring speculative real estate booms. A more sophisticated version of this proposal would be to assess a bank's portfolio in terms of the covariance of individual loan default probabilities. The score in this exercise would then produce an adjusted capital adequacy requirement. The main problem is that the internationally agreed system of risk-weighted capital adequacy assessment is already too complicated for most developing economies to implement effectively. Adding yet more complexity may have to wait. Meanwhile, the PBC may simply have to resort to the tried and true technique of moral suasion.

Given the moral hazard problem created by deposit insurance, the PBC might kill two birds with one stone by introducing risk-weighted deposit insurance premia. These would address not only the moral hazard problem but also could deter excessive lending concentration or excessively risky lending.

Tighter Monetary Control through Treasury Bill Auctions and a Three-Tranche Advance Facility

The imposition of a maximum loan to deposit ratio is inconsistent with the PBC's general objective of moving toward a system of monetary control based on the use of indirect market-based instruments. Nevertheless, the PBC could certainly use such instruments to achieve a target loan-to-deposit ratio by establishing regular weekly auctions of treasury bills. At some price or yield that is unknown in advance, a sufficient tender of treasury bills will reduce the loan-to-deposit ratio because banks would necessarily be holding a volume of liquid assets that kept the loan-to-deposit ratio below any set required minimum. Such holdings of liquid assets would also make the required excess reserve ratio redundant. Naturally, the use of market-based instruments, such as auctions of treasury bills, would be used to ensure that the abolition of balance-sheet ratio constraints imposed for monetary control rather than prudential purposes was not accompanied by any undesired expansion in domestic credit.

To achieve this outcome, the PBC must persuade the commercial banks to hold treasury bills *voluntarily*, a goal that is fully consistent with the objective of moving toward monetary control through the use of indirect market-based instruments of monetary policy. Were all balance-sheet ratio constraints—such as the require reserve ratio, the required excess reserve ratio, and the maximum loan-to-deposit ratio—currently imposed for monetary policy purposes to be abolished, a market-based mechanism must be used to persuade the banks to take up a sufficient volume of treasury bills to mop up excess liquidity that would otherwise result in excessive growth in domestic credit and the monetary aggregates.

This can be accomplished through the regular weekly auction arrangement, with the understanding that the auction rates would have to offer competitive yields. Of course, some price floor can be set in advance so that the PBC would take up treasury bills were the auction price to fall embarrassingly low (that is, an excessively high yield). Indeed, as banker to the government the PBC should smooth out fluctuations in the government's financing requirements by taking up treasury bills at some times of the year with the intention of selling them again through open-market operations at other times of year. The substitution of the PBC's loans to the government for treasury bills would provide the PBC with a sufficient portfolio of securities to start such active open-market operation.

Ideally, the treasury bill auction should be open to all on an entirely voluntary basis. Deposit holders would soon realize that treasury bills offered an attractive alternative to deposits. Should the banks offer prices that are too low compared to prices offered by depositors, banks will lose deposits that in turn will drain their liquid asset holdings. In this case therefore both quasi money and liquid assets will fall by the same amount, again leaving the crucial variable for monetary control, domestic credit to the private sector, unchanged.

As well as raising revenue for the government, sales of treasury bills can be used for monetary policy purposes. The essential aim must be to make treasury bills compete with deposit money in order to establish a critical mass of voluntary holders of treasury bills that, in turn, will enable an active secondary market to develop. It is in this market that the PBC will then be able to conduct open market operations.

The ideal arrangement would be for the PBC to offer treasury bills for monetary policy as well as budgetary purposes. There are no *net* financial implications to government finances from an overissue of treasury bills as opposed to the same issue of PBC bills. In the former case, either PBC profits (accruing to the government) rise from its eventual investment of the proceeds of the excess issue of treasury bills in foreign assets or the PBC could pay interest on the government's balance at the PBC exactly equal to the treasury bill yield, thus self-financing the overissue. In the latter case, the PBC's profits are unchanged because it pays interest on its issue of its own bills and eventually invests the proceeds as before.

Such a system will deliver five benefits: (1) it removes rigidities in the form of unnecessary balance sheet restrictions imposed on the banks; (2) it promotes the use of market-based monetary policy instruments; (3) it stimulates competition for deposit money; (4) it creates the critical mass of voluntary holders of treasury bills for an active secondary market to develop, so enabling open-market operations; and (5) it removes an implicit discriminatory tax on the banks.

With excessive inflationary pressures at present, active monetary control is imperative. Therefore, the PBC might adopt a more formal, frequent, and active monetary policy-making mechanism involving the following steps:

1. A bank rate could be set automatically equal to the latest treasury bill auction rate plus a 1 percent margin. The new bank rate can be announced each week along with the auction results. The bank rate would apply to the advance or rediscount facility made available by the PBC to the commercial banks. This advance facility would be available automatically on demand to each bank at the bank rate. However, it should be limited by a formula based on both the value and volatility of each bank's deposits. Each bank's advance line could be set equal to the coefficient of variation of its end-of-day (end-of-week or end-of-month, if daily or weekly data are unavailable) deposit volume over the past 12 months multiplied by its present deposit volume. With a coefficient of variation of 3 percent, for example, a bank would be entitled to an advance facility equal to 3 percent of its present deposit volume. Of course, this advance line could be set at half or twice or any other fraction of the basic formula suggested here. Alternatively, a simpler formula using a uniform ratio or a ratio based on each bank's relative size could be adopted.
2. The PBC also could offer an emergency overnight facility at penal rates in two tranches. The first tranche of such an emergency over-

night facility could be offered at the bank rate plus an administrative charge equal to perhaps one-tenth of a percentage point (equal to an annual compound rate of 43.3 percent based on a 360-day year). This might be limited to 5 percent of a bank's total deposits. The second tranche would be unlimited but incurs an administrative charge equal to one-half of a percentage point (equal to an annual compound rate of 502.3 percent based on a 360-day year). The levels of these emergency rates are not substantially different from emergency rates offered in Singapore and Switzerland. It is essential for effective monetary control that the PBC should *not* provide any unlimited borrowing facility to financial institutions at a fixed rate or at a rate approximately of the same magnitude as short-term market rates.

3. Active monetary policy must be made on a month-to-month basis. Targets for money and credit aggregates designed to contain inflation (the target could be the weighted average inflation rate of China's trading partners, since this would remove the necessity for eventual devaluation) and maintain a reasonable level of foreign-exchange reserves must be set. Each month current developments must be reviewed against these monetary policy objectives and the implementation of monetary policy over the following month agreed. A *pro forma* briefing paper for such policy making activity could be drafted by the PBC's Research Department after it has forecast money demand and prepared financial projections for the ensuing twelve months.
4. Determine the tightness of monetary control. Looseness at the expense of tight control can be introduced to any desired degree through the severity of the penalties for reserve shortfalls, the length of the averaging period used to calculate cash reserve requirements, and the width of the band around the target growth rate for reserve money established to produce desired growth in domestic credit and the money supply. The higher the penalties, the shorter the averaging period and the smaller the tolerance band, the tighter will be control over the money supply at any point in time. Tighter monetary control implies more volatility of overnight interest rates. It is important to understand that the tightness of monetary control is entirely independent of the required reserve ratio. Exactly the same tightness can be obtained with a required reserve ratio of 10, 5, or zero percent.
5. The PBC should conduct auctions of and open-market operations in treasury bills to ensure that domestic credit targets are achieved.

Six Perceived Obstacles to Interest-Rate Liberalization

Some fear interest-rate liberalization because they do not understand it, while others understand it but perceive six obstacles to its implementation. This section examines each of these perceived obstacles in turn.

State-Owned Enterprises

The perilous financial state of many state-owned enterprises (SOEs) is perceived as a major impediment to interest-rate liberalization. This view holds that higher interest rates would hasten their demise.

The problem of highly indebted or insolvent SOEs is all too familiar not only in economies in transition but also in many developing countries. The solution to this problem can be separated from the issue of interest-rate liberalization. In the first place, SOEs that are too fragile to face interest-rate liberalization must be cordoned off from the financial markets. This means that some form of hard budget constraint other than that imposed through the normal workings of the commercial market is required immediately for all such enterprises.

The second step is to weed out those SOEs that are not only loss-making and likely to continue to be loss-making but are also insolvent. These should be wound up as soon as possible. Those SOEs that can sell their output at prices covering costs but cannot meet accumulated debt service burdens must be restructured. As soon as they have been recapitalized, they can be launched into the market environment produced by interest-rate liberalization. Any further subsidies deemed necessary for noneconomic reasons must be provided directly from the budget rather than from the PBC in the form of subsidized interest rates.

In conclusion, access to financial markets by SOEs that cannot withstand interest-rate liberalization must be restricted to funds provided under temporary conditions by a specially constituted disability fund. Those SOEs producing negative value added should be closed as soon as possible, while viable ones should be restructured before being launched into the new commercial financial market place. Since these actions are required in any event, they need not precede and therefore need not delay interest-rate liberalization, provided the vital step of ensuring that such SOEs do not have access to the commercial financial markets is taken immediately. At the same time, some encouragement to the establishment of new small and medium-size enterprises could be provided to reduce dislocation in the labor market.

Regional Disparities

The second main concern is that interest-rate liberalization will exacerbate the growing regional disparity caused by rapid growth along the coastal areas and economic stagnation in some of the China's more backward regions. The concern here is that interest-rate liberalization will result in funds' being sucked out of the depressed areas into the booming ones.

Restricting financial flows or even reversing financial flows is not the answer, as the case of Southern Italy so clearly demonstrates. Riccardo Faini, Giampaolo Galli, and Curzio Giannini (1993, p. 158) state: "Almost half a century of development policy, fostering large-scale transfer of income and capital to Southern Italy, has failed to narrow in any significant manner the output gap between North and South." Public policy ensured that investment in the south was high, but productivity in both the public and private sectors was low. "As a result, 36 percent of the Italian population live in a region that has become heavily dependent on public subsidies" (Faini, Galli, and Giannini, 1993, p. 158).

After providing a detailed analysis of finance in Southern Italy, Faini, Galli, and Giannini (1993, pp. 197–199) conclude:

> The protection of local banks, the promotion of specialized regional institutions, interest subsidies and interest rate ceilings were essential ingredients in a global development strategy aimed at overcoming the lack of saving and of long-term capital, which were perceived as the key obstacles to growth. . . . These motivations now appear outdated. For one thing, low productivity, not lack of capital is the key impediment to growth in today's Mezzogiorno [Southern Italy]. . . . Overall, there is good cause to complain about the state of finance in the Mezzogiorno. Banks have certainly not performed the Schumpeterian role of promoting large-scale development projects. And the same goes for special credit institutions, even though these were created specifically to perform this function on behalf of the public sector. Intermediaries have also displayed shortcomings in such less ambitious but nonetheless important tasks as screening and monitoring. At best, they have played the role of followers, providing finance when it was demanded in the private and especially the public sector.

To improve the situation, Faini, Galli, and Giannini (1993, pp. 197–199) proffer various remedies:

> In our view, one feature of overriding importance concerns competition. Slack competitive pressure affects not only costs and prices but also the "quality" of the banking product. In this regard, financial liberalization (which started slowly in the early 1980s and has recently accelerated) will prove to be of major benefit to the efficiency of the entire Southern economy, not just the financial system.

Their final comment is this (p. 200):

> The final feature on which we focus is the system of financial subsidies, which greatly impairs the efficiency of the special credit institutions. On the one hand, it burdens them with functions and responsibilities, including legal ones, that are typical of government (judging whether a project is eligible for subsidies); on the other it tends to relieve them of the main responsibility of the banker: evaluating the economic merits of a project. Administered interest rates on subsidized loans, besides impairing competition among intermediaries, also downgrade the screening function of the institutions. When the interest rate is fixed exogenously by a government agency, the banker will only be concerned with the lower tail of the distribution of returns: he has to make sure that bad outcomes have a low probability and that the risk is covered by collateral. As we have seen, risky projects tend to be rejected, regardless of expected returns. As a consequence, what is sometimes called "development finance" (relating to projects with high return and high risk) is virtually nonexistent: new product and technology ideas, growth-oriented firms, etc., have little or no access to long-term capital. This is a most unfortunate situation. Development needs development finance, for at least two reasons. First, in an area that is totally open to external trade, local firms cannot grow simply by copying what is done in mature areas. They must generate new ideas, in terms of technology, organization, products, etc.: in a word, they must take risks. Second, in the Mezzogiorno, and presumably in the less developed areas of other industrial countries, firms are either very large (typically outside or public corporations) or very small (typically the local firms). While efficiency does not always grow in direct proportion to size, it is clear that very small firms may not be able to develop the technical structures, marketing organization and so on that are required to survive and, *a fortiori*, to prosper. Moreover, expanding a firm's size usually requires a discontinuous jump with the financing of new projects that are large compared to the existing concern. Once again, risk-taking emerges as an important feature of development.

In sum, the recommendations for the development of a backward area in Italy comprise a thorough transformation of the financial system, "for which liberalization and increased competition are necessary but not sufficient conditions" (Faini, Galli, and Giannini, 1993, p. 201). Virtually all these arguments appear to apply *mutatis mutandis* to the backward regions of China.

Inadequate Payments System

Some claim that China's payments system is too underdeveloped to enable interest-rate liberalization to transmit funds efficiently across the country. In fact, all financial systems in market economies, whether they are developed or developing, perform two basic functions: (1) administering the country's payments mechanism and (2) intermediating between savers and investors.[5] The main aim of interest-rate liberalization is to improve the financial sector's ability to and efficiency in intermediating between savers and investors. Interest-rate liberalization can certainly improve this function whether or not it also enables the stance of monetary policy to be transmitted rapidly across financial markets and across regions of the country. In other words, interest-rate liberalization does not jeopardize the equally important work needed to improve the ability of China's financial system to administer the country's payments mechanism. Both interest-rate liberalization and payments system improvements can usefully proceed in step with one another.

Lack of Competition

The statement that there is little competition within China's financial sector is undisputed. International experience does indeed suggest that competition is a prerequisite for interest rate liberalization to produce a competitive free-market interest-rate structure of interest rates. Without competition, a cartel is likely to take over the present arrangements for setting interest rates, but for the benefit of the banks rather than the economy.

Possibly the most appropriate objectives of interest-rate policy in China are the efficient mobilization and allocation of domestic resources. Efficiency of both the mobilization and allocation of saving is maximized when institutional interest rates are set at their free-market equilibrium levels and discriminatory taxes on financial intermediation are removed. With an oligopolistic financial system, the competitive solution may well have to be imposed. Provided adequate bank supervision is in place, there is probably little point in attempting to set loan rates of interest; they can be evaded so easily through compensating deposits. Instead, the monetary authorities might set deposit rates at levels that approximate the competitive free-market rates. Specifically, banks might be required to offer indexed six- or twelve-month deposits with a modest (perhaps 3 percent) real return at their own expense.

One way of stimulating rather than simulating a competitive interest-rate solution is for the government to issue treasury bills and bonds with attractive yields. Typically, government securities are held only by financial institutions as part of their required liquidity ratios and by business firms required to hold them in order to bid on government contracts. Yields on government securities are so low that voluntary holdings are nonexistent.

The appropriate interest-rate structure, however, applies equally to the government and the private sector. Indeed, if the government is unwilling to compete in this way, financial development is doomed.

The sale of government securities with attractive yields could start with fixed-price sales at post offices. The next stage would be auction sales at which direct investors as well as dealers and brokers might bid for securities. This scheme has the double advantage of ensuring that both the government as well as the banking system offers competitive returns to savers. An experiment along these lines in Turkey succeeded in raising real deposit rates of interest by 20 percentage points in 1981. The rate of economic growth accelerated sharply in that year.

Directed or selective credit policies go hand in hand with interest-rate policies. The defects of low interest-rate policies are compounded by selective credit policies that differentiate and subsidize interest rates charged to particular categories of borrowers. The most obvious disadvantage of selective credit policies is that capital rather than labor is subsidized. Where an economic activity is deemed worthy of subsidy, a fiscal subsidy that subsidizes the use of labor by at least as much as it subsidizes the use of capital must be preferred. Fiscal subsidies have the added advantage that they must be budgeted; financing through a consumption tax would probably be least distortionary. The cost of interest-rate subsidies is usually concealed and ignored. Abandoning directed credit programs must constitute one of the first steps of any sensible financial development program. If the government is too weak to take this step, it may well be too weak to implement any well-conceived macroeconomic policy.

Markets in which interest rates are freely determined by the interaction of supply and demand are few and far between in the developing world. The PBC can offer education in and experience with the market determination of interest rates in a few easy stages. Logical progression in financial development programs is crucial. It is important to start the process by introducing short-term financial assets with no risk other than a small amount of interest risk. Prices must be determined in the market through the free interplay of demand and supply. Since 1984 Indonesia has provided some excellent examples of how to introduce and develop markets in short-term financial claims. Bank deposits are a bad example because their price does not change. Treasury bills, central bank negotiable certificates of deposit (NCDs), and interbank money markets are good examples. After experience has been gained in these simple, low-risk, transparent markets, then and only then does it makes some sense to turn to equity market development.

The PBC could also develop a treasury bill market. The development of such a market would provide some salient competition with the banking system. Negotiable treasury bills with short maturities of 30, 60, and 180 days could be sold by the PBC on behalf of the government. These bills might be sold at auction once a week. The amount to be sold (and possibly also a reservation price below which sales would not be made) would be announced by the PBC during the preceding week. Bids for treasury bills would be placed prior to the actual auction. The bids might take the form of quantities to be bought at prices ranging from the reservation price to the face value of the bill in standard increments. At the time of the auction, the bids would be totaled and the ruling price would be the lowest at which supply exceeded or equaled demand. A small quantity of bills would therefore be unsold after each auction.

The PBC could also establish an open market for the resale of treasury bills. Initially, the PBC might offer to repurchase treasury bills, using some formula with which to calculate an offer price. By establishing a physical marketplace and by offering to buy at a price somewhat unattractive to potential sellers, the PBC could attract other buyers, including dealers and brokers, into the market.

Another instrument in which initial experience with market determination of interest rates can be gained is the NCD. It can serve three purposes. First, NCDs stimulate competition among the issuing banks. Second, they lengthen the maturity of banks' liability portfolios, so enabling them to increase their medium- and long-term lending activities without undue interest-rate risk. Third, trading in NCDs produces a simple market in which experience with market determination of interest rates can be gained with minimum trauma. Conditions of supply of NCDs are critical. Clearly, if NCDs are issued on tap at a fixed price with the same fixed guaranteed repurchase price, they will be indistinguishable from savings deposits. The market price would be tied rigidly to the redemption price, and no trading would occur. The ideal solution is sale by auction. Provided the dividend is sufficiently attractive, the market price can be kept above the floor at which banks guarantee repurchase. Then, provided supply is regulated in one way or another, market trading at prices above the price floor will take place.

High Inflation

High and persistent inflation certainly prevents interest-rate liberalization from operating effectively, since positive real interest rates would imply nominal interest rates that are probably too high to be sustainable even by many solvent firms in China. The basic problem of high nominal interest rates lies in the effective shortening of a loan's maturity. Under inflationary conditions, the inflation premium in the nominal interest rate compensates for the erosion in the real value of financial claims and is, therefore, principal repayment in real terms. Hence, high nominal interest rates reflecting high inflation can turn a twenty-year loan into a five-year loan. If the investment that is financed by such a loan has an expected life of twenty years and income from it would sustain interest and amortization payments adequately in the absence of inflation, the effective shortening of the loan's maturity under high inflation and high nominal interest rates inevitably creates a liquidity problem.

There are two questions here. The first is whether or not the competitive free-market equilibrium interest rate in China would be positive in real terms if measured against the consumer price index. Apart from a number of administered price increases, there must also have been large price increases in nontradable goods (real estate, and so on) in 1994. That pressure on the exchange rate is in the direction of appreciation rather than depreciation is another indicator that price increases in the tradable goods sectors have not been nearly as pronounced as the CPI inflation rate might suggest.

China may resemble Hong Kong with respect to its equilibrium real interest rate. The Hong Kong dollar is pegged to the U.S. dollar and Hong Kong imposes no controls on capital movements. Therefore, interest rates in Hong Kong necessarily deviate very little from interest rates in the United States. Because of much faster growth, which always increases prices of nontraded goods in fixed supply, however, inflation in Hong Kong has been considerably higher than inflation in the United States (Balassa, 1964). Hence, competitive free-market equilibrium real interest rates in Hong Kong have been negative when measured against the CPI. In fact, the wholesale or producers' price index is a far better measure of inflation for the assessment and measurement of real interest rates (McKinnon, 1973, pp. 96–97; 1979, pp. 234–236; 1993, pp. 31–38).

With China's spectacular growth, CPI inflation may well continue in double digits even if tradable goods prices are stable. In such case, the competitive free-market equilibrium real interest rate in China could be negative by 5 to 10 percentage points when measured using the CPI. Measured using a wholesale price index, however, real interest rates would be positive.

The second question is whether inflation is high in China. Certainly recorded CPI inflation in 1994 exceeded 20 percent. However, it has fallen since then and could well continue to fall further in the future. It is neither a persistent inflation to which the population has adapted, nor is it driven by hard-to-correct macroeconomic imbalances. For these reasons, China appears to meet the prerequisite of reasonable price stability for a successful interest-rate liberalization.

Excessive Capital Inflows

There is a fear that interest-rate liberalization could make inflation worse by encouraging capital inflows that have already caused problems for monetary control. While it is certainly true that recent capital inflows increased net foreign assets of China's banking system in 1994, much of this capital took the form of foreign direct investment and portfolio investment. Neither are influenced directly by the level of institutional interest rates. Furthermore, portfolio investment inflows are likely to be *negatively* affected by higher institutional interest rates in China to the extent that such interest rate increases dampened equity prices.

The real danger lies in capital inflows attracted by fixed-interest financial assets, such as treasury bills or bank deposits, or in the form of foreign borrowing by Chinese enterprises. Without exchange rate guarantees and other forms of government guarantee of repayment, which should only be provided with the greatly care and reluctance, the probability of any large capital inflow into China before property rights are better established and its legal system improved considerably seems remote in the extreme. Hence, the fear of an unmanageable and disruptive surge of capital inflows following interest-rate liberalization in China under present circumstances appears unwarranted.[6]

Conclusion

As enumerated at the outset, China is now in a position to benefit from interest-rate liberalization in the following ways:

- Better monetary control and hence lower and more stable inflation,
- Improved allocation of scarce investible funds, and
- Higher levels of saving, which, in turn, permit more investment without accelerating inflation.

With careful implementation, there appear to be no valid reasons why China should not proceed to reap these benefits by pursuing a policy of interest-rate liberalization.

Acknowledgments

My thanks go to Andy Mullineux for extremely useful comments on an earlier draft. This paper is based on seminars held in Beijing as part of a technical assistance program provided by the Monetary and Exchange Affairs Department of the International Monetary Fund to the People's Bank of China in January 1995. While I am most grateful to the International Monetary Fund for inviting me to join their team on this occasion, the views expressed in this chapter do not necessarily reflect those of the International Monetary Fund, its Board of Directors, its management, or any of its member countries. MicroTSP, version 7.0, was used for the regression and CorelDraw for the graphics presented in this chapter.

Notes

1. See David Begg and Richard Portes (1992) for a more detailed discussion of the debt overhang problem in economies in transition.
2. For details of what constitutes improved prudential regulation and supervision, see Dimitri Vittas (1992).
3. These data were used in the money demand estimates reported in Wanda Tseng et al. (1994, app. IV).
4. I am grateful to Andy Mullineux for providing this analogy.
5. Mark Gertler and Andrew Rose (1994) provide a nontechnical exposition of the theory of financial intermediation. Gertler (1988) offers a more technical analysis.
6. For further analysis of excessive capital inflows, see Susan Schadler et al. (1993).

References

Arndt, Heinz W., and Peter J. Drake. (1985). "Bank Loans or Bonds: Some Lessons of Historical Experience." *Banca Nazionale del Lavoro Quarterly Review* 155 (December): 373–392.

Balassa, Bela. (1964). "The Purchasing-Power Parity Doctrine: A Reappraisal." *Journal of Political Economy* 72(6) (December): 584–596.

Begg, David, and Richard Portes. (1992). "Enterprise Debt and Economic Transformation: Financial Restructuring of the State Sector in Central and Eastern Europe." London: Centre for Economic Policy Research, Discussion Paper No. 695, June.

Calvo, Guillermo A., and Fabrizio Coricelli. (1992). "Stagflationary Effects of Stabilization Programs in Reforming Socialist Countries: Enterprise-Side vs. Household-Side Factors." *World Bank Economic Review* 6(1) (January): 71–90.

Cuddington, John T., and Gordon W. Smith. (1985). "International Borrowing and Lending: What Have We Learned from Theory and Experience?" In Gordon W.

Smith and John T. Cuddington (eds.), *International Debt and the Developing Countries* (pp. 3–17). Washington, DC: World Bank.

De Gregorio, José, and Pablo E. Guidotti. (1993). "Financial Development and Economic Growth." Washington, DC: International Monetary Fund, July.

Errunza, Vihang R., and Joseph P. Ghalbouni. (1986). "Interest Rates and International Debt Crisis." *Banca Nazionale del Lavoro Quarterly Review* 157 (June): 225–245.

Faini, Riccardo, Giampaolo Galli, and Curzio Giannini. (1993). "Finance and Development: The Case of Southern Italy." In Alberto Giovannini (ed.), *Finance and Development: Issues and Experience* (pp. 158–214). Cambridge: Cambridge University Press.

Fry, Maxwell J. (1994). "Direct and Indirect Effects of Financial Repression on Saving and Growth: A Simultaneous-Equation Model of Saving, Investment, Exports and Growth." Birmingham: University of Birmingham, International Finance Group, IFGWP-94-05, November.

Fry, Maxwell. (1995). *Money, Interest, and Banking in Economic Development* (2nd ed.). Baltimore: Johns Hopkins University Press.

Gertler, Mark. (1988). "Financial Structure and Aggregate Economic Activity: An Overview." *Journal of Money, Credit and Banking* 20(3, ii) (August): 559–588.

Gertler, Mark, and Andrew Rose. (1994). "Finance, Public Policy and Growth." In Gerard Caprio, Jr., Izak Atiyas, and James A. Hanson (eds.), *Financial Reform: Theory and Experience* (pp. 13–48). New York: Cambridge University Press.

Jappelli, Tullio, and Marco Pagano. (1994). "Saving, Growth, and Liquidity Constraints." *Quarterly Journal of Economics* 109(1) (February): 83–109.

Liu, Liang-Yn, and Wing Thye Woo. (1994). "Saving Behaviour under Imperfect Financial Markets and the Current Account Consequences." *Economic Journal* 104(424) (May): 512–527.

McKinnon, Ronald I. (1973). *Money and Capital in Economic Development.* Washington, DC: Brookings Institution.

McKinnon, Ronald I. (1979). *Money in International Exchange: The Convertible Currency System.* New York: Oxford University Press.

McKinnon, Ronald I. (1991). "Monetary Stabilization in LDCs." In Lawrence B. Krause and Kim Kihwan (eds.), *Liberalization in the Process of Economic Development* (pp. 366–400). Berkeley: University of California Press.

McKinnon, Ronald I. (1993). *The Order of Economic Liberalization: Financial Control in the Transition to a Market Economy* (2nd ed.). Baltimore: Johns Hopkins University Press.

Morris, Felipe, Mark Dorfman, José Pedro Ortiz, and Maria Claudio Franco. (1990). "Latin America's Financial Systems in the 1980s: A Cross-Country Comparison." Washington, DC: World Bank, Discussion Paper 81, May.

Patrick, Hugh T. (1994). "Comparisons, Contrasts and Implications." In Hugh T. Patrick and Yung Chul Park (eds.), *Financial Development of Japan, Korea, and Taiwan: Growth, Repression, and Liberalization* (pp. 325–371). New York: Oxford University Press.

Schadler, Susan, Maria Carkovic, Adam Bennett, and Robert Kahn. (1993). *Recent Experiences with Surges in Capital Inflows.* Washington, DC: International Monetary Fund, Occasional Paper 108, December.

Talley, Samuel H., and Ignacio Mas. (1992). "The Role of Deposit Insurance." In Dimitri Vittas (ed.), *Financial Regulation: Changing the Rules of the Game* (pp. 321–351). Washington, DC: World Bank, EDI Development Studies.

Tseng, Wanda, Hoe Ee Khor, Kalpana Kochhar, Dubravako Mihaljek, and David Burton. (1994). "Economic Reform in China: A New Phase." Washington, DC: International Monetary Fund, Occasional Paper 114, November.

Villanueva, Delano P., and Abbas Mirakhor. (1990). "Strategies for Financial Reforms: Interest Rate Policies, Stabilization, and Bank Supervision in Developing Countries." *International Monetary Fund Staff Papers* 37(3) (September): 509–536.

Vittas, Dimitri (ed.). (1992). *Financial Regulation: Changing the Rules of the Game.* Washington, DC: World Bank, EDI Development Studies.

5 FINANCIAL REFORM, INSTITUTIONS, AND MACROECONOMIC ADJUSTMENT

The Destabilizing Effects of Financial Liberalization in the Philippines, 1970 to 1992

Rob Vos

Introduction

The experience of developing countries has shown that successful financial liberalization is not a simple matter of "getting the prices right." Attempts toward financial liberalization in several Latin American countries in the 1970s and 1980s have provoked major banking crises and related economic recessions, requiring subsequent government interventions at considerable economic cost. Financial reforms in various East Asian countries have been rated more successful, but the common denominator to this success appears to be a very gradual and cautious approach toward financial liberalization. In these cases good economic performance preceded the liberalization process, and heavy government controls of the financial sector played (and still play) a key role in successful industrial development.

Analysis of the experience from developing countries seems to point out that the success or failure are closely related to (1) the timing and sequencing of financial liberalization measures in relation to the overall macroeconomic conditions and other economic reforms, (2) the institutional structure of the financial sector, and (3) the effectiveness of government interventions and adequacy of financial-sector supervision.

The developing country experience shows that reform measures, in lieu of enhancing economic efficiency, may create severe macroeconomic problems when implemented in an unstable macroeconomic environment and where supervision and regulation of financial institutions is inadequate (Vos, 1995). Perhaps at least equally important, failures of financial liberalization attempts often also stem from an insufficient understanding of prevailing market imperfections. Of the typical imperfections, some are inherent to the functioning of financial markets such as asymmetric information and problems of moral hazard, while others are rooted in the historical development of financial institutions, such as bank concentration and interlocking interests between bank and nonbank firms.

In this chapter, I analyze the importance of these factors in explaining the destabilizing impact of financial reform policies implemented in the Philippines during the 1970s and the 1980s. The dismal performance of the Philippine economy over the past decades gives it a status of a stray cat among the neighboring economic tigers and tiger cubs in the East Asian region, and its macroeconomic disequilibria, debt problems, sluggish growth, and failed financial liberalization during the 1970s and the 1980s have given the economy more a Latin American standing than a rank among the fast-growing East Asian miracle countries. The Philippine financial system featured credit and interest-rate controls not unlike those of its neighboring economies. However, the overall institutional structure of bank-firm conglomerates tied to political elites and an economic incentive structure made the financial system prone to crises. Various attempts toward financial reform and liberalization during the 1970s and the 1980s were not able to overcome the structural problems of the Philippine financial system. The World Bank–supported financial reform, implemented in the early 1980s amid major macroeconomic disequilibria, made these problems manifest rather than resolving them. The domestic financial system fell subsequently into a severe crisis thereby deepening the macroeconomic problems. The cost of adjustment to the financial crisis were still being paid in the mid-1990s.

The Philippine Financial System and Macroeconomic Disequilibria

The development of the financial system of the Philippines over the past two decades does not provide an exemplary case of smoothly operating financial markets fueling investment and growth. On the contrary, structural features of the process of financial intermediation have been sources of recurring liquidity and solvency crises in various parts of the Philippine banking system and capital markets. Instead of providing channels to alleviate financial constraints, the malfunctioning of the financial system has been a source of macroeconomic problems. As discussed below, the structural problems relate to the segmented nature of Philippine financial markets, the lack of competition among financial institutions, wide-ranging interlocking directorates and ownership patterns across the banking industry and other economic sectors, the shallowness of financial markets, and the unresolved external debt overhang.

The Philippine financial system has a strongly dualistic nature with an important informal financial market segment coexisting with the formal banking system (Vos and Yap, 1996). Informal money lenders fund, at relatively high cost, small businesses and household firms that have little or no access to the formal banking system. Large private corporations are the preferential borrowers of the highly concentrated formal banking system. Interlocking interests of banks and corporate enterprises strongly direct the allocation of funds, often overriding normal financial risk assessment. Overleveraged firms and bad loan problems have been systemic problems requiring Central Bank and government intervention to bail out ailing financial institutions, often at substantial macroeconomic costs. At the same time, financial markets have remained rather thin. While financial deepening has proceeded at an accelerated pace in its neighboring Asian countries, the mobilization of savings through the financial system has stagnated in the Philippines. The main causes can be found in the lack of institutional development of the financial system and low degree of competition within the banking industry, a prolonged period of financial repression policies that kept down real rates of return on financial assets, low interest-rate elasticities of the demand for financial savings, and the structural determinants of real savings.

The consequent lack of credit availability has constrained investment spending. During the 1970s, many financial institutions resorted to foreign borrowing to enhance their domestic lending capacity making the system vulnerable to external shocks. A subsequent financial crisis in the early 1980s forced the Central Bank of the Philippines to save the system by taking over most of the banks' external debt and nonperforming loans. This weakened the balance sheet of the monetary authority and formed the major source of huge losses of the Central Bank affecting its capacity to control monetary aggregates. The external debt of the Central Bank and the rest of the public sector remained a major factor in sustaining a large public sector deficit. IMF agreements conditioned restrictive monetary policies to keep inflation down; combined with the shallowness of Philippine capital markets this required the financing of fiscal deficits through high-yielding, short-term government securities. Toward the end of the 1980s, this led to a vicious circle of a persistent external debt overhang and continuous domestic public debt accumulation that has continued to burden economic adjustment in the 1990s. The buildup of domestic public debt at high interest rates led to a further widening of fiscal deficits, more government demands on the domestic capital market and back to higher interest rates, and so on. At the same time, the external debt overhang has made the monetary authorities reluctant to adjust the exchange rate as a devaluation would raise the domestic currency cost of debt and thus the fiscal deficit. The cost of this attempt to stick to fiscal targets has been a tendency toward currency overvaluation, which in turn has affected export performance and has sustained incentives toward capital flight by the private sector. On the other hand, the high domestic real interest rates worked in the opposite direction and provoked some return of capital flight toward the end of the 1980s. However, this did not help to boost private investment in productive assets due to the government's drain on domestic financial resources.

Various attempts toward financial reform and liberalization during the 1970s and 1980s were not able to overcome the structural problems of the Philippine financial system. It is even fair to conclude that these reforms have exacerbated the mentioned weaknesses, such as the increase in concentration of the banking sector after the financial liberalization measures of 1981. Adjustment policies in the 1980s and early 1990s primarily sought to resolve the economy's fiscal and foreign-exchange constraints. It seems that even if the government manages to overcome these problems, an increase in private-sector savings and investment will not be immediate or automatic. The structural problems of the financial sector will also have to be dealt with.

Philippine Financial Development

Financial development in the Philippines mimics the performance of the real economy. Where neighboring economies have witnessed substantia financial deepening during the last quarter century, indicators for the Philippines show only a slow pace of financial growth. Figures 5.1 and 5.2 illustrate this. The level of currency plus financial savings relative to GNP (M3/GNP) remained relatively stable in the Philippines over the past two decades (between 25 and 30 percent), while that in neighboring countries like South Korea, Thailand, and Indonesia increased considerably, particu-

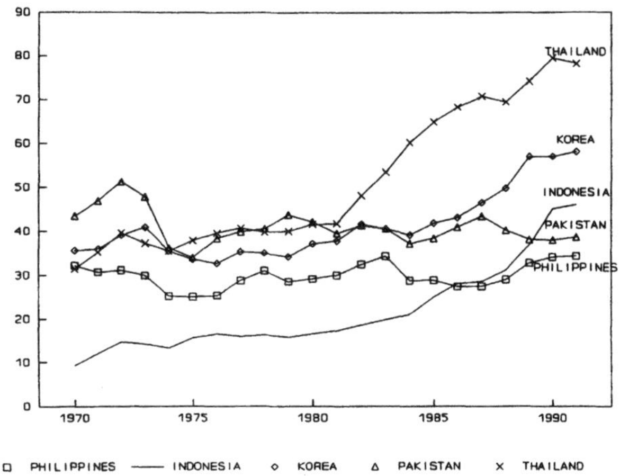

Figure 5.1. Broad money to GNP ratio (M3/GNP) in selected Asian countries (percent)

Source: IMF, *International Financial Statistics.*

larly during the 1980s. Financial development was particularly spectacular in Thailand with the M3/GNP ratio doubling from 40 to 80 percent in a decade. The ratio for low-income Pakistan also has been relatively stable over the period but is higher than that of the Philippines. The M3/GNP ratio may be somewhat misleading as a measure of financial deepening as the composition of the money supply matters also.

With economic development one expects the importance of currency and demand deposit holdings (M1) to decline and that of time and savings deposits (quasi-money) and other liabilities of the financial system to increase. Figure 5.2 shows that in Pakistan the financial intermediation ratio (M3/M1) is quite low (only slightly above 1), implying that the relatively high M3/GNP ratio mainly reflects a high M1/GNP ratio and thus a low income velocity of money (V = GNP/M1). The degree of financial intermediation in Indonesia is similar to that of Pakistan but has increased sharply after the financial reform reform policies initiated in the early 1980s. The ratios for Korea and Thailand follow the pattern of the M3/GNP ratio showing substantia financial deepening.

In the Philippines, the financial intermediation ratio (M3/M1) went up considerably during the 1970s, peaking at around 4 in the early 1980s. However, the economic crisis and the related financial crisis of the 1980s provoked a tendency toward financial *dis*intermediation. From the early 1970s onward, there have been several financial reform programs attempt-

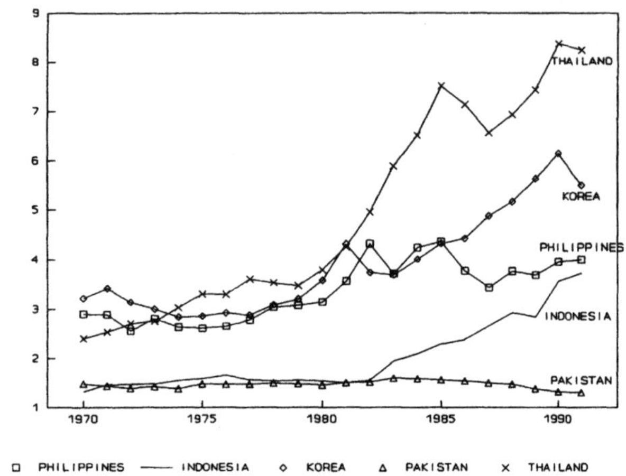

Figure 5.2. Financial intermediation ratio (M3/M1) in selected Asian countries (percent)

Source: IMF, *International Financial Statistics.*

ing to liberalize and strengthen the financial system. This created institutional changes and financial growth but often not in desired directions. For instance, the accelerated growth of M3 in the 1970s was largely driven by growth of deposit substitutes (such as promissory notes, certificates of assignment, repurchase agreements), which provided an alternative to time and savings deposits that carried negative real interest rates due to the financial repression policies. The funds raised in this market provided a source of relending to firms and owners and directors of bank-firm conglomerates that had already exhausted exposure limits as per Central Bank regulations (Lamberte, 1989). Such financial innovations mainly worked to strengthen the central features of the Philippine financial system, which can be characterized by high degrees of market segmentation, bank concentration, and interlocking directorates and ownership patterns.

Weaknesses of the Financial System

The Philippine financial system experienced three major crises since 1970: the first in the mid-1970s, the second in 1981; and the third in 1983 to 1984. The principal weaknesses underlying the system's fragility relate to (1) low capacity of the financial system to mobilize private savings, (2) credit rationing practices, (3) a heavy segmentation and concentration of the sector, (4) interlocking interests of banks and nonfinancial enterprises, (5) external vulnerability built up during the 1980s, and (6) weak enforcement of bank supervision and prudential regulations and credit and banking policies of the government. These factors have led to inadequate domestic resource mobilization and excessive exposure of banks to single borrowers, and hence a financial system prone to crises.

Low Capacity to Mobilize Private Savings

Financial deepening stagnated in the Philippines during the 1980s, partly because of the overall economic crisis affecting the real savings rate and partly because of the low (even negative) responsiveness of household savings to higher interest rates. Vos and Yap (1996, ch. 4) present econometric evidence showing both household and private enterprise savings respond negatively to the real interest rate. In the case of household savings, the negative link is small and barely significant.[1]

Interest rates may be a more important determinant of financial savings. Evidence for the Philippines suggest, however, that the expansion of financial savings in the 1970s was mainly driven by income growth and, more in particular, the expansion of branching by the banking system making it more accessible to consumers of financial services. Real deposits rates were negative as a result of the financial repression policies of fixed nominal interest rates. Financial liberalization in the early 1980s lifted interest-rate ceiling but did not lead to a boost in financial savings. Regression analysis confirms that income growth, institutional development (bank density), and confidence in the financial system (Central Bank's operations as lender of last resort) are important determinants of the demand for time and savings deposits (Table 5.1). However, the interest-rate elasticity of the demand for savings and time deposits is quite low. Table 5.1 shows no significant relationship between real interest rate and the demand for savings deposits. In the case of time deposits there is a positive and significant relation with the nominal interest rate and a negative one with the rate of inflation, but the implicit elasticity for the real interest rate is low.[2] A low interest-rate elasticity of the demand for financial savings, means that large interest-rate shifts are required for any new demands for funds, if the market is to clear through the interest rate.

However, despite the lifting of the interest-rate ceilings, financial markets in the Philippines are not price-clearing, as follows from the observed oligopolistic pricing policies of the banks and credit-rationing practices

Table 5.1. Estimated demand for savings and time deposits.

	Savings Deposits			*Time Deposits*
	SD (Real)	*SD/GNP*	*TD (Real)*	*TD/GNP*
Constant	15,886.6	13.2	17,779.1	20.4
	(7.02)*	(6.56)*	(1.41)	(1.57)
Interest rate:				
Nominal	—	—	1,648.0	1.583
			(2.69)**	(2.33)**
Real	98.6	0.067	—	—
	(1.56)	(1.16)		
Inflation rate	—	—	–356.0	–0.376
			(–2.18)**	(–1.94)**
Real GNP growth	827.7	0.639	428.2	0.162
	(3.43)*	(2.91)*	(0.92)	(0.35)
Banking density[a]	–781.5	–0.419	–1,690.9	–1.633
	(–5.65)*	(–3.33)*	(–2.39)**	(–2.27)**
Incidence of bank failure	–2,597.0	–2.164	1,137.9	1.418
(Dummy)	(–1.96)**	(–1.79)**	(0.49)	(0.52)
Central Bank intervention	268.3	0.223	–48.2	–0.075
(Dummy)	(3.86)*	(3.53)*	(–0.39)	(–0.56)
Adjusted R^2	0.65	0.44	0.71	0.71
Durbin Watson	1.75	1.83	2.19	2.20
F-value	8.06	3.95	6.19	5.53
Sample period	1970–89	1970–89	1976–89	1976–89

Source: Vos and Yap (1996, Table 5.5). T-statistics are in parentheses.

a Defined as population per bank branch. Thus, a negative coefficient means that an expansion of bank branching enhances demand for time and savings deposits.

* Significant at 1% level.

** Significant at 5% level.

discussed below. The point made about low interest-rate elasticities is nevertheless important because it highlights the thinness of financial markets in the Philippines. Issuance of new financial instruments, like the deposit substitutes in the 1970s and government securities in the 1980s, required very high yields in order to attract enough investment funds. In the case of the domestic borrowing by the government this did not attract more household savings but rather investment funds of private corporations and commercial banks, thereby crowding out funds available for productive investment.

Credit Rationing and Excessive exposure

Credit allocation in the Philippines is subject to various rationing rules. The practice of credit rationing did not alter under the liberalized interest-rate regime established in 1980 (see Lapar and Graham, 1988). The existence of imperfect information on credit markets creates risk and, therefore, makes credit rationing a rational form of behavior for banks, even in competitive credit markets.[3] As we have seen, however, financial markets in the Philippines are far from competitive and are highly segmented. Households and unincorporated businesses are by and large rationed out of the formal market for commercial bank loans (see Vos and Yap, 1996, Table 5.1). They have to rely on informal money lenders and credits from specialized government banks. The latter, including the Development Bank of the Philippines (DBP), the Philippine Amanah Bank (PAB), and particularly the Land Bank (LBP), in principal are to play a major role in providing the agricultural sector with adequate credits. However, these institutions allocated at best one-quarter of total credits to agriculture, but the share fell dramatically in the first half of the 1980s, recovered during 1986 and 1988 and then fell off again to below 10 percent. More important, the total loan supply from state-owned development banks, including the government-owned commercial Philippine National Bank (PNB), fell dramatically between 1985 and 1989. This is largely due to the severe financial problems encountered by the DBP caused by ill management. Lending to the industrial sector suffered most when DBP reduced its loan portfolio. Lending to this sector witnessed a remarkable recovery starting in 1988 as DBP was successfully rehabilitated. Loans to agriculture from LBP stabilized explaining the falling share for agriculture.

Commercial banks also have been supplying a declining share of credits to agriculture (Vos and Yap, 1996, Table 5.7). This might be a normal event given the sector's (albeit slowly) declining share in total output. However, credit allocation is influenced by government policies, as all banks operating in the Philippines are subject to the so-called agri/agra law, which requires all banks to allocate 25 percent of their loanable funds to agriculture and agrarian reform beneficiaries. But banks may satisfy this requirement by buying eligible government securities. In effect, the agri/agra law thus works more as an additional reserve requirement than as an effective means to provide agriculture and rural unincorporated businesses with credits. This agri/agra reserve requirement comes on top of already high reserve requirement ratios, which in the Philippines has tended to be highest within the ASEAN region. Obviously, this continuing financial repression has limited bank lending to productive sectors. As noted, following the crisis of the early 1980s the commercial banks themselves exacerbated credit constraints on the economy by heavily engaging in the purchase of high-yielding government securities.

Concentration and Oligopolistic Banking

The Philippine commercial banking system is highly concentrated. Concentration increased during the 1980s despite financial reform measures aiming at the stimulation of bank competition. In 1991, 52 percent of the total assets of the commercial banking system were owned by five largest banks, up from 30 percent in 1980. As shown in Figure 5.3, the Herfindahl concentration index almost doubled during the decade (from 0.044 to 0.074).[4] Yap et al. (1990) also noted that in the money market, four large banks directly accounted for 13.3 percent of the total deposit substitutes of all financial institutions with quasi-banking licenses, while their affiliates accounted for 34.7 percent.

The increased concentration of the banking sector following the financial reforms of 1980 is a typical result of ill-conceived and badly timed liberalization measures. As discussed further below, the financial reforms were introduced at a point when banks suffered from severe financial distress caused by external shocks (higher world interest rates) and a huge portfolio of nonperforming loans with overleveraged large private corporations. The liberalization measures pushed up real lending rates, thus creating the bad loan portfolios of the banks. To save the system, the Central Bank of the Philippines (CB) successfully persuaded commercial banks and quasi-banks to merge and consolidate their institutions, in particular among financial institutions belonging to the same conglomerate (Lamberte, 1989, p. 50). Similar tendencies of increased bank concentration following financial liberalization and subsequent financial distress have been reported in other developing countries, particularly in Latin America (Morris et al., 1990; Fischer, 1993; and Vos, 1995).

Competition among banks has been further reduced after the financial rehabilitation of two ailing, large government-owned banks, PNB and DBP. After their rehabilitation, to avoid competition with private banks, the government-owned banks moved away from retail lending and now focus instead on wholesale lending (Lamberte, 1992).

Bank concentration in the Philippines is not worse than in other developing countries with apparently better functioning financial systems (Vos, 1995, Table 5.1). Bank concentration by itself thus not necessarily condi-

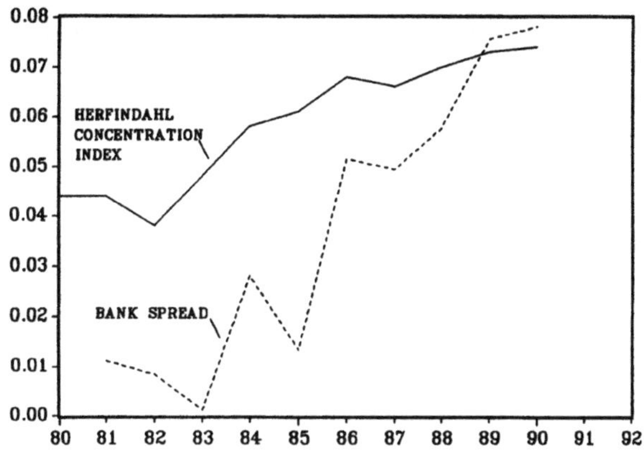

Figure 5.3. The Philippines: all commercial banks—Herfindahl concentration index of deposit liabilities and bank spread

Source: Data adapted from Lamberte (1992).
Note: A regression analysis of the Herfindahl concentration index (*H*) on bank spread (*SPREAD*) gave the following result:

$$SPREAD = -0.08 + 2.046H - 0.03\text{DUM85}$$
$$(-4.01) \quad (6.46) \quad (-8.81)$$
$$R^2_{adj} = 0.88 \quad \text{D.W.} = 1.69 \quad F = 35.1$$

t-statistics are in parentheses; all coefficients are significant at the 1 percent level. DUM85 is an intercept dummy for 1985. The regression results should be taken with caution as the number of observations is only ten (years).

tions an ill-performing financial sector, but it can be an important contributing factor. One of the effects of the increased bank concentration seems to have been a boost in oligopolistic pricing practices. Figure 5.3 shows the close relationship between the increase in bank spreads during the 1980s (from 1.1 to 7.8 percent). Bank spreads declined in the early 1980s. This was not caused by increased competition, but by losses incurred by some banks as a result of the financial crisis that struck in 1981.[5] The bank spread continued to increase after 1983 despite the deep economic crisis in 1984 to 1985 and the deceleration growth starting in 1990. Widening spreads while credit demands are low can be a result of oligopolistic pricing practices. This seems a much more plausible explanation than the suggestion of some studies (e.g., World Bank, 1993) that taxes on financial intermediation have driven up spreads, since gross receipt taxes on interest income of banks have remained the same (5 percent) during the 1980s. It should be added, however, that most likely at least some of the major banks that entered into financial problems (such as the PNB) also widened their profit margin in order to provide means of covering losses.

Interlocking Interests

A former CB governor, Gregario Licaros, observed cunningly that the "average Filipino banker is in the banking business not for banking profits; he uses his bank for allied business."[6] Philippine industries and banks exhibit a high degree of interlocking interests. Even before the advent of universal banking, a bank and its directors would have equity participation in other financial and nonfinancial enterprises. Lamberte et al. (1992), Floro and Yotopoulos (1991) and Kunio (1988) describe concrete examples of such conglomerates in the Philippines, while De Dios (1994) gives an analysis of their emergence.

Interlocking interests and lending to directors, officers, stockholders, and other interests are common characteristics in many developing countries (Leff, 1976; Fischer, 1993). Such in-house lending practices also tend to be the main channel in diverting bank funds to affiliated companies in the Philippines. The obvious problem with such lending practices in conjunction with the concentrated nature of the banking system is that it can easily drive banks toward overexposure to a limited number of activities and borrowers, while the near coincidence of creditor and borrower can easily lead to a lax stance with regard to normal risk assessment of loans, as well as to excessive distress lending to allied companies when facing liquidity problems. Moreover, interlocking ownership strengthens domestic lobbies against free entrance of banks enabling doubtful lending practices to continue.

The Philippine financial system forms a clear-cut example of such practices and its financial crises bear similar characteristics as those witnessed in various Latin American countries, despite the existence of fairly tight CB regulations to counteract bank-firm group related lending.[7] Weak monitoring of in-house lending practices turned the CB regulations into a soft instrument. Moreover, particularly in the 1970s, the bank-firm conglomerates used the quasi-banks they had acquired or set up primarily to service their own financing requirements by borrowing funds from the money market or underwriting commercial papers issued by their own affiliates (Lamberte, 1989). Combined with the financial repression policies that kept real lending rates down, this practice stimulated heavy borrowing by the major firms. The average debt-equity ratio of the 1,000 largest private corporations went up from 1.7 in 1975 to 4.7 in 1981 and 5.8 in 1983. The financial system encountered a full-scale liquidity crisis. The default of textile entrepreneur Dewey Dee triggered a series of bankruptcies and exposed the weakness of the investment and broker houses allied to the commercial banks, which often carried large exposures to single borrowers. Investment houses affiliated to the Herdies conglomerate of companies had lent huge sums to Dewey Dee and their affiliates with funds mainly sourced from deposit substitutes in the money market. The Dewey Dee scandal unraveled this as a widespread practice.

The post-1981 increase in firms' debt-equity ratio should be seen as a typical sign of distress lending to avoid a widespread crisis in the productive sector. The financial crisis precipitated the earlier indicated changes in the sector, merging commercial banks and affiliated quasi-banks. Banks also entered into more conservative lending practices as already signaled by their stake in the acquisition of government securities. The 1980s have seen the emergence of tax-free trust operations managed by the banks and increased from a negligible amount in 1980 to 12.5 percent of commercial bank assets in the early 1990s. Nearly 60 percent of trust assets are in the form of corporate loans and discounts and likely forms the new channel of banks to divert loans to affiliated companies.

External Vulnerability

Along with the rest of the economy, the financial sector exposed itself to external shocks during the 1970s, and the toll was still being paid in the early 1990s. Banks engaged themselves in heavy external borrowing, while government financial institutions (PNB and DBP) also granted quite liberally public guarantees to foreign loans contracted by private corporations; many of these eventually ran into debt-servicing problems. The vulnerability of the financial system (that is, deposit money banks and the CB) to foreign-exchange crisis and global financial shocks may be seen from Figure 5.4. Growth of foreign liabilities of the commercial banks strongly outpaced that of foreign-asset holdings leading to a large negative net foreign-asset position between 1970 and 1983. The CB incurred foreign liabilities at a rapid pace, starting in 1980 with enhanced borrowing from the IMF to cope with the second oil price shock and the world interest-rate shock and subsequently through the takeover of the foreign liabilities of the banking system to avoid the system from collapse.

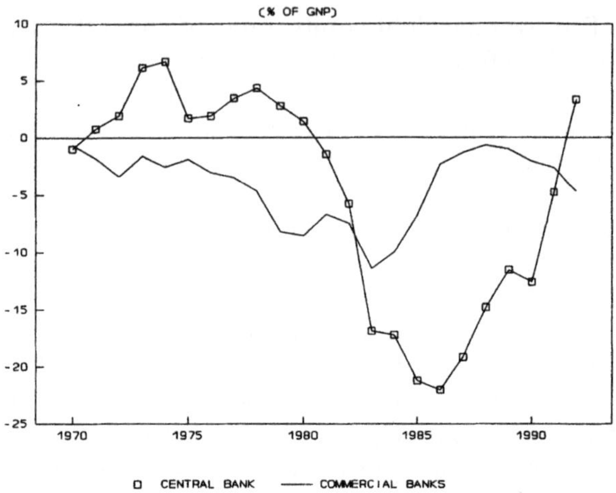

Figure 5.4. The Philippines: net foreign assets of the banking system (percent of GNP)

Source: Central Bank of the Philippines.

Financial Crisis and Its Macroeconomic Consequences

Bad Loans, Central Bank Losses and Monetary Policies

By the beginning of the 1980s, several large corporations, specifically those that grew fast in the 1970s,[8] suddenly found themselves in financial difficulty as a result of the economic slump brought about by the second oil shock and raising interest cost on their domestic and external liabilities. In the early part of 1981, a bank that had heavy exposure to a large mining firm that collapsed, experienced a run on deposits. The run spilled over to other banks. Then, as mentioned earlier, a prominent businessman, Dewey Dee, suddenly left the country leaving behind 90 million pesos of unpaid debts. Financial institutions that were heavily involved in the money markets suffered irreversible runs that eventually led to their collapse. Reeling from the painful effects of the 1981 liquidity crisis for two consecutive years, the first quarter of 1983 began with optimism, only to be frustrated by the balance-of-payments crisis that struck toward the first quarter of that year. Between 1983 and 1987, the CB closed down a total of 131 banks. The government used two of its financial institutions, DBP and PNB, in bailing out financial institutions and large corporations that collapsed right after the second oil chock. The 1983 to 1984 foreign-exchange crisis further aggravated their already tainted loan and investment portfolios. Both assumed privately contracted foreign loans that they guaranteed since corporations that obtained those foreign loans could no longer repay their foreign creditors. The losses they incurred during the period 1984 to 1986 amounted to 29.8 billion pesos. In 1986, both institutions underwent a rehabilitation program that involved the transfer to the national government of their nonperforming liabilities and related accounts, burdening the fiscal balance.

Besides adding to the fiscal deficit, the financial-sector crisis saddled the CB with a large negative net foreign-asset position. This has been the main source of losses (negative savings) of the Central Bank. These losses became a major macroeconomic burden towards the end of the 1980s. As explained in the Appendix, the sources of Central Bank losses stem from an excess of interest outlays over income on both domestic and foreign liabilities and assets and further from losses on foreign-exchange operations due to exchange-rate changes. Besides the losses due to excessive foreign liabilities, also interest income from *net* domestic assets turned negative starting in 1985. This is the result of interest subsidies provided by the CB to many government institutions because many of the CB's loans have gone bad during the economic crisis and further because the interest obligations on foreign liabilities were increasingly financed through domestic borrowing in the form of high-yielding CB bills. Table 5.2 shows that CB losses reached a staggering 5.3 percent of GNP in 1984 and remained around 2.0 percent of GNP from 1986 onward. Over the period as a whole the CB contributed one-third to one-half of the total public sector deficit.

By 1992, as shown in Figure 5.4, the situation seemed to have improved as net foreign assets turned to a positive position and, as shown by Table 5.2, the negative net interest income from net foreign assets fell from 1.4 to 0.7 percent of GNP. The adjustment has been largely cosmetic, however, and problems remain. In 1992, the CB's external debt was reduced from U.S. $5 billion to $2 billion in one year's time due to debt-buybacks and debt conversions totalling U.S. $0.75 billion in debt reduction and the remaining U.S. $2.25 billion corresponded to a debt rescheduling operation whereby CB external debt was transferred to the national government in exchange for domestic liabilities of the CB with the national government. Though adding to the domestic liabilities of the CB they are due in foreign currency and explains about half of the increase in net interest payments on domestic liabilities in 1992. The other half is explained by the new issuance of CB bills to cover CB losses and to finance the debt-reduction operations.

The recurrent losses of the CB are of serious concern not just for their public finance consequences but also for their implications for monetary

Table 5.2. Central Bank of the Philippines: income and outlay statement (percentage of GNP).

	CB Surplus (+) / Deficit (–)	Net Interest Income		Foreign Exchange Dealings	
		On NDA[a]	On NFA[b]	Forward Cover	Swap Cover
1980	–0.1%	0.3%	–0.5%		
1981	–0.4	0.6	–1.0		
1982	–2.3	0.9	–1.6	–0.4%	–1.2%
1983	–3.8	1.0	–1.5	–1.9	–1.4
1984	–5.4	0.4	–2.1	–2.8	–1.0
1985	–2.8	–0.8	–2.0	1.4	–1.4
1986	–3.1	–0.6	–2.5	–0.1	0.2
1987	–1.6	0.2	–1.7	–0.0	–0.1
1988	–2.1	–0.4	–1.7	–0.0	–0.1
1989	–2.3	–0.6	–1.6	–0.0	–0.1
1990	–2.0	–0.4	–1.3	–0.0	–0.3
1991	–1.7	–0.7	–1.2	–0.0	0.2
1992	–1.6	–1.4	–0.4[c]	0.0	0.2

Source: Vos and Yap (1996, Table 5.8), based on primary data from Central Bank of the Philippines, DER-Domestic, unpublished, for 1986 to 1992; and World Bank (1993) for 1980 to 1985.

a Interest income on domestic assets less interest payments on domestic liabilities. Includes Peso Differential (MAAB 43), which refer to peso gains realized from foreign-exchange swap transactions. As defined in the Memorandum for Authorized Agent Banks (MAAB) No. 43, this differential is equal to the difference between the official guiding rate (on the renewal date) and the original forward rate of the maturing swap contract multiplied by the foreign-currency volume of the swap contract being renewed.

b Interest income on foreign assets less interest payments on foreign liabilities.

c In 1992 the external debt of the Central Bank was reduced by about U.S. $3 billion (to U.S. $2.2 billion outstanding debt at the end of 1992). This debt reduction was partly due to debt buybacks and debt swaps totalling about U.S. $0.75 billion. The remainder is explained by debt rescheduling agreement through which part of the Central Bank's external debt is taken over by the national government against an increase in domestic liabilities of the Central Bank with the national government, but payable in US dollars. The decline of net interest payments on foreign liabilities in 1992 is mirrored by an increase in payments on domestic liabilities. The latter increase consists in part of an increase in interest payments on CB bills issued to finance losses and the external debt-reduction operations and in part of an increase in foreign-currency denominated obligations to the national govenment.

policy. First, the financing of foreign interest payments by domestic borrowing has raised interest rates as the already shallow domestic capital market had to deal with excess demand for funds from national government demands for securities. Second, CB losses contribute to the expansion of the money supply (see Appendix). Being strict on monetary targets in the second half of the 1980s, the CB kept its policy of sterilization operations. But these became increasingly costly with the higher interest rates. The condition has also raised the cost of sterilization operations needed to avoid excess money creation that might result from external debt-swap operations.[9] Third, the CB concern with its own losses and financing requirements has affected the appropriate use of monetary instruments. Issuance of short-term CB bills was deployed for CB revenue purposes, instead of monetary control and development objectives. The CB has employed reserve requirements and other regulatory measures, like the awarding of licenses to new commercial banks, essentially with the CB's cash flow in mind rather than with the objective of developing and protecting the financial system.

The Public Debt Overhang and Financial Reform

Fiscal imbalances have been a key problem in the adjustment process in the Philippines in the 1980s. For long policy makers have blamed part of the problem on the large external debt service obligations burdening the budget. However, during the 1980s persistent fiscal deficits, the poor functioning of financial markets and the priority given to monetary restraint, obliged the government to recur to costly domestic financing. This led to an increasing domestic public debt overhang with interest payment constituting over 40 percent of total government spending by the early 1990s (see Vos and Yap, 1996, for details).

The *domestic* debt overhang is not merely a problem of too high government spending and too low tax incomes. As became overly clear in the 1980s, the tight, IMF-conditioned monetary policies, combined with the structurally shallow basis of Philippine financial markets, required very high interest rates to attract enough funds to finance fiscal deficits through government securities. Figure 5.5 shows that the outstanding domestic public debt doubled as a share of GNP to 40 percent in 1992, up from around 20 percent between 1970 and 1983. Such a size of domestic public debt might seem far from excessive by international standards. The member states of the European Monetary System target a "manageable" public debt to GNP ratio of 65 percent under the Maastricht agreement, but most have a ratio much higher than that. Malaysia's domestic government debt reached 70 percent of GNP in 1989 without putting excessive pressure on domestic capital markets. In other words, a moderate-sized domestic public debt in the Philippines produced considerable financial strain because of the generally low capacity of the financial system to mobilize financial savings, which in turn is related

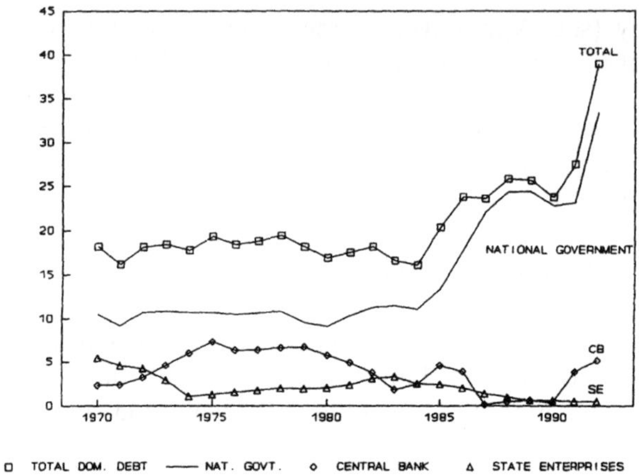

Figure 5.5. The Philippines: domestic public debt by borrower (percent of GDP)

Source: Central Bank of the Philippines.

to the wide income disparities, low interest-rate sensitivity of savings and investment demand, and the lack of bank competition. High-yielding government securities crowd out private investment, not so much because they raise the cost of borrowing to investors but because they have provoked shifts in the portfolios of private companies and commercial banks. The agri/agra law has formed to date a policy-driven preference of banks to hold government securities, while fears for a new financial crisis has further restricted lending to the private sector. Weak economic performance has provoked many firms to engage in investment in short-term financial securities to the detriment of investment in productive assets.

Cutting the fiscal deficit and domestic public debt will likely help to bring down interest rates on government securities. This will not lift the structural weaknesses of the financial system, however. Banks may continue to prefer relatively risk-free government securities over lending to the agricultural sector under the agri/agra law, while nonbank private investors may well shift back into the purchase of foreign financial assets if the exchange-rate risk-adjusted return on those assets exceeds again domestic returns.

Banking Supervision and the Handling of the Crisis

As indicated, the freeing of interest rates in the early 1980s provoked a financial crisis as most industrial and commercial firms had highly indebted themselves under the low real interest-rate conditions and uncontrolled in-house lending practices through allied finance companies. The Central Bank's reaction to attempts to circumvent its rules and regulations and endanger the viability of the financial system has been slow and weak (Lamberte, 1989). Nevertheless, the Philippine monetary authorities did a good job in containing the effects of bank failures in the 1980s. Between 1983 and 1987, the Central Bank closed down a total of 131 banks. The bankruptcy affected among others a number of government-owned banks and the Royal Savings Bank, one of the leading thrift banks. However, the larger commercial banks and development banks that entered into solvency problems, including the government-owned Philippine National Bank (PNB) and Development Bank of the Philippines (DBP), were rehabilitated. The direct costs of the bankruptcies were shared by depositors, bank owners, and the government, but losses to depositors have been most considerable (Lamberte, 1989; Nascimiento, 1991). Less than half of the deposits of the banks that went bankrupt were insured through the Philippine Deposit Insurance Corporation (PDIC), and the heavily under-capitalized PDIC was only capable of refunding two-thirds of the amount of insured deposits and could only do so by heavily borrowing from the Central Bank.

Prior to their rehabilitation, the government used PNB and DBP in bailing out financial institutions and large corporations that collapsed right after the second oil shock. PNB and DBP assumed huge foreign liabilities contracted by private corporations that could no longer repay, but for which the state banks had provided the public guarantees. As indicated above, the losses incurred by PNB and DBP during the period 1984 to 1986 amounted to 29.8 billion pesos (about 5 percent of 1986 GNP) and in 1986, both institutions underwent a rehabilitation program that involved the transfer to the national government of their nonperforming liabilities and related accounts, burdening the fiscal balance.

Reforms to the structure of the Philippine banking system have not been effective to reduce systemic risk. The reforms of the early 1970s regulated an *Anglo-American system*, while those of the beginning of the 1980s moved toward a system of *universal banking* (Lamberte, 1989; Vos and Yap, 1996). Starting in 1972, authorities encouraged financial development through nonbank financial institutions (NBFIs) engaging in issuance of deposit substitutes and short-term money-market instruments and underwriting corporate securities. Interest-rate controls and reserve requirements were much less tight in this separate market segment than in the market for bank deposits and loans. Less than a decade later, in 1980, a financial reform under auspices of the World Bank and the IMF completely reversed the policy of financial specialization and a system of universal banks was introduced and interest rates were freed. In the 1970s, bank-firm conglomerates used the largely unregulated finance companies they owned to serve their own financing requirements. These finance companies would underwrite commercial papers issued by allied companies and provide loans to managers, owners, and officers associated with affiliated banks and firms. As it turned out, the NBFIs proved an effective mechanism to circumvent Central Bank regulations that were meant to restrict in-house lending practices of commercial banks and their exposure to single borrowers.[10] The regulations did not apply to NBFI operations. The interest-rate liberalization, in combination with a number of external shocks (oil price increase, increase in world interest rates), triggered a full-scale liquidity crisis. As indicated above, the default and fled from the country of a major entrepreneur, Dewey Dee, provoked a series of bankruptcies and exposed the widespread weakness of the investment and broker houses, allied to the commercial banks, which carried large exposures to single borrowers.

The financial crisis precipitated the move toward a universal banking system, and many commercial banks were forced to merge with their affiliated investment houses. Under the circumstances, the interest-rate liberalization of the early 1980s was a key factor in triggering the financial crisis (though not the fundamental cause). As shown above, the financial crisis and the move toward universal banking in fact enhanced the concentration of the banking sector and reduced competition in financial markets, instead of making it more competitive, which was the main objective of the 1980 financial reform. The concentration of the Philippine bank industry and its interlocking interests with large conglomerates of firms formed the preconditions for a heavy concentration of lending with a limited number of borrowers. By the early 1990s, these conditions had not fundamentally changed, indicating that it could happen again. Unregulated, off-balance trust fund operations of commercial banks now appear to form the new channel to circumvent restrictions on in-house lending and potentially could grow out to excessive bank exposure to nonperforming loans of its allied companies.

Conclusions

In sum, attempts toward financial liberalization in the 1980s were not successful in enhancing the efficiency of financial intermediation in the Philippines. The reform policies failed to deal with the high degree of segmentation and concentration of the financial system. An initial problem was that the financial liberalization measures were taken when the financial system was under considerable stress due to the overexposure of banks and related quasi-banks to allied companies, officers, and owners and to foreign creditors. The almost simultaneous occurrence of the second oil price shock, the steep increase in world interest rates, and the liberalization of domestic interest rates led to a liquidity crises manifesting the insolvent asset-liability structures of many firms, commercial banks, and quasi-banks. A large number of banks went bankrupt. The merging and consolidation of the banks and quasi-banks that were helped back into solvency, as well as the stepping up of reserve requirements and the maintenance of the agri/agra law led to increased bank concentration and financial repression, instead of promoting bank competition and financial deepening as targeted through the financial reforms. Credit constraints on firms were tightened as a consequence, while bank spreads and borrowing costs went up. Government-owned banks were also part of the financial crisis due to the same external shocks and severe mismanagement by the political protegees of president Marcos. Small-scale businesses and household firms suffered an even more restrained access to bank credits as the loan portfolios of the development banks were severely cut in the mid-1980s as they had to clean their accounts from bad loans. All these factors exacerbated the recessionary impact of the external shocks.

Reduced bank competition, lower real incomes, and increasing income inequality further contributed to the tendency toward financial *dis*intermediation that took place during the 1980s. The shallowness of the segmented financial market and low interest-rate sensitivity of savings and investment demand pushed up lending and T-bill rates when the government and the CB tried to finance their persistent deficits through domestic borrowing. Fiscal deficits remained up because tax revenues could not be stepped up adequately (see Vos and Yap, 1996, ch. 4) but also because of a continuously increasing public debt. Initially, the external debt of the government and the CB increased after taking over such liabilities from ailing government enterprises and from private corporations. With strict monetary targets, issuance of high-yielding government securities were required to cover increased public-sector borrowing requirements, leading to a rapid build up of domestic public debt. A vicious circle emerged of domestic public debt accumulation, high interest rates, high government deficits and CB losses, and crowding out of private investment in productive assets. The structural factor underpinning this vicious circle is the segmented and concentrated character of the shallow domestic financial and capital markets.

The structural problems underlying Philippine financial development are not dissimilar to those found in other countries that suffered from banking crises following financial reforms (Vos, 1995; Fischer, 1993). Where things went wrong, it has usually been a combination of macroeconomic instability and several institutional weaknesses that made deregulation policies create banking crises. A proper ordering and coordination of financial reform policies is therefore required to avoid such upheavals. The main lessons that can be drawn from the Philippine case, and benefiting from knowledge of the experience elsewhere, are presented below.

1. The importance of macroeconomic stability. From the literature on the sequencing of adjustment policies in developing countries, it is clear that financial liberalization, particularly freeing of interest rates, is hazardous under conditions of great macroeconomic imbalances and related unsound portfolio positions of private and public agents. As in the case of the Philippines, savings may show little responsiveness to higher real interest rates, or may even respond negatively if the increase leads to a substantial redistribution of income from debtors to creditors. Company profits may decline and public finances come under stress, with severe macroeconomic consequences if both private corporations and the public sector have large financial liabilities. Lower savings availability and emerging bad loan problems may put financial markets under further stress and push up real interest rates. Under the circumstances, government recurring to domestic financing of fiscal deficits will have to guarantee very high yields on securities to attract private savings, thereby likely exacerbating macroeconomic and bad loan problems. Governments recurring to the money printing press will have to face an acceleration of inflation and the loss of private sector confidence due to the erosion of financial asset values. The role of financial liberalization in macroeconomic stabilization thus seems very limited, and it may well work in the wrong direction. Financial-sector policies should be based on a cautious assessment of savings and investment behaviour and of the other structural features listed below. Deregulation of financial institutions are best conducted after macroeconomic stability has been achieved.

2. Be aware of the degree of bank competition. Concentrated banking sectors and interlocking ownership patterns have been causes of allocative and productive financial inefficiencies throughout the developing world. Much of the bad loan problems found in the Philippines and elsewhere have roots in (1) unsound bank behavior related to the colliding interests of proper bank management and easy loan provisioning to allied firms and (2) ineffective bank supervision. But, of course, these institutional factors alone do not explain the emergence of bad loan problems, rather their presence in combination with macroeconomic instabilities due to external shocks and ill-conceived liberalization policies appear to underlie such financial crisis. Measures to stimulate bank competition include freeing of interest rates, privatization of government-owned banks, establishment of direct securities markets, and lifting barriers on new bank entry. However, when taken in isolation, such measures may fail to enhance competition. Freeing of interest rates may trigger a banking crisis under the conditions specified above. Bank consolidation and merging, and thus larger bank concentration, may be required as part of the solution of the crisis. The Philippine experience of the 1970s and 1980s exemplifies the case. The development of a securities market and other NBFI activities may be effective ways to stimulate competition, but if financial markets are shallow because of a weak savings performance of the economy as a whole, it may rather be a source of high interest rates and speculative behavior. With wealth concentrated in the hands of a limited number of investors, expansion of NBFI activities may center around agents with a stake in existing commercial banks and economic groups. Problems of interlocking interests do not disappear but are reinforced as happened in various Latin American countries and in the Philippines. Privatization of state banks not necessarily leads to enhanced competition for the same reasons.

Allowing foreign bank entrance may become an important option if chances to enhance domestic competition are remote. To ensure competition at an equal footing and minimize the risk of massive takeovers of weaker domestic financial institutions, balance sheets of domestic banks may need to be cleaned first from nonperforming loans, and high minimum reserve requirements may have to be reduced to give domestic banks more competitive edge to compete with foreign banks that can more easily raise funds abroad (see also Fischer, 1993).

3. Take account of credit rationing practices and its consequences for allocative efficiency. Problems of risk, imperfect information and credit market segmentation inherently lead to credit-rationing mechanisms. In financial markets that are not fully developed and that have only a reduced number of financial instruments on offer, it may imply that certain groups of borrowers are excluded from market access. Developing country experience is that small-scale farms and small- and medium-scale industries find difficulties in obtaining adequate amounts of credit. Specialized, government-owned financial institutions have been usually set up to fill the gap. Subsidized loans and poor management of such institutions have generated high costs to taxpayers in many cases. Nevertheless, if—because of imperfect risk assessment—markets fail to meet credit demands of important parts of the productive sector, the development of specialized financial institutions (such as savings and loan cooperatives) through government stimulus is justified, although the government need not take control or subsidize credits.

Allocative inefficiencies related to in-house lending practices require adequate measures enhancing bank competition (see above) and improving prudential regulation and bank supervision (see below).

The choice between an Anglo-American or a German type financial system, or some intermediate form, is relevant for the development of market institutions and regulations, but—as the Philippine case shows—neither form of financial arrangement is a guarantee to eliminate financial inefficiencies. Under both forms bank concentration, interlocking interests, in-house lending practices may persist.

4. The importance of adequate prudential regulation and bank supervision. Bad loan problems and financial crises could emerge in developing countries because of inadequate supervisory regulations, but probably most of all because implementation of existing regulations was weak. Lack of sufficient autonomy of supervisors from political interference has been one issue of concern. One option is to establish an autonomous agency (as in many Latin American countries), but this is no guarantee for better bank supervision. It can be done by the Central Bank (as in most countries), but competent staff should be able to apply a set of sound rules, have authority to enforce decisions and to intervene in ailing institutions, and be able to focus on the soundness of individual institutions and the financial system as a whole without interference of other policy objectives. Regulations on in-house lending practices may have to be made enforceable by disclosing certain bank secrecy regulations (as in the Philippines). Further, coverage of prudential regulations should extend to the whole financial system (banks and NBFIs) and off-balance-sheet financial transactions of banks. In the Philippines, in-house lending practices have found effective channels through the largely unregulated finance companies and off-balance-sheet transactions, undermining the effectiveness of existing prudential regulations limiting lending to single borrowers and allied firms.

The role of deposit insurance systems is controversial. Full explicit deposit insurance may form grounds for excessive risk taking by bank managers, as does the expectation (usually based on experience) of de facto insurance by the monetary authorities. Some differentiated form, as introduced for instance in Chile in the late 1980s (see Morris et al., 1990; Vos, 1995), which penalizes moral hazard and encourages depositors to assess the viability of financial institutions, may be recommendable in situations with underdeveloped financial markets. For the well-functioning of such a system, minimum requirements will include the *publication of credit ratings and quality of asset structures* of financial institutions and the adequate capitalization of the deposit insurance system to ensure confidence and full compensation of insured deposits held in failed banks.

5. Provide clear mechanisms for resolving bad loan problems. The domestic debt overhang in the public sector and widespread nonperforming assets of the banking system have formed an important barrier to successful financial liberalization. Solving the bad loan problem is essential for a proper functioning of the financial system. Across-the-board bailouts of banks and borrowers by the monetary authorities have been extremely costly and in some countries, as we have seen in the case of the Philippines, have contributed to Central Bank losses, accelerated growth of domestic pubic debt, and loss of monetary control. Proper guidelines of how to deal with bad loan problems should form part of the system of prudential regulations. Clear loan performance criteria should be in place and should form the basis of the identification of the magnitude of the damage and the decision to liquidate or recapitalize ailing financial institutions. The cost of bailouts and bank rehabilitations will depend to a great extent on the importance of the structural problems listed above. Questions should be raised: Is the bad-loans problem widespread and a systemic cause of in-house lending practices and ineffective bank supervision? Will the financing of bailouts require the issue of high-yielding CB bills and government securities because of the shallowness of domestic capital markets and thereby exacerbate the domestic debt crisis? In other words, the measures to be taken to resolve bad loan problems should be well coordinated with macroeconomic stabilization measures and should address the issue of moral hazard (that is, avoid across-the-board bailouts) to reduce the risk that it may happen again.

Obviously, the above lessons provide no blueprint for financial reform. However, since bankers and financial markets have shown weak memories where it comes to recollect financial crises (cf. Kindleberger, 1978), tales from the distant and recent past and from different country situations cannot be told often enough.

Appendix: The Relationship between Central Bank Losses and Money Supply[11]

Central Bank losses can be shown to lead to monetary expansion. The money supply may be defined as

$$M = m \cdot RM \tag{5.1}$$

where M = money supply, m = money multiplier, and RM = reserve money.

For any value of m, the money supply expands with the level of reserve money. Losses of the Central Bank may be derived from income and outlay statement of the Central Bank, which can be specified in simplified form as shown in Table 5.A1.

From the above the surplus (deficit) of the Central Bank for a given period is

$$S = Y - E. \tag{5.2}$$

The Central Bank's balance sheet may be specified as shown in Table 5.A2.

Thus,

$$L + eFA = RM + Q_G + eFL + LB_O + W_n. \tag{5.3}$$

Table 5.A1. Income and outlay statement of the Central Bank.

Income (*Y*):	
$i_L L$	Interest income on loans (i_L is interest rate and L is outstanding loans by Central Bank)
ERG	Exchange-rate gains on foreign assets and gains or losses on foreign-exchange dealings (forward cover, swaps, etc.) $[(e_t - e_{t-1})\ FA]$
Expenditures (*E*):	
$i_d Q_G$	Interest payments on government deposits (Q_G) held in Central Bank, where i_d is the interest rate on government deposits)
ERL	Exchange-rate losses on foreign liabilities $[(e_t - e_{t-1})\ FL]$
$i_d LB_O$	Interest payments on other liabilities (LB_O)
Surplus (*S*):	
S	Surplus = Income – Expenditures

Table 5.A2. Balance sheet of Central Bank.

Assets:	
L	Loans and discouts to banks
$e \cdot FA$	Foreign assets converted to local currency value using exchange rate e
Liabilites:	
RM	Reserve money (currency in circulation and reserves of commercial banks against deposits)
Q_G	Deposits of national government
$e \cdot FL$	Foreign liabilities converted to local currency at exchange rate e
LB_O	Other liabilities (CB bills, reverse repurchase, and so on)
W_n	Net worth

Rearranging (5.3):

$$RM = (L + eFA) - (Q_G + eFL + LB_O + W), \tag{5.4}$$

where W_n is the net worth of the Central Bank. Equation (5.4) can be simplified to

$$RM = NFA + NDA - W_n, \tag{5.5}$$

where $NFA = e(FA - FL)$ = net foreign assets and where $NDA = L - (Q_G + LB_O)$ = net domestic assets.

Any surplus of the Central Bank will be added to its net worth, so that

$$S = \Delta W_n. \tag{5.6}$$

We can now link Central Bank losses to the conduct of monetary policy. Taking first differences of (5.5):

$$\Delta RM = \Delta NFA + \Delta NDA - \Delta W_n = \Delta NFA + \Delta NDA - S. \tag{5.7}$$

Equation (5.7) states that any surplus realized by the Central Bank will lead to a reduction in reserve money and hence in the money supply. Conversely, any deficit will lead to an increase in reserve money. The equation brings out the important point that the money supply may change even in the case that NFA and DNA remain unchanged.

Acknowledgments

Part of this chapter draws on a larger study, coauthored by Rob Vos and Josef Yap, *The Philippine Economy: Stray Cat of East Asia?*

(London and New York: Macmillan and St. Martin's Press, 1996). I am nevertheless solely responsible for any errors. The views expressed in this chapter do not necessarily coincide with those of the Inter-American Development Bank.

Notes

1. In Vos and Yap (1996, ch. 4), econometric tests for a large number of hypotheses derived from alternative savings theories are discussed. The more robust results presented in the final analysis gave the following specifications (time series for 1970 to 1992; t-statistics are in parentheses):

$$\begin{aligned} S_H/Y &= \underset{(.08)}{0.069} - \underset{(-0.09)}{0.008} \ln YPC + \underset{(3.38)}{0.009} \ln y - \underset{(1.67)}{0.001}\, r + \underset{(1.39)}{0.351}\, \Delta F/Y - \underset{(2.51)}{0.686}\, W/Y \\ &\quad + \underset{(4.23)}{0.911} \left(S_H/Y\right)_{-1} \\ &\quad R^2(\text{adj}) = 0.542 \quad F = 7.05 \quad \text{D.W.} = 1.76 \\ S_{PE}/Y &= \underset{(-0.12)}{-0.078} + \underset{(0.17)}{0.012} \ln YPC + \underset{(4.09)}{0.004} \ln y - \underset{(-3.31)}{0.002}\, r + \underset{(-0.25)}{0.038}\, \Delta F/Y \\ &\quad - \underset{(-2.62)}{0.004}\, r^* \\ &\quad R^2(\text{adj}) = 0.639 \quad F = 7.0 \quad \text{D.W.} = 1.45 \end{aligned}$$

where. S_H = household savings, S_{PE} = private enterprise savings, Y = GDP, YPC = income per capita, y = GDP growth, r = real domestic interest rate (T-bill rate), r^* = real foreign interest rate (LIBOR), ΔF = foreign savings, and W = wage bill.

2. The regression coefficient in Table 5.2 indicates the marginal rate of change of deposit demand (relative to GNP, d) with respect to increases in the real deposit rate (r). The elasticity is defined by

$$\varepsilon_d = \frac{\Delta d}{\Delta r} \cdot \frac{\bar{r}}{\bar{d}}.$$

For savings deposits the elasticity is zero because of the insignificant regression coefficient. For time deposits the derived elasticity is 0.3.

3. Stiglitz and Weiss (1981) have provided a solid theoretical basis for this point.

4. The Herfindahl concentration index is defined as the sum of the squared market shares of the top five banks:

$$H = \sum_i^n m_i^2.$$

The data in Figure 5.3 relate to the concentration index of deposit liabilities of the top five commercial banks, excluding the government-owned PNB and LBP.

5. The bank spread as reported in Figure 5.3 is affected by such factors given the way these were estimated. Data are derived from Lamberte (1992). The calculation of the bank

spread was based on reported income earnings and payments of the income and outlay accounts of the commercial banks. The interest rate on bank loans (deposits) was computed by dividing interest income (payments) on outstanding loans (deposits) adjusted for the 5 percent gross receipts tax (reserve requirement ratio).

6. Interview in the *Far East Economic Review*, April 7, 1978, p. 80; cited in Lamberte (1989, p. 8).

7. See Lamberte (1989) and Vos (1995) for more detailed further discussions. As documented by Lamberte (1989), CB regulations applicable in the 1970s stipulated that lending to directors, officers, stock holders, and related interests could not exceed the value of their respective outstanding deposits and the book value of their paid-in capital. In addition, outstanding loans to a single borrower could not exceed 15 percent of the net worth of the bank. These regulations were tightened after the 1980 financial reforms, including the rule that the in-house loans could not exceed 30 percent of total outstanding credit. As indicated in the text, the CB had difficulty enforcing these regulations.

8. Most of these were firms owned by Marcos's cronies (see Lamberte, 1989).

9. See Dytianquin (1989) for an analysis of the monetary implications of the Philippine debt-equity swap programme.

10. The Philippine Central Bank applicable in the 1970s stipulated that bank lending to directors, officers, shareholders, and related interests could not exceed the value of their outstanding deposits and the book-value of their paid-in capital. In addition, outstanding loans to a single borrower could not exceed 15 percent of the net worth of the bank. These regulations were tightened after the 1980 reforms, including the rule that the in-house loans could not exceed 30 percent of total outstanding credit. As indicated in the text, the Central Bank had difficultly enforcing these regulations. See Lamberte (1989) for further details.

11. Taken from Vos and Yap (1996) and adapted from Lamberte (1992).

References

De Dios, E. (1994). "Resource Mobilization and Industrial Organization." In R. Febella and H. Sakai (eds.), *Resource Mobilization and Resource Use in the Philippines* (pp. 55–82). Tokyo: Institute of Developing Economies.

Dytianquian, N. (1989). "The Economics of Debt-Equity Swaps." ISS Working Paper Series No. 69. The Hague: Institute of Social Studies.

Fischer, B. (1993). "Impediments in the Domestic Financial Sector to Financial Opening." In H. Reisen and B. Fischer (eds.), *Financial Opening: Policy Issues and Experience in Developing Countries* (pp. 119–132). Paris: OECD Development Centre.

Floro, S., and P. Yotopoulos. (1991). *Informal Credit Markets and the New Institutional Economics: The Case of Philippine Agriculture.* Boulder: Westview Press.

Kindleberger, C. (1978). *Manias, Panics and Crashes: A History of Financial Crises.* New York: Basic Books.

Kunio, Y. (1988). *The Rise of Ersatz Capitalism in South-East Asia.* Manila: Ateneo de Manila University Press.

Lamberte, M. (1989). "Assessment of the Problems of the Financial System: The Philippine Case." PIDS Working Paper Series, No. 89-18. Manila: Philippine Institute for Development Studies.

Lamberte, M. (1992). "Assessment of the Financial Market Reforms in the Philippines, 1980–1992." Paper presented at Third Convention of the East Asian Economic Association, Seoul, August 20–21.

Lapar, L., and D. Graham. (1988). "Credit Rationing Under a Regulated Financial System." PIDS Working Paper Series No. 88-19. Makati: Philippine Institute for Development Studies.

Leff, N. (1976). "Capital Markets in Less Developed Countries: The Group Principle." In R.I. McKinnon (ed.), *Money and Finance in Economic Development* (pp. 97–126). New York: Marcel Dekker.

Morris, F., with M. Dorfman, J.P. Ortiz, and M.C. Franco. (1990). *Latin America's Banking System in the 1980s: A Cross-Country Comparison.* World Bank Discussion Papers No. 81. Washington, DC: World Bank.

Nascimiento, J.-C. (1991). "Crisis in the Financial Sector and Authorities' Reaction: The Philippines." In V. Sundararajan and T. Baliño (eds.), *Banking Crises: Cases and Issues* (pp. 175–233). Washington, DC: IMF.

Stiglitz, J., and A. Weiss. (1981). "Credit Rationing in Markets with Imperfect Information." *American Economic Review* 71(2): 393–410.

Vos, R. (1995). "Financial Liberalisation, Growth and Adjustment: Some Lessons from Developing Countries." In S. Griffith-Jones and Z. Drabek (eds.), *Financial Reform in Central and Eastern Europe* (pp. 179–220). London: Macmillan.

Vos, R., and J. Yap. (1996). *The Philippine Economy: Stray Cat of East Asia?* London and New York: Macmillan and St. Martin's Press.

World Bank. (1993). *The Philippines: An Opening for Sustained Growth.* Country Operations Division, East Asia and Pacific Region. Washington: World Bank.

Yap, J.T., et al. (1990). "Central Bank Policies and the Behavior of the Money Market: The Case of the Philippines." PIDS Working Paper Series No. 90-24. Makati: Philippine Institute for Development Studies.

6 FINANCIAL LIBERALIZATION AND STABILIZATION POLICIES

The Experience of Chile

Kate Phylaktis

Introduction

Chile stands out as one of the first countries in Latin America to have embarked on an ambitious liberalization program. Its experiment started in 1973, and the events that followed during the first decade convinced many observers at the time to pronounce it a big failure (see, e.g., Corbo, 1985; Corbo and de Melo, 1987; Edwards and Edwards, 1987). The development of the economy since then has produced a different picture.

The purpose of this chapter is to examine this experiment by placing it in historical perspective. As Table 6.1 shows, Chile's economic performance varied enormously since 1960. During the period 1960 to 1973, the economy was characterized by chronic inflation, relatively low to moderate growth, and frequent balance-of-payments crises. The 1970s saw a big increase in inflation and a worsening in economic growth. In the first half of the 1980s inflation came under control but at a cost. The economy plunged into a deep recession with negative economic growth. Since 1985, the economy was revived, while inflation remained low. Chile's extensive structural reform finally paid off, and by 1991 the country was at the most advanced stage in the process of return to sustainable growth.

Table 6.1. Per capita growth and inflation, 1960 to 1994.

	Growth	*Inflation*
1960–1973	1.8%	50%[a]
1973–1980	1.1	138
1980–1985	–2.1	22
1985–1991	4.4	20
1992–1994	4.0	12

Sources: Growth (per capita) for 1960 to 1980 from Summers and Heston (1991); growth for 1980 to 1994 from International Financial Statistics (IFS); inflation (CPI) from IFS.

a 1963 to 1973.

The chapter is structured as follows. In the next section, I present historical background prior to the beginning of the big experiment of 1973. Then I examine the liberalization program and stabilization policies. Finally, I analyze some of the effects of these policies on the domestic and foreign financial markets and draw some policy lessons.

Historical Background: 1960 to 1973

During the period 1960 to 1973 Chile enjoyed a stable democratic political system and a shift from right-wing to socialist governments. Until 1964, Chile was ruled by a conservative and center-right coalition that emphasized inflation stabilization and assumed that macrostability would automatically generate growth as well as redistribution.

In 1964, the coalition was replaced with a Christian Democratic administration that had an absolute majority and emphasized structural changes such as land reform and Chilean participation in the foreign-dominated (mainly U.S.) ownership of the country's large copper mines. Purchase of 51 percent of the mines was carried out, social expenditure toward enhancement of low and middle-income groups was increased, and 100 percent backward cost of living indexation on wages was introduced. This latter policy was to create problems when the government tried to reduce the escalating rate of inflation during the late 1970s and early 1980s.

During the office of this government, average GDP growth was about 4 percent, average inflation was 23 percent, while the fiscal deficit was 2 percent; unemployment was 6 percent, and real wage growth was at high

Table 6.2. Macroeconomic indicators for Chile, 1965 to 1990.

	Fiscal Deficit/ GNP (%)	CPI Inflation (%)	GDP Growth Rate (%)	Gross Fixed Investment (growth rate)	Unemployment Rate (%)	Real Wage Index (1969 = 100)	Terms of Trade	Current Account Deficit (1987 = 100) ($ bn.)
Democracy								
Import substitution, 1965–1970	2.1%	23%	4.1%	5.3%	6.0%	98	306	—
Allende socialism, 1971–1973	16.1	150	1.3	−9.8	4.6	98	271	$0.3
Military government								
Reform:								
1974–1976	5.1	358	−1.8	−7.8	14.2	69	140	0.2
1977–1978	1.3	79	7.8	16.7	13.6	82	122	0.8
Tablita, 1979–1981	−2.1	26	6.9	17.8	12.2	100	111	2.9
Debt crisis, 1982–1983	3.1	22	−7.4	−26.6	22.2	82	110	1.7
Recover, 1984–1985	3.7	27	4.4	11.8	17.8	91	102	1.7
Normalization,[b] 1986–1990	−2.2	19	6.2	11.8	11.1	95	132	0.7

Sources: 1965 to 1983: based on Corbo and de Melo (1987); 1984 to 1990: based on Bruno (1993).

b Chile returned to democracy in December 1989.

annual rate of 10 percent (see Table 6.2). At the same time, Chile did not face a balance-of-payments constraint as increases in the real price of copper kept exports high. In fact, total exports rose to over $1 billion, and foreign exchange reserves quadrupled to $400 million (five months' worth of imports) during the period 1968 to 1970.[1]

In 1970, a left-wing and center-left coalition (Unidad Popular) was democratically elected headed by Salvador Allende. The objective of the new administration was to transfer power from the dominant capitalist group to the workers and peasants. This was to be achieved (1) through nationalization of the copper mines, other basic resources (coal, nitrates, and iron), industrial enterprises, and banks; (2) by aiming to increase nominal wages, which together with price controls and fixed exchange rates would have increased real wages; and (3) by expanding government expenditure, while giving monetary policy a passive role. The high international reserves were to fund any possible increase in imports. The macropolicy stance was based on a structuralist theory of inflation whereby the ownership reform, the elimination of monopolistic profit margins, and the existence of price controls would allow growth without further inflation.

The effects of the above policies were as follows: the share of public ownership increased from around 14 percent in 1965 to 39 percent by 1973 (85 percent in mining and in the financial sector) (see Larrain and Meller, 1991); the economy enjoyed an 8 percent growth, a relatively low inflation of 22 percent, an unemployment rate of less than 4 percent, and an amazing 22 percent increase in real wages in 1971. In the two years 1972 and 1973, however, there was a dramatic increase in inflation by 2,400 percent, while economic growth fell so much so as to produce a stagnant economy over the three years of the Allende administration (see Table 6.2). The increase in inflation was due to the monetization of the public sector deficit, which was on average 16 percent of GDP during the period 1971 to 1973. At the same time, all aspects of the economy were distorted. About 3,000 prices were set by the government, and there were multiple exchange rates and very low labor mobility.

The Allende government was displaced by the military in September 1973.[2]

Economic Reforms

The military coup of 1973 marked an important turning point in Chile's economic and political history. The new government embarked on the most ambitious plan to reform a financially repressed and isolated economy into a world-integrated market-oriented economy. It aimed to reinstate economic incentives, restore economic growth, rationalize resource allocation, and decrease the budget deficit. The economic reforms can be examined under four categories: external-sector reforms, financial reforms, fiscal-sector reforms and labor reforms.

External-Sector Reforms

In late 1973, Chilean foreign trade was subject to heavy restrictions, and trade policies distorted the signals transmitted to the market. Of a total of 5,125 tariff items, 63 percent were subject to direct or indirect prohibitions (advance import deposits or official permits). The highest tariff rate was 750 percent of the c.i.f. value. The initial goal was to eliminate all quantitative restrictions and to lower the highest tariff to 220 percent with an average level of 94 percent. It the succeeding months the highest tariffs and the respective classes were lowered further, and by June 1979 there was a uniform tariff of 10 percent (except on motor vehicles) (see Pietrobelli, 1994; Edwards and Edwards, 1987).

Following the crisis of 1982, there was a temporary increase in tariffs. The basic tariff was increased to 20 percent in March 1983 and 35 percent in September 1984. It was then lowered to 30 percent (March 1985), 20 percent (June 1985), and 15 percent (January 1988).

The liberalization of the capital account started in 1974 but intensified in 1979. The purpose of the deregulation was to give the banking system greater autonomy in borrowing and lending foreign funds subject to certain restrictions. The latter referred to the terms of foreign credits and the maximum amounts the banks could borrow and lend to their customers. In general, the objective was to encourage credits with longer terms. For example, staring in 1979 there was a mandate deposit from the credits of 25 percent for terms of less than thirty-six months and of 15 percent for terms longer than thirty-six months. These percentages and conditions were subsequently reduced. The minimum term on the maturity of the loan was twenty-four months, reduced, however, to zero in early 1981. Another type of restriction affected the foreign exposure of the banks. The banks could borrow a percentage of their capital and reserves, which stood at 215 percent in early 1979 prior to its abolition.[3]

There was also a gradual increase in the amount of foreign currency that could be bought without a written declaration of purpose starting in mid-1976. This restriction was tightened up in the third quarter of 1982 following the financial crisis.

Measures to increase direct foreign investment were also taken. There was a complete relaxation of the restriction affecting the amount of profits, dividends, and royalties repatriated in 1977.

Financial Reforms

The financial system in Chile prior to the reforms was characterized by segmentation. There was a group of specialized entities that allocated resources for specific purposes within the framework of very generalized state regulations, which had a direct or indirect bearing on the determination of the amounts, conditions, and costs of the various lines of credit available in the market.

The financial reforms were initiated in early 1974, when reserve requirements, which stood at 100 percent in 1973,[4] were lowered, and new nonbank finance institutions (*financieras*) were permitted to operate. In May of that year, *financieras* were allowed to freely determine interest rates in short-term financial operations. A year later, in October 1975, interest rates charged by the commercial banks and SINAP—the National Savings and Loan System, which was organized to finance housing credits through mutual savings banks—were also decontrolled. The freeing of interest rates represented a major change in a country where for more than twenty years financial operations had been tightly controlled, and it meant a move from negative to positive and very high real interest rates.

Along with these reforms the government began a process of privatization of banks, which had been nationalized during the Allende administration. A number of these banks were bought by private conglomerates (the *grupos*) (see Munoz, 1992).

Fiscal-Sector Reforms

In 1975, the government undertook a massive government expenditure cut and a rationalization of its tax system to try to reduce the chronic fiscal deficit that had built up during the Allende regime. It introduced a value-added tax system, a one-year surcharge on personal income tax, and a 10 percent consumption tax on luxury goods. It replaced the high social security taxes that were used to run its social security scheme with fully funded privately operated bodies. The financing of the educational system was also revised, and the number of the state enterprises was gradually reduced, which resulted in a fall in government employment. However, sixteen of the largest state enterprises were retained, and so the public sector still remained significant.

Labor Reforms

Reforms in the labor market were initiated in 1981. Legislation was enacted allowing workers to negotiate fringe benefits and employers to fire workers without giving cause. A major change took place in June 1982 with the suspension of the wage indexation system (see Munoz, 1992).

The Stabilization Program: 1973 to 1983

The above liberalization policies together with a series of stabilization programs brought the economy to a standstill by 1983. Three different phases can be distinguished. The first one covers the period September 1973 through to early 1978 and was characterized by an attempt to correct the most serious economic distortions introduced during the Allende regime and by the adoption of an orthodox closed-economy stabilization program based on tight monetary policy and the elimination of the fiscal deficit. The second phase covers the period from early 1978 to the first half of 1981 and the change to open economy monetarism. Finally, the third period begins in late 1981 to 1983 and covers the collapse of the economy. Table 6.2 presents developments in macroeconomics indicators during these three periods.

The Orthodox Close-Economy Stabilization Policies: 1973 to 1978

The government's main objective during this period was the reduction of inflation, which had exceeded 600 percent during the previous twelve months. Other important objectives were the eradication of black markets and food shortages, the reduction of government controls, the reorganization of the productive sector, and the avoidance of balance-of-payments crises. In order to achieve those objectives the government rationalized the exchange-rate system, reducing the fifteen multiple exchange rates to three and implementing a massive devaluation in late 1973.[5] It also decontrolled the prices of 3,000 goods and took measures to reduce tax evasion. At the same time, it started its liberalization program of reducing tariffs and privatizing firms.

The government implemented a gradual approach to reducing inflation. The rate of money supply growth was only slightly less expansionary than during the Allende regime—333 percent as opposed to 342 percent. The government concentrated more on reducing the government budget deficit, which came down from 24.6 percent to GDP in 1973 to 10.5 percent by 1974. This was achieved through the privatization, the firing of a substantial number of civil servants, and the elimination of most subsidies.

The result of these tight fiscal measures was a decline in industrial production and an increase in unemployment. On the other hand, the relatively lax monetary policy limited progress in reducing inflation, which at the end of 1974 stood at 370 percent. On the external sector, the high inflation (influenced adversely by the first oil price shock), in combination with a 50 percent fall in copper prices, caused the biggest deterioration in the terms of trade in Latin America and a worsening balance-of-payments situation. The Chilean economy was paying the costs of the stabilization effort in terms of negative effects on economic activity and unemployment without reaping the benefits of a reduction in inflation.

In April 1975, the government embarked in a "shock" anti-inflationary program. The main characteristics were (1) an across-the-board reduction in government expenditure (between 15 percent and 25 percent), (2) a 10 percent temporary hike in income tax, (3) an acceleration of the program to reduce the public sector and the budget deficit by implementing a drastic tax reform, and (4) a tight monetary policy.

The shock stabilization program had an initial success in reducing inflation. It came down to 26 percent by the end of 1975. At the same time, however, there was a steep fall in economic activity and a steep rise in unemployment. In the first quarter of 1976, inflation started to gain the old momentum. Having got the fiscal deficit under control and reduced the rate of growth of the money supply, the government realized that the behavior of the exchange rate had become an important element in the process of formation of inflationary expectations. Through as series of minirevaluations it hoped to break the inflationary expectations. Although some progress was made in reducing inflation, the inflation rate was still 84 percent in late 1977. A drastic change in the orientation of the stabilization policy was required to make further progress against inflation.

The Tablita: 1978 to 1981

In February 1978, an active crawling peg (*tablita*) exchange-rate system was established as the main anti-inflationary policy tool. This was a preannounced decreasing rate of crawl, below the previous month's inflation rate, gradually leading to a fixed exchange rate in June 1979, when inflation was still running at 2.5 percent a month. This system, in conjunction with the reduced tariffs, was expected to reduce the prices of tradable goods and inflation expectations downward.

The new open-economy approach to stabilization policies was based on the simple version of the monetary approach to the balance of payments (see Frenkel, 1976; Johnson, 1977). This approach is based on the purchasing power parity (PPP) and on money-market equilibrium holding continuously. Monetary policy has no effect on inflation or on the rest of the economy, even in the short run. All the monetary authorities can hope to do is to affect the composition of high-powered money; changes in domestic credit result in instantaneous and opposite changes in the stock of international reserves, with total money supply being unaffected. PPP entails that the domestic rate of inflation will be equal to the world rate of inflation plus the rate of devaluation.

Convergence of the two inflation rates was assumed to be fast. Integration of Chile's capital markets, which was taking place around the same time, under the assumption of interest-rate parity, was supposed to lower domestic interest rates by reducing the expected rate of devaluation.

Contrary to what was expected domestic inflation did not converge to world inflation (see Table 6.3). The rate of domestic inflation exceeded the rate of U.S. inflation plus the rate of devaluation over the period 1978 to 1981. In fact, the real overvaluation of the peso affected adversely the tradable sector. The main reason for the nonconvergence was the ex post 100 percent wage indexation, which had been in place since 1964. This

Table 6.3. The rate of devaluation on the peso, and inflation rates in Chile and the United States.

	Annualized Rate of Devaluation with Respect to U.S. $	*Annualized U.S. Rate of Inflation (CPI)*	*Annualized Chilean Rate of Inflation (CPI)*
1978	21.4%	9.1%	37.2%
1979	14.9	13.3	38.0
1980	0	12.4	31.2
1981	0	8.9	9.5
1982	88.3	3.9	20.7
1983	19.2	3.8	23.1

Notes: The rate of change refers to end of year calculation. Data were taken from the IFS.

meant an increase in real wages, which in turn generated a real overvaluation. In this case, even if PPP holds for tradable goods, the convergence of domestic to international inflation can be very slow (see Edwards and Edwards, 1987, pp. 42–44). Furthermore, the prices of many nontradables (housing rentals, mortgages, tuition fees) were likewise indexed to ex post inflation.

There was another problem that was overlooked in Chile. The lifting of controls on capital movements enabled Chile to finance the increased demand for nontradable goods. The active crawl further enhanced capital inflows because it increased the spread between domestic and foreign interest rates. These huge capital inflows, which totalled $5 billion over the period 1977 to 1979, postponed the inevitable balance-of-payments crisis, since in the meantime the current account deficit was increasing very fast.

During this period the Central Bank followed a "neutral policy" where its stock of domestic credit would remain unchanged in nominal terms and where increases in demand for money were satisfied by the accumulation of international reserves that, in turn, would be the reflection of higher international loans.

The Confidence Crisis: 1982 to 1983

In late 1981 and early 1982, there was a general expectation of a devaluation as the rate of real overvaluation reached considerable proportions. The speculation against the peso and the halt of international inflows as a result of the difficulties that the international banks were beginning to face in other Latin American countries, caused interest rates to rise. The result was a dramatic fall in industrial production and an increase in unemployment. The squeeze in companies' operational profits caused many bankruptcies and eventually a banking crisis. There was a run on the banks leading the government to take over (in 1983) the two largest commercial banks.

In June 1982, the peso was devalued by 18 percent, and a partial reversal of the liberalization policies took place. There was a temporary increase in import tariffs and a reimposition of severe exchange controls. There were further devaluations that amounted to the Chilean peso being devalued by 100 percent between June 1982 and June 1983. Inflation, on the other hand, was back to its long-term historical average of around 22 percent. The years 1982 to 1983 saw a deep recession, with GDP dropping by 7 percent, investment dropping even more sharply and the unemployment rate rising to 22 percent. Finally, Chile was in a debt crisis, having almost tripled its external debt during 1979 to 1983.

By 1984, observers could pronounce the Chilean structural reform an almost complete failure.

Effects of Reforms

This section attempts to analyze the effects of the reforms on certain aspects of the domestic and foreign financial sector[6]—for example, the effects on interest rates, on the behavior of the exchange rates, and on the financial structure. The effects in each of these areas highlight some of the mistakes and the lessons that can be learned from the liberalization and stabilization policies in Chile.

Interest Rates

Interest-rate behavior constitutes one of the major puzzles of the Chilean reforms and stabilization policies (see, e.g., Harberger, 1982; Sjaastad, 1983; Calvo, 1982). During most of the experiment both nominal and real interest rates remained very high in relation to those on dollar deposits (and the London interbank offer rare, LIBOR), even after the beginning of the relaxation of capital controls and the pegging of the exchange rate in June 1979 (see Table 6.4).

Various explanations have been put forward for this bizarre behavior of the interest rates. The first is the ever-expanding demand for credit by the groups and the public in general as a result of the optimistic views concerning the economy. The groups, after acquiring some of the newly privatized banks, started to use the funds obtained through them to finance the purchase, modernization, and expansion of other firms that were privatized. This initial demand for credit by the groups soon became an ever-growing "false demand" consisting of the rolling over of bad loans. Many of the firms acquired by the groups did not turn out to be profitable, and in order to avoid bankruptcy they continued to borrow from the banks (Munoz, 1992). On the other hand, the public encouraged by expectations of high long-run growth in the economy increased their spending, which was largely financed by the banking sector. The higher demand for credit not only put pressure on domestic interest rates but also increased foreign indebtedness because it was cheaper to borrow abroad and put off problems to the future.

Table 6.4. Interest rates, the rate of devaluation, and the rate of inflation, 1977 to 1983.

		Annualized Nominal Deposit Interest Rate	*Annualized Rate of Devaluation*	*LIBOR Interest Rate*	*Annualized Rate of Inflation*
1977	Q1	124.6%	71.4%	6.3%	103.2%
	Q2	83.6	23.4	6.8	100.0
	Q3	70.8	71.9	7.0	61.2
	Q4	99.8	85.5	7.8	57.4
1978	Q1	70.7	57.4	8.0	37.9
	Q2	55.6	33.1	8.5	41.2
	Q3	55.5	19.7	9.3	43.0
	Q4	70.0	11.2	11.5	28.1
1979	Q1	47.3	14.3	11.8	24.9
	Q2	44.1	18.7	11.8	32.9
	Q3	42.7	33.8	12.3	48.8
	Q4	46.1	0	15.5	39.2
1980	Q1	52.1	0	16.3	28.5
	Q2	32.7	0	14.0	32.0
	Q3	31.8	0	11.5	27.0
	Q4	34.2	0	17.8	33.0
1981	Q1	45.0	0	19.0	18.0
	Q2	40.9	0	20.5	11.6
	Q3	38.8	0	20.5	8.5
	Q4	38.5	0	16.0	7.4
1982	Q1	38.9	0	15.6	7.0
	Q2	32.4	14.3	16.2	4.2
	Q3	37.8	245.1	12.1	26.1
	Q4	73.2	152.0	9.5	55.8
1983	Q1	33.1	36.9	9.5	18.7
	Q2	28.9	1.3	9.7	25.4
	Q3	25.0	26.2	10.5	26.8
	Q4	24.9	30.8	9.9	26.5

Source: Edwards and Edwards (1987).

This view is confirmed in a paper by McNelis and Schmidt-Hebbel (1993), who show the importance of domestic factors in keeping domestic interest rates higher than foreign interest rates (adjusted for exchange-rate changes). They develop a portfolio model that is based partly on Dornbusch and Fisher (1980) and partly on Kouri and Portes (1974). The goods are, however, divided between traded and nontraded, and there are three assets—money, domestic, and foreign bonds. They assume imperfect capital mobility in response to domestically imposed restrictions on flows or on holdings of foreign capital or debt. They define imperfect capital mobility by the speed that the interest arbitrage condition is established following a shock.[7] The uncovered interest-rate arbitrage condition is modified to take account of the legal restrictions and country risk. Imperfect capital mobility thus allows for short-run deviations of domestic interest rates from their long-run equilibrium levels.

They distinguish between instantaneous and long-run asset market equilibria. The domestic financial markets (for money and government bonds) and the nontraded goods market clear instantaneously, determining the nominal interest rate and the real exchange rate (nominal exchange rate is assumed fixed, and prices of nontraded goods are determined in the nontraded goods sector). When capital mobility is low and domestic asset holders cannot quickly change their portfolio composition by buying or selling foreign assets, there will be short-run deviations of domestic interest rates from their long-run equilibrium levels consistent with covered interest-rate arbitrage. During that transitional period the domestic interest rates are determined by the monetary flow equilibrium condition—that is, by domestic factors.

I will concentrate on the results found for Chile for the nominal interest rate i (and the real exchange rate p in the next section). They use a general-to-specific approach (see Hendry, 1986) assuming first constant coefficients and then time-varying coefficients (the Kalman filter two-stage process), for the period 1975Q3 to 1982Q4. The results for the first case are presented below:

$$\Delta i = \underset{(-1.21)}{-0.0062} + \underset{(2.46)}{0.349}\Delta\left(i^* + \hat{E}^e\right)_{t-2} - \underset{(-1.04)}{0.00071}\Delta f_{t-4} + \underset{(1.75)}{0.0032}\Delta r_{t-2} - \underset{(-2.23)}{0.0004}\Delta z_{t-2},$$

where $(i^* + \hat{E}^e)$ is the foreign interest rate adjusted for expected exchange rate, f is holdings of foreign assets, r holdings of international reserves, and z ex ante monetary base. The numbers in parentheses are t-statistics. The specification pass the usual diagnostic tests.

The foreign interest rate and the ex ante domestic money supply have a dominant influence, while foreign assets are not significant. In contrast, holdings of international reserves are significant. When the Kalman filter technique was used, the domestic interest rate became less responsive to domestic credit expansion, while the effects of foreign interest rates at the end of the sample period were stronger than at the beginning. This shows that the effects of the opening of capital account took their time to be felt and during that period domestic factors were dominant.

Another explanation for the behavior of interest rates, which also has implications for the liberalization and stabilization process, relates to the various effects of capital controls. Although, the authorities started to open the capital account in 1979, the lack of confidence in the stabilization policies pursued at the time increased the political risk associated with prospective controls and kept a wide spread between domestic and foreign interest rates adjusted for expected exchange-rate changes.

It should be noted that capital controls give rise to three effects on international interest-rate parities: a political risk premium that results from the possibility of imposing controls and affects the variance of an asset's return (Aliber, 1973), an effective tax that refers to the existing controls (Aliber, 1973; Phylaktis and Wood, 1984), and an exchange-risk premium that is associated with prospective controls and affects the confidence with which exchange-rate expectations are held.

In Phylaktis (1990), these different effects are estimated for Chile on the basis of a simple portfolio balance model developed in Phylaktis (1988) for the case of Argentina. The effect on the interest-rate differential due to political and exchange-risk premia is found to depend mainly on the gross stock of outside claims against residents of the country in question and on the distribution of world wealth between residents and nonresidents. The effective tax is represented by multistep dummy variable, and the signs are derived using a partial equilibrium analysis.

The following result is obtained using OLS corrected for serial correlation on quarterly data for the period 1975 to 1984 (the numbers in parentheses are t-statistics).

$$\begin{aligned} i_t - i_t^* - \dot{e}_t = {} & \underset{(1.32)}{1.13523} + \underset{(2.00)}{0.00010\overline{B}} - \underset{(-2.49)}{0.00008W} - \underset{(-2.17)}{0.00008W^*} + \underset{(1.78)}{0.12DA} + \underset{(2.51)}{0.20DD} + \underset{(3.20)}{0.33DE}, \\ & \overline{R}^2 = 0.370 \quad DW = 1.86 \quad \underset{(-2.25)}{\rho = -0.32} \end{aligned}$$

where i_t is the yield on domestic assets, and $(i_t^* + \dot{e}_t)$ is the sum of the foreign interest rate i_t^* and the expected rate of depreciation $\dot{e}_t$, $\overline{B}$ denotes the real domestic and foreign holdings of domestic government debt issued in domestic currency, and W and W^* denote domestic and foreign real financial wealth, respectively.[8] DA, DD, and DE represent the dummies for the various types of capital controls: DA the amount of profits as a percent of capital that can be repatriated, DD the minimum maturity on foreign loans, and DE the exchange-rate guarantee on foreign loans.

The results are very interesting. The variables representing the political and exchange-rate risk premia associated with prospective controls are statistically significant. Three of the capital controls tested were also found to be statistically significant. Two of the controls, *DA* and *DD*, have the expected sign since they increase the interest rate that residents have to pay in the domestic financial market, while *DE* has the opposite sign to the one expected. The exchange-rate guarantee on foreign loans to residents represents an implicit subsidy on the cost of foreign borrowing, increasing capital inflows, and reducing the domestic interest rate. The positive sign could be explained, however, by a simultaneous reduction in new foreign lending by the international banks in the early 1980s as the external foreign debt of Chile was rising.

The empirical evidence suggests that the abolition of restrictions on international capital flows was not sufficient for integrating the domestic capital market with international markets. Even when the existing level of controls was not high, prospective controls created political and exchange-risk premia that kept the domestic interest rate at a different level from the foreign interest rate after adjusting for exchange-rate changes. The failure of the authorities to reduce the rate of inflation, which led to real exchange-rate appreciation, weakened the credibility of the stabilization and consequently that of the liberalization effort.

The Liberalization of the Capital Account, Capital Inflows, and the Real Exchange Rate

Following the liberalization of the capital account, which started in June 1979, the foreign indebtedness increased substantially. Between 1978 and 1982 it increased from U.S. $6,664 million to $17,153. At the same time, the relative importance of the private debt, and especially that of the banking sector, grew rapidly. Two factors encouraged the substantial increases in foreign borrowing. First, the market-oriented policies adopted encouraged the perception of profitable domestic investment opportunities over the long-run. That encouraged foreign investors to want to hold a significantly higher fraction of Chilean assets as part of their portfolio. Thus, when capital controls were reduced, they adjusted their portfolios, giving rise to a jump in capital inflows.

The second factor that explains the increase in capital inflows relates to the interest-rate differential adjusted for expected devaluation. We have already shown that this differential, although variable, was most of the time positive, implying that foreign borrowing was cheaper.

The increase in capital inflows, following the opening of the capital account, resulted in an increase in the money supply under the pegged exchange-rate regime and an increase in inflation. In particular, the increase in expenditure had increased the demand for both traded and nontraded goods. The excess demand for the latter type of goods increased their relative prices and caused a real appreciation. At the same time, a fall in real wages, which could have initiated an automatic adjustment process, was hampered by the backward wage indexation.

The above events highlight the possible destabilizing effects of capital inflows following the liberalization of the capital account and raise questions concerning the timing and the speed of the liberalization. It will be helpful, however, to bear in mind the following before one draws any conclusions. First, the authorities encouraged this increase in private foreign indebtedness. For example, private loans were not required to have government guarantee. Second, rigidities in the labor market and the backward wage indexation were partly to blame for the real appreciation. Third, the connection between real appreciation and capital inflows has not been confirmed by empirical estimation. For example, in McNelis and Schmidt-Hebbel (1993) the following real exchange-rate equation is reported for Chile:

$$\underset{}{\Delta p} = \underset{(1.63)}{-0.027} + \underset{(2.23)}{0.448\Delta p_{t-1}} + \underset{(2.94)}{0.673 ir_{t-1}} - \underset{(3.17)}{0.772 ir_{t-2}} + \underset{(2.58)}{0.673 ir_{t-3}},$$

where *ir* is the real interest rate. The specification passes the usual diagnostic tests. Neither foreign assets, nor international reserves (domestic wealth), nor government spending was found to be statistically significant when included in the estimation.

In a different paper by Edwards and Edwards (1987), lagged net capital flows were found to affect the real exchange rate in Chile in an OLS estimation in levels for the period 1977 to 1982. These results, however, could be spurious as the real exchange rate is not a stationary series.

In conclusion, the capital inflows that Chile experienced following the opening of the capital account were huge in quantity and with possibly destabilizing effects because of other policies. The lessons that can be drawn from this experience relate to the speed of the liberalization. A gradual liberalization can spread a possible increase in the stock of foreign debt through time, reducing the degree of possible real appreciation. In addition, a gradual liberalization is advisable in the presence of other distortions like legally imposed real wage rigidity.

Financial Liberalization and the Financial Crisis

In this section, I discuss the role of financial liberalization on the development of the financial sector in Chile—particularly how the interest-rate policies and the lack of banking supervision contributed to the financial crisis that started in November of 1981 when two major banks, the Banco Espanol and Banco de Talca, ran into serious problems and had to be rescued. That was preceded by the collapse of one of the medium-sized conglomerates, the CRAV grupo, which could not pay its debts. The situation became worse in 1982, when the foreign banks reduced lending to Chile. Many banks were badly affected.[9] In January 1983, the government stepped up its degree of intervention and liquidated two banks. At the end of 1983 it nationalized the banking sector. Thus, the banking sector stood at the same position as it did ten years previously, before the reform.

The following analysis shows how the lack of adequate banking supervision interacts with freely market-determined interest rates to produce a fragile banking sector. The market for bank credit, whether in an industrial or developing country, differs in one important respect from any other spot market for a commodity or other financial asset. In these other markets the seller of the instrument receives a rate of return exactly equal to the price of the commodity or the foreign exchange or the interest rate on the bond. In the market for bank credit there is a difference between the interest rate charged on the loan and the expected return to the bank. This is because the latter is equal to the product of the interest rate and the repayment probability of borrowers, which is less than 100 percent because of imperfect or asymmetric information between banks and their borrowers.

The probability of repayment itself is negatively related to the interest rate charged. As the interest rate on loans increases, the probability of repayment declines. At a certain interest-rate level, the fall in the probability is greater than the increase in the interest rate, and the expected return to the bank may actually decline with further increases in the interest rate. The bank may turned down borrowers even if they are willing to pay higher interest rates. The analysis shows that banks charge an interest rate below the level that would clear the market. This rate is both optimal and efficient for the bank because profits are at a maximum level and risky borrowers are rationed out (see Stiglitz and Weiss, 1981).

In the case of macroeconomics instability (in the form of big changes in the prices of goods and factors of production that will affect investment adversely), and in the presence of official supervision and prudential regulation, the banks will increase their reserves against loan losses. That would lower the expected profit function of the bank at given levels of the loan interest rate. The response of the bank is to lower interest rates on loans further and to ration credit much more.

In the case, however, of weak bank supervision and prudential regulation (either in design or enforcement or both) such that the levels of bank capital (in relation to risk assets) and provisions for loan losses are inadequate, and in conjunction with free state deposit insurance (implicit or explicit), the problem of moral hazard intensifies. The banks have an incentive to provide high interest rates and high-risk loans, since they can keep extraordinary profits in good times without having to pay the full cost of large losses in bad times (see McKinnon, 1988, p. 388; Villanueva and Mirakhor, 1990).

The experience of Chile provides a good illustration of the analysis above. Chile adopted a strategy of complete interest-rate liberalization in a very short period of time and relaxed government supervision over the banking system, when there was macroeconomics instability.[10] These measures were accompanied by the provision of free deposit insurance. The result was excessively high interest rates, which forced many low-risk firms to leave the market, and the quality of bank loans suffered. In their place, high-risk firms were prepared to pay high interest rates for loans to finance riskier projects with higher expected rates of return. These firms, however, had high default probabilities (see Velasco, 1988). In addition, as high macroeconomics instability became worse, and real interest rates rose, firms kept increasing their borrowing. The rising indebtedness reflected distress borrowing just to pay interest, and many firms eventually went bankrupt. In fact, the number of bankruptcies reached 810 in 1982, with adverse effects in bank incomes, cash flows, and financial positions.[11]

Lessons from the Chilean Experience

The first decade of the Chilean experiment with free-market policies ended in major disappointment. Instead of the country entering a new phase of prosperity and continuous growth, the economy collapsed with negative economic growth, high unemployment, a huge current account deficit, and a collapse of the financial sector. This section summarizes the policy mistakes made and discusses the lessons that have emerged from this experience. First, however, we look into the adjustment of the economy after 1983 to get a better perspective of the benefits of the reforms, however, costly they had been.

Recovery and Normalization: 1984 to 1994

In early 1984, although the country was in deep crisis, its economy had been radically transformed following the economic reforms. For example, domestic interest rates were market determined, a distorted sales tax had been replaced by a uniform 20 percent value added tax, employment in the public sector had substantially been reduced, there was a homogeneous tariff of 35 percent, that by 1988 was reduced to 15 percent, the labor market had become much more flexible, there were no unions and no collective bargaining power, and nonwage labor costs had been reduced.

Chile embarked on a major stabilization program backed by substantial IMF, World Bank, and inter-American loans. It aimed at reducing the current account deficit, which had reached 123 percent of exports in 1981, by following a crawling peg with a series of substantial discrete devaluations (1982, 1984, and 1985). These doubled the real exchange rate and resulted in a substantial switch of production to tradable goods. It also reduced domestic absorption sharply, through fiscal and monetary stringency with wage deindexation and a sharp real wage erosion.

At the same time, various steps were taken to rehabilitate the financial sector. These steps included the liquidation of eight of the commercial banks and all the private investment banks that had been taken over, two programs to sell bad loans to the Central Bank, a number of massive debt reschedulings, and the recapitalization of the banks. The process of returning financial activity to normal culminated in late 1986 with the promulgation of the New Banking Law. It was only at this point in time that Chile can be said to have put in place a regulatory framework for financial activity designed for the functioning of free credit markets, without quantitative restrictions and with the minimum of state interference. State insurance for time deposits was eliminated, and a procedure was established to classify the risks of the loans made by financial institutions. From mid-1987 the assessments were made public. In addition, problem situations were defined that automatically require the creation of reserves, capital increases, and even the liquidation of the bank (see Munoz, 1992).

Finally, a major social security reform took place in 1981, which helped the development of capital markets. The system of state-administered pay-as-you-go pension funds were replaced by privately run and capitalized pension funds, financed by a mandatory 10 percent tax on wages paid by the government into funds. While this generated an extra fiscal deficit (about 3 to 4 percent of GDP, to be eliminated gradually) that had to be covered from other cuts in expenditure, it also turned the pension funds into a source of funding in the capital market, including the purchase of equity in privatized state-owned enterprise.

During the five-year period 1986 to 1990, Chile enjoyed substantial growth (over 6 percent per annum), reduced its unemployment rate, kept inflation below 20 percent, and reduced its current account deficit to low manageable levels. In addition, the economic transition has been successfully sustained as Chile has reverted to a democratic electoral system in December 1989. During the period 1992 to 1994 the average rate of inflation was reduced to 13 percent, while the rate of economic growth increased to 7 percent. The observers of 1984 thus proved wrong, but the costs and the policy lessons for subsequent reforms processes remain. We turn now to summarize some of the lessons.

The Lessons

Our analysis has shown that the order of liberalization and stabilization policies is crucial for a successful outcome. One major lesson that has emerged is that the stabilization of the economy should precede any liberalization attempts. We have seen, for example, that the abolition of restrictions in international capital flows was not sufficient for integrating the domestic and international capital markets. Even if the existing level of controls is not very high, prospective controls can create political and exchange-risk premia that keep the domestic rate at a different level from the foreign interest rate after adjusting for exchange-rate changes. Since the political and exchange-risk premia relate to the possibility of imposing controls, tackling inflation and improving the balance of payments will be reducing the risk premia. That leads to the policy implication that countries should embark on the liberalization of international capital flows after they have stabilized their economies.

Another lesson that has emerged from the Chilean experience relates to the order of liberalization of the domestic and foreign sectors. We have seen how the backward indexation of wages has hampered the efforts to reduce the rate of inflation, especially after the opening of the capital account and the huge increase of capital inflows. It should be said, however, that the Chilean government did adopt the right policy of liberalizing the domestic financial market by freeing interest rates first, before abolishing foreign-exchange restrictions. The abolition of these restrictions should be gradual in order to spread a possible increase in the stock of foreign debt through time and reduce the degree of possible real appreciation.[12]

In liberalizing the financial markets and freeing interest rates, the government made a mistake. It did not previously strengthen its supervision and regulation of the banks. These preconditions are necessary in order to minimize moral hazard in the banking system. That is, the tendency to provide risky loans at high rates in the expectation that large losses will be covered by deposit insurance, explicitly or implicitly provided by the government. Strong supervision and regulation entail the provision of reserves against bad loans, capital accumulation, and measures that facilitate the flow of information, credit appraisal, and rating.

Finally, a major lesson that can be learned from the Chilean experiment is the government's passive macroeconomics policy. For example, it refused to act in the face of macroeconomics disequilibria such as the steep increase of interest rates,[13] the increase in bankruptcies, the sustained real overvaluation, and the massive increase in the current account deficit in the first half of 1981, causing a deepening in the recession. The government's stance resulted in a loss of credibility on the long-run viability of the experiment and created growing expectations of a reversal of the liberalization policies.

The recovery of Chile since 1986 puts another perspective to the Chilean experiment with liberalization policies. Mistakes were made and lessons have been learned. But if it was not for the reforms, the stabilization policies of recent years would not have been successful.

Notes

1. Copper constituted the major part of Chilean Exports (around 70 percent).
2. The U.S. government withdrawal of aid might have contributed to Allende's downfall.
3. For an account of the capital controls over the period 1975 to 1984, see Phylaktis (1990).
4. In 1979, reserve requirements stood at 42 percent, and by late 1980 by they were only 10 percent.
5. In late 1975, the three rates were unified to one.
6. See, e.g., Pietrobelli (1994) for the effects of trade liberatlization on the industrial sector.
7. A similar definition of capital mobility has been adopted in Phylaktis (1997).
8. The exchange rate is defined as domestic currency per unit of foreign currency.
9. The backward indexing of wages and the fixed exchange rate were hindering the adjustment of prices to affect a real depreciation following the decline in capital inflows.
10. The concentration of loans to the financial and manufacturing conglomerates, groups (20 percent of the banking system's portfolio), reflected the lack of adequate bank supervision of bank lending (see Velasco, 1988).
11. The number of bankruptcies showed a steady increase over the years: 1977, 224; 1978, 312; 1979, 344; 1980, 415; 1981, 431 (see Munoz, 1992).
12. In fact, when Chile faced substantial capital inflows in the early 1990s, it introduced some capital controls to reduce the impact on the real exchange rate. It imposed a 20 percent

reserve requirement against foreign holdings of bank deposits in 1991, which was subsequently raised to 30 percent in 1992. It also imposed a tax of 1.2 percent on short-term external credits. See Calvo, Leiderman, and Reinhart (1993) for a discussion of the various policy options open to country with substantial capital inflows.

13. See McKinnon (1991, pp. 66–83) for a discussion of the reasons for intervening to slow down the increase in interest rates.

References

Aliber, R. (1973). "The Interest Rate Parity Theorem: A Reinterpretation." *Journal of Political Economy* 81: 1451–1459.

Bruno, M. (1993). *Crisis, Stabilization and Economic Reform.* Oxford: Clarendon Press.

Calvo, G. (1982). "The Chilean Economy in the 1970's." In K. Brunner and A. Meltzer (eds.), *Economy Policy in a World of Change.* Carnegie Rochester Conference Series on Public Policy. Amsterdam: North Holland.

Calvo, G., L. Leiderman, and C.M. Reinhart. (1993). *Capital Flows and Real Exchange Rate Appreciation in Latin America*, Staff Papers, International Monetary Fund 40, 152–177.

Corbo, V. (1985). "Reforms and Macroeconomic Adjustment in Chile during 1974–1984". *World Development* 13: 893–913.

Corbo, V., and Jaime de Melo. (1987). "Lessons from the Southern Cone Policy Reforms." *Research Observer* (International Bank for Reconstruction and Development) 2(2): 113–142.

Dornbusch, R., and S. Fisher. (1980). "Exchange Rates and the Current Account." *American Economic Review* 70: 960–971.

Edwards, S., and A.C. Edwards. (1987). *Monetarism and Liberalization: The Chilean Experience.* Cambridge, MA: Ballinger.

Frenkel, J.A. (1976). "A Monetary Approach to the Exchange Rate: Doctrinal Aspects and Empirical Evidence." *Scandinavian Journal of Economics* 78(2): 200–224.

Harberger, A.C. (1982). "The Chilean Economy in the 1970's: Crisis, Stabilization, Reform." In K. Brunner and A. Meltzer (eds.), *Economic Policy in a Wrold of Change.* Carnegie-Rochester Conference Series on Public Policy, 17. Amsterdam: North Holland.

Hendry, D.A. (1986). "Econometric Modelling in Cointegrating Variables: An Overview." *Oxford Bulletin of Economic Statistics* 48: 201–212.

Johnson, H.Q. (1977). "The Monetary Approach to the Balance of Payments. A Non-technical Guide." *Journal of International Economics* 7: 251–268.

Kouri, P., and M. Porter. (1974). "International Capital Flows and Portfolio Equilibrium." *Journal of Political Economy* 86 (May/June): 443–468.

Larrain, F., and P. Meller. (1991). "The Socialist-Populist Chilean Experience: 1970–1973." In R. Dornbusch and S. Edwards (eds.), *The Macroeconomics of Populism in Latin America* (pp. 175–222). Chicago: University of Chicago Press.

McKinnon, R.I. (1988). "Financial Liberalization in Retrospect: Interest Rate Policies in LDCs." In G. Ranis and T. Paul Schultz (eds.), *The State of Development Economics: Progress and Prospectives* New York: Basil Blackwell.

McKinnon, R.I. (1991). *The Order of Economic Liberalization: Financial Control in the Transition to a Market Economy*. Baltimore: John Hopkins University Press.

McNelis, D., and K. Schmidt-Hebbel. (1993). "Financial Liberalization and Adjustment: The Cases of Chile and New Zealand." *Journal of International Money and Finance* 12(3): 249–277.

Munoz, O. (1992). "Economic Reforms in Chile." *Occasional Papers* (Inter-American Development Bank).

Phylaktis, K. (1988). "Capital Controls: The Case of Argentina." *Journal of International Money and Finance* 7: 303–320.

Phylaktis, K. (1990). "Capital Controls in Argentina, Chile and Uruguay." In K. Phylaktis and M. Pradhan (eds.), *International Finance and the LDCs*. London: Macmillan Press.

Phylaktis, K. (1997). "Capital Market Integration in the Pacific Region: An Analysis of Real Exchange Linkages." Working Paper 95/133. Washington, DC: International Monetary Fund. Pacific Basin Finance Journal (forthcoming)

Phylaktis, K., and G. Wood. (1984). "An Analytical and Taxonomic Framework for the Study of Exchange Controls." In J. Black and G.S. Dorrance (eds.), *Problems of International Finance*. London: Macmillan Press.

Pietrobelli, C. (1994). "Trade Liberalization and Industrial Response: The Case of Chile (1974–1987)." *Banco Natsionale de Lavoro Quarterly Review* 191 (December) 431–468.

Sjaastad, L.A. (1983). "Failure of Economic Liberalsim in the Core of Latin America." *World Economy* 6: 5–26.

Stiglitz, J., and A. Weiss. (1981). "Credit Rationing in Markets with Imperfect Information." *American Economic Review* 71: 394–410.

Summers, R., and A. Heston. (1991). "The Penn World Table: An Expanded Set of International Comparisons." *Quarterly Journal of Economics* 106: 327–368.

Velasco, A. (1988). "Liberalization, Crisis, Intervention: The Chilean Financial System, 1975–1985." Working Paper 88/22. Washington, DC: International Monetary Fund.

Villanueva, D., and A. Mirakhor. (1990). "Strategies for Financial Reforms." *Staff Papers, International Monetary Fund* 37(3): 509–536.

III THE CENTRAL AND EAST EUROPEAN EXPERIENCE

7 RUBLES, RUBLES, EVERYWHERE . . .

Cash Shortages and Financial Repression in the Economies of the Former Soviet Union

Patrick Conway

Introduction

Cash shortages were a persistent and recurrent phenomenon in many of the economies of the former Soviet Union during the two-year period after the dissolution of the Soviet Union in 1991. These were largely, but not exclusively, shortages of ruble bank notes and were coincident with a period of rapid commodity price increases. The shortages exacerbated the difficulties of economic transition in the productive sectors, caused a decline in the faith of citizens in their governments' ability to manage the economies, and greatly increased political tensions among these economies.

Cash shortage is defined here as an inability of individuals or firms to obtain desired nominal balances of cash. Given the rapid growth in cash in circulation in these economies during this period, the persistence of cash shortages is striking. These were not transitory random shortfalls due to faulty distribution algorithms but were shortages that spanned six-month periods and that recurred in the same countries with regularity. Explanations of the phenomenon have in the past focused on two supposed features of these economies: their common membership in the ruble monetary union that limited access to cash and the supply-side shocks driven by market liberalization that caused consumer prices to rise more rapidly than the money supply. In other words, these explanations focus on an excess demand for cash for commodity transactions.

I argue in this chapter that the causes of cash shortage lay more in the financial markets than in the commodity markets. The excess demand for currency was due not only to transactions requirements but also to demand for currency as a financial asset. This demand for currency was increased by increased public-sector deficit spending and by a "repressive" financial-market policy. I support this explanation with both analytical modeling and empirical evidence, while recognizing that a statistical test requires more evidence than is presently available.

Recognition of the financial-market roots of the phenomenon provides an explanation for the pathological results some transition economies achieved in combating cash shortage. Currency emission is only a short-term panacea, while early initiation of financial-market reform becomes central to ending the phenomenon in a noninflationary manner.

Cash shortage can exist only in a rationing equilibrium, although this rationing scheme binds financial-market behavior. Earlier analyses have laid out in detail the implications for individual choice and macroeconomic equilibrium of commodity rationing in the command economies of the Soviet bloc, including the seminal work of Kornai (1980) and the later discussion of Weitzman (1991). The links between this rationing and observed holdings of financial instruments are found in the studies of the ruble overhang: Cottarelli and Blejer (1992) and Lin (1993) are interesting examples of these. The structure of this chapter examines economies with liberalized commodity markets, as have existed since early 1992 in the economies in question. Conway (1997) makes the case that the ruble overhang of the commodity rationing period and the cash shortage discussed here were really two facets of the same phenomenon; I refer those interested in the similarities to that paper. Hardy and Lahiri (1992) present a model of financial sectors in transition economies with some similarities to those observed here and explore the possibility of banking-system illiquidity—a type of cash shortage.

In the first section of the chapter I define the phenomenon of cash shortage and derive a model that illustrates its financial-market roots. The fiscal position of the government and the intermediating role of the banking system prove crucial in explaining a persistent cash shortage: the phenomenon is shown to be a product of persistent financial repression. The second section provides available evidence on cash shortages in the former Soviet Union. The third section marshals the evidence to indicate the consistency of observed behavior with the financial-market explanation of cash shortages when contrasted with explanations rooted in the commodity markets. The fourth section provides concluding comments.

The Analytics of Cash Shortage

Existing explanations of cash shortage in the former Soviet Union focus on its role in goods-market transactions—that is, given levels of real transactions and commodity prices, the supply of cash is insufficient. In this section I begin with an illustration of this logic. I then continue with a more fully specified model of the desired holding of cash within the context of portfolio allocation among domestic and foreign assets. It will allow for equilibrium holdings of real cash balances as a possible outcome and will link cash shortage to relative price rigidity in the financial markets. The relevant opportunity costs of cash in financial markets will be the interest rate on bank deposits and the inflation rate. Within the complete model, the phenomenon of cash shortage will be shown to be an effect of financial repression.

I consider an economy with three sectors. The public sector includes both government and state enterprises. The banking sector includes both the central bank and the formal commercial banking system. The private sector combines households with private enterprises. There will be economic transactions within each of these sectors, but those transactions are not of immediate interest: the focus will be on the cash and credit flows among sectors.

The public sector will have a net expenditure position relative to the other sectors. When its wage, pension, and other payments exceed goods purchased by and tax payments from the private sector, it has a real budget deficit ω: given the combination of government and state enterprises in this sector, it also could be thought of as the public-sector borrowing requirement. The banking system here does not have a net position other than zero, for it acts simply to intermediate between private and public sector.[1] The private sector will have a net surplus position that will be called private saving s. One other source of saving will be the rest of the world. Real net exports nx during the period indicate an alternative use of available saving.

Alternative Explanations of Cash Shortage

Cash shortage has typically been described as a central bank failure to provide adequate supply to service goods and market transactions. Consider the quantity equation as a representation of the transactions demand for nominal money balances *M*, with total real transactions *T*, the commodity price index *P*, and the velocity of money *v*. If velocity and the quantity of real transactions are held constant, the transactions demand for money balances is a function of *P* as illustrated in Figure 7.1.[2] A rise in *P* for any reason, without a consequent rise in *M*, will lead to a shortage of money.[3] If currency is the primary type of money, then the shortage will be a cash shortage. Sources of this exogenous rise in *P* have been postulated to come from the supply side of the economy: mark-up pricing by firms (Taylor, 1983), the impact of exchange-rate depreciation on producer pricing, or the removal of government subsidies to producers.

A variant of this explanation posits that price increases follow money creation (as in Irving Fisher's logic) but cash is only one component of money. Lipton and Sachs (1992) and Easterly and Vieira da Cunha (1993), for example, explain the price increases observed in Russia in terms of money creation to finance government budgetary deficits. Sachs and Lipton (1992) and Ickes and Ryterman (1994) note the unusual dichotomy between cash and noncash components of money in the former Soviet economies; if the money creation is predominantly in noncash form, there is so little substitutability that a cash shortage can result. The explanation of Gros (1995) based on the insufficient emission of rubles within the ruble

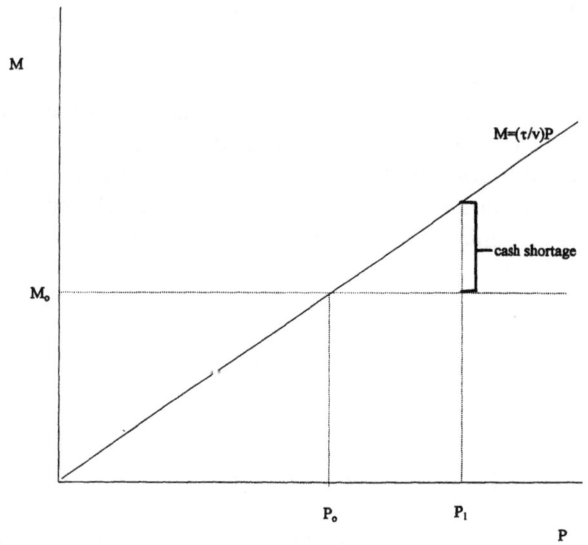

Figure 7.1. Cash shortage due to supply shortfall

currency area has this feature as well. In each of these explanations price increases apparently lead to cash shortages primarily by decreasing the supply of currency in real terms, with the demand for real cash balances largely unchanged.

This supply-based explanation has been the basis of policy intervention in the post-Soviet economies where such shortages have been observed recently. These policy interventions have worked at cross-purposes to the removal of the causes of cash shortage. To understand properly the causes of cash shortage in the post-Soviet economies, it is important to look as well to determinants of the demand for real cash balances within the portfolio of available financial instruments.

Cash Shortage in a Model of Portfolio Allocation

Suppose that the private sector can allocate its wealth to three instruments: cash h, deposits a, and foreign exchange f.[4] Cash shortage in this framework is defined as an excess demand for cash real balances. Following portfolio-balance theory, its real demands could be represented as functions of the real interest rate ($i - \pi$), the interest rate on foreign exchange holdings (i^f), the value of real private-sector income ($y = \omega + ia$), and real wealth (θ).[5] The functions α, β, and γ represent the shares of real wealth placed in the various instruments:[6]

$$h^d = \alpha(i - \pi,\ y)\theta \qquad \alpha_1 < 0,\ \alpha_2 > 0 \tag{7.1}$$

$$a^d = \beta(i - \pi,\ i^f,\ y)\theta \qquad \beta_1 > 0,\ \beta_2 < 0,\ \beta_3 < 0 \tag{7.2}$$

$$ef^d = \gamma(i - \pi,\ i^f,\ y)\theta \qquad \gamma_1 < 0,\ \gamma_2 > 0,\ \gamma_3 > 0 \tag{7.3}$$

$$h^d + a^d + ef^d = \theta \tag{7.4}$$

The interest rate on foreign exchange may be zero, or it may be positive corresponding to an interest rate on deposits denominated in foreign currency. The partial derivatives with respect to real economic activity are assumed as above since both domestic and foreign cash are often used for transactions; by the adding-up constraint, then, the derivative in the accounting-credit equation must be negative.

A private sector with constant real income and facing a given i^f has portfolio preferences for cash and bank deposit holdings as a proportion of total portfolio that will vary with the real interest rate. This covariation is derived in equation (7.5) for the ratio of cash to bank deposit holdings (h^d/a^d) and is illustrated in Figure 7.2:

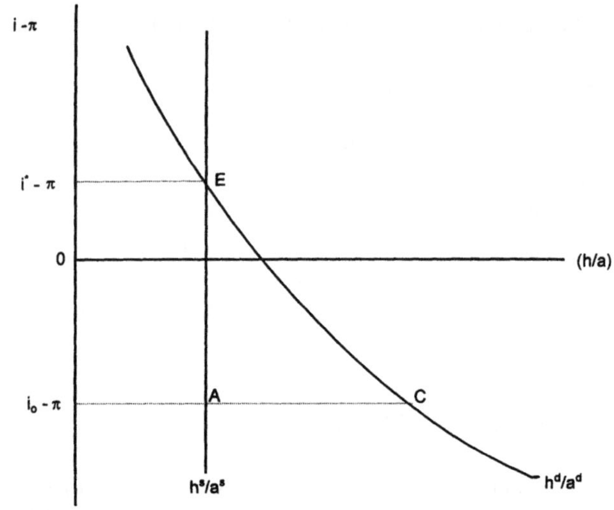

Figure 7.2. Cash shortage as an outcome of portfolio choice

$$d\left(h^d/a^d\right)=\left(1/\alpha\right)\left[\dot{h}^d-\left(h^d/a^d\right)\dot{a}^d\right]=\left(1/\beta^2\right)\left[\beta\alpha_1-\alpha\beta_1\right]d\left(i-\pi\right). \quad (7.5)$$

This demand ratio will be decreasing in the real interest rate as the private sector prefers to hold a greater share of wealth in domestic-currency deposits. Cash shortage characterizes those combinations of public supplies of real balances and real interest rates in Figure 7.2 that fall below the curve. For these, $h^s < h^d$ (and $a^d < a^s$).[7]

Financial repression is characterized, according to McKinnon (1973, p. 69), by "unduly low return to depositors—one that may well be negative in real terms if inflation is significant." It is maintained by induced bank financing of public-sector borrowing requirements at concessional nominal interest rates; this low return on the banks' assets implies a correspondingly low return on the deposits that make up the banks' liabilities. The ratio h^s/a^s of public-sector supply of cash and accounting credit to the banking system can be represented by a vertical line. There is a real interest rate $i^* - \pi$ that sets equal these two ratios: this interest rate i^* is consistent with financial deepening.[8] An equilibrium with financial repression is represented by a lower nominal interest rate i^o. In this framework, therefore, financial repression and cash shortage are equivalent outcomes, as for example at point A in Figure 7.2. Each represents a rationing equilibrium at which the private sector is constrained to hold a combination of cash and deposits that it would prefer not to hold.[9] There must also be a rigidity of the nominal interest rate on deposits that prevents a rise in this interest rate to clear the excess demand for cash.

Outcomes with cash shortage are not stock equilibria. In these outcomes with excess demand and relative price rigidity, usual rationing rules indicate that the short side of the market will be observed.[10] The excess demand for cash continues, with a rule for allocating the scarce currency. However, this implies necessarily a continuing excess supply of bank deposits. Here, the long side of the market is observed through banking-system imposition of inconvertibility of deposits into cash and mandatory deposits of wages to bank accounts. In the absence of such restrictions, the banking system could not finance the government deficit in each period through accounting credits and would be forced to issue additional currency.

Such inconvertibility will lead to the growth of a parallel market in exchange of deposits for cash at a discount. The private sector will be unwilling to make deposits into these accounts once an excess supply develops, and the public sector must have methods to ensure that these deposits are made into and retained by the banking system. There will also be nonacceptance of deposits as media of exchange for commodities at par with currency: this will be a consequence of nonconvertibility. The implicit discount ρ on bank deposits in the private portfolio can be derived from the rationing equilibrium.[11]

$$\rho = (\beta/\alpha)(h^s/a^s). \tag{7.6}$$

The banking system does not incorporate this discount in its own valuation and exchange of cash and bank deposits but continues to promise conversion at par of the two liabilities.

The Coincidence of Cash Shortage and Inflation

Inflation and cash shortage do not necessarily occur together, but they are commonly observed concurrently. In the hypothesis advanced by this chapter, the relation to financial repression makes the rationale clear: elevated inflation is a common path to financial repression. In the alternative supply-side explanations, inflation acts by (in the absence of central bank activity) reducing the real value of the supply of currency while leaving demand unaffected.

Inflation is the product of excess demand in commodity markets. Given the netting out of transactions within the sectors, excess demand for commodities can be stated as the sum of the public, private, and foreign-sector excess demands. This excess demand causes an increase in inflation π.

Equation (7.7) provides a simple statement of this dynamic for constant parameter ϕ:

$$\pi = \phi(\omega + nx - s). \tag{7.7}$$

The deficit ω is the excess demand for the public sector, while $-s$ is the excess demand for the private sector. The net export position represents another excess demand for domestic goods and services. Although the three must sum to zero ex post, in ex ante terms they can diverge. If the budget deficit exceeds desired private saving, the resulting inflation will cause the ex post excess demands to equalize by discouraging real private consumption and thus raising realized private saving.

The banking system provides the usual channel for mobilizing private saving. This can be stated in algebraic form with $\dot{h}^s$ representing the increase in real cash stocks, $\dot{a}^s$ representing the increase in real accounting (or bank) credits and $e\dot{f}$ representing the increase in real claims on foreign countries. The real deficit ω becomes the increment to the asset base of the banking sector, which creates new liabilities by either issuing cash or creating accounting credits.[12] The demands for the liabilities of the banking sector are the increments to the real quantities of cash and bank credit (deposits) that the private sector is willing to hold. These plus desired increments to the value of foreign-currency holdings are equal to the desired saving s of the private sector:

$$\omega = \dot{h}^s + \dot{a}^s + (h^s + a^s)\pi \tag{7.8a}$$

$$s = \dot{h}^d + \dot{a}^d + e\dot{f}^d + (h^d + a^d + ef^d)\pi \tag{7.8b}$$

$$nx = e\dot{f}^s + ef^s\pi. \tag{7.8c}$$

Inflation can be restated in terms of banking-system flows using the definitions of (7.8):[13]

$$\pi = \phi((\dot{h}^s - \dot{h}^d) + (\dot{a}^s - \dot{a}^d)). \tag{7'}$$

Inflationary pressure will be positive for excess supplies of these banking-system liabilities.

Note that if the money supply is defined (in real balances) as $m = h^s + a^s$, then this explanation of inflation nests the supply-based explanation above: increased real supplies of either instrument will ceteris paribus have an inflationary effect.[14] The innovation of considering the portfolio-balance effects is to introduce the possibility that inflation is associated with an ex ante flight from holdings of domestic assets. This will introduce a possibly destabilizing dynamic to cash shortage discussed below.

The rationing rule imposed by the banking system to bring demand and supply of financial instruments into line also plays a role in the determination of inflation. If inconvertibility of accounting credits to currency is imposed on the private sector, then this places a restriction on the purchasing power of the private sector. Those selling commodities will be unwilling to accept payment in accounting credits at par with currency, since the inconvertibility would then bind the seller. Those with holdings of accounting credits in bank deposits will have reduced purchasing power relative to those with holdings of currency—the shadow valuation of that reduced purchasing power is the premium ρ derived above. The inflation-generation process when this inconvertibility is used to support the excess demand for cash is presented in (7.9):

$$\pi = \phi\left(\left(\dot{h}^s - \dot{h}^d\right) + \rho\left(\dot{a}^s - \dot{a}^d\right)\right). \tag{7.9}$$

Other things equal, a deficit financed through issuance of accounting credit is less inflationary than one financed through cash emission; this is due to the fact that a portion $(\dot{a}^s - \dot{a}^d)$ of the increment to accounting credits is not willingly held but is in fact forced saving. Note that a stock shift of deficit finance from accounting credit to cash for a constant deficit will increase the inflation rate for small induced increases in ρ; this is an implication that will be explored more fully later.

$$d\pi = \phi\left(\dot{h}^s(1-\rho) - \left(\dot{a}^s - \dot{a}^d\right)d\rho\right) > 0 \qquad \text{for } \dot{h}^s = -\dot{a}^s. \tag{7.10}$$

Examination of (7.7′) illustrates that positive inflation is neither a necessary nor sufficient condition for a cash-shortage economy. However, cash shortage (or more properly the inconvertibility associated with it) serves as a brake on the degree of inflation observed.

Evidence of Cash Shortage in the Former Soviet Union

Cash shortages were reported throughout the ruble area shortly after the dissolution of the Soviet Union. The features were strikingly similar across countries: producers and government had too little access to currency through their financial accounts and thus could not pay wages, pensions, and intermediate-input suppliers in currency. Wage earners and pensioners then received insufficient currency to make necessary purchases, while producers shut down or ran arrears with suppliers. These suppliers in turn had no currency and either shut down or ran arrears with their labor and suppliers. The problem was exacerbated by the rapid rise in retail prices throughout the ruble zone. A premium arose in the financial intermediaries, with noncurrency rubles (that is, accounting credits at financial intermediaries) selling at a discount to currency rubles. In this section I provide both direct evidence of the scope and duration of cash shortages and indirect evidence of the phenomenon through examination of the premium offered for cash in various financial markets.

Direct Evidence

From the dissolution of the Soviet Union, severe cash shortages were observed periodically in the republics. Table 7.1 provides a chronology of cash shortages in seven of the republics. As noted there, the incidence of cash shortage is associated with an inability of enterprises to pay wages and of the governments to pay pensions, benefits, and other transfers. There is as well a secondary effect in purchase of consumer goods, as consumers request to purchase on account because of the incidence of wage arrears.

The countries under study can be separated into two groups. In the first, cash shortages were endemic throughout 1992 and 1993. The countries in which these sustained shortages were observed are Ukraine and Georgia. In Belarus, Kazakhstan, Lithuania, and Russia the shortage of rubles became acute in April 1992 and continued until the fall; there was a further episode of cash shortage in May and June 1993 for Belarus, Kazakhstan, and Lithuania. Estonia provided a third model. As Hansson (1992) notes, ruble shortages existed there prior to the introduction of a new currency in June 1992; after that time, there were no such shortages.

Premia for Cash over Other Financial Assets

A necessary condition for cash shortage is that the supply of other goods or assets be in excess supply and that there be less than perfect convertibility of these other goods or assets into cash.[15] One such asset is the bank deposit. In conditions of cash shortage the cash ruble will trade on informal markets at a premium to the bank deposit.

Such evidence of ruble shortages predates the dissolution of the Soviet Union. During the period of stable prices (that is, pre-1991) there was nevertheless an excess demand for cash rubles relative to bank (or accounting) rubles. This pressure came in large part from the value of cash rubles in untraceable or black market transactions and led to a premium estimated to be roughly 10 percent.

Table 7.1. Chronology of cash shortages: selected republics.

Country	*Period*	*Source and Magnitude of Shortage*
Belarus	May 1992	4 billion rubles, wage arrears
	March 1993	Ruble shortage, cash flight
	May to July 1993	Reported wage arrears
Estonia	March 1992	Ruble shortage requires sale of hard cash reserves
Georgia	May to December 1992	Severe arrears on wage and pension payments
	January to April 1993	4 months of wage and pension arrears, widespread efforts of consumers to purchase on account for lack of rubles (60–80 percent of potential purchasers)
Kazakhstan	February to March 1992	Ruble shortages lead to Cabinet of Ministers edicts 148 and 300 limiting withdrawals of cash from bank accounts
	May to August 1992	Wage and benefit arrears building from 6 billion to 15.4 billion rubles
	May to September 1993	Ruble shortfall. Many firms in July were in prestrike situation due to wage arrears. "New" Russian rubles not yet accepted as legal tender despite entry into circulation through trade with Russia
Lithuania	February 1992	Monthly salaries not paid to government officials (including prime minister)
	May 1992	3 billion rubles in wage and pension arrears
Russia	December 1991 to January 1992	CBR short 12 billion rubles. Russian Supreme Soviet places restrictions on cash use and withdrawals
	May 1992	2 trillion rubles in wage and benefits arrears
	June 1992	Kuzbass workers and trade union FNPR threaten strike over nonpayment of wages
Ukraine	January 1992	Ruble shortage equal to 25 percent of wage payments leads to introduction of coupon
	June to August 1993	Widespread cash shortages lead to restrictions on cash withdrawal and use

Sources: Data-collection network (see Conway, 1995a) and news accounts. Individual months indicate a news account, while ranges indicate a series of accounts or reports from data collectors begun in 1993.

After independence there were substantial premia for cash over accounting credits. Table 7.2 illustrates this point with premia drawn from the foreign-exchange markets in Belarus, Georgia, and Kazakhstan: these were the premia implied by enterprise transactions to convert both cash and credits to foreign exchange. Similar premia existed for the direct conversion of accounting credits to cash. In Belarus, for example, *obnalichka* dealers

Table 7.2. Premium of cash over accounting credits in foreign-exchange markets.

Country	*Period*	*Foreign-Exchange Price Ratio: Cash/Accounting Credit*
Belarus	June 12, 1993	1.80
	August 15, 1993	2.52
	November 3, 1993	6.10
Georgia	April 1, 1993	7.69
	June 18, 1993	2.21
	October 4, 1993	2.54
Kazakhstan	June 16, 1992	1.35
	December 15, 1992	1.15
	May 20, 1993	1.34
	August 24, 1993	1.37

Source: Data-collection network (see Conway, 1995a, for a discussion of this network).

converted bank credits to cash for a 30 percent fee.[16] These dealers had established personal contacts with the management and staff of banks and exploited those contacts to circumvent the regulations or to "jump the queue" among those legally entitled to the scarce cash.

The nonconvertibility of bank deposits to cash can take the form of rationing of conversion through availability of cash. Alternatively, nonconvertibility may be stated explicitly in regulations. In 1992 in Georgia, for example, the ability to convert bank credits (deposits) to cash was regulated by the National Bank of Georgia. State enterprises faced minor restrictions in access to cash while households were in most cases denied convertibility of existing deposits. Kazakhstan introduced similar restrictions on the availability of cash for deposits in February 1992 and renewed them in June 1993. One feature of the former restrictions was the automatic deposit of 30 percent of private wage earnings in banking system deposits; these were then inconvertible into cash in most cases. The innovation of the latter restrictions was the declaration that all shops must introduce cash registers for cash trade, with the evident hope that the machines would allow a more accurate tracking of cash flows.[17]

Evidence on the Causes of Cash Shortage in the Former Soviet Union

There are three competing explanations for cash shortage. The first relies on the exogeneity of inflation and the lag in currency emission to keep up with that inflation. The second is the explanation with endogenous inflation but an inappropriate mix of supply emission. The third is the explanation based on financial repression and a shifting mix of financial assets demanded by the private sector.

The first step of this empirical work will be to discuss causes of inflation in these countries. Easterly and Vieira da Cunha (1993) and Sachs (1994) have made the case that inflation in Russia is largely a phenomenon of public-sector deficits; I will present evidence for all countries under consideration to support that explanation. The second step is to distinguish between the supply-based and portfolio-balance explanations for cash shortage. Beginning from equilibrium as illustrated in equations (7.1) to (7.4), cash shortage develops if

$$\dot{h}^s - \left(\left(1-\theta\right)/\theta\right)\dot{a}^s < \left[\dot{h}^d - \left(\left(1-\theta\right)/\theta\right)\dot{a}^d\right], \tag{7.11}$$

where $\theta = (h/(a+h))$ is evaluated at the initial equilibrium. The left side of the inequality represents the "inappropriate supply mix" argument of Sachs and Lipton (1992) and Gros (1995): if the share of increments to accounting credits from ω exceeds the share observed in equilibrium, cash shortage will occur. The right side of the inequality indicates the inappropriate portfolio demand determinants of cash shortage: if the economic environment changes to such an extent that the increment to demand for cash real balances from increased income is greater than the share observed in equilibrium, cash shortage will occur. The obvious change in economic environment that could lead to such an outcome is the dramatic fall in the real interest rate and the consequent financial repression, although restrictions on convertibility of bank deposits to cash could also play a role.

Budget Deficits and Inflation

Bruno, di Tella, Dornbusch, and Fischer (1988) and Dornbusch, Sturzenegger, and Wolf (1990) illustrate the interaction of public-sector borrowing requirements and inflation for Latin American countries and others (for example, Israel) outside the region during the 1970s. Extreme inflation was the norm for large public-sector borrowing requirements in those countries at that time. It also became a staple of the transition economies of the former Soviet Union.

The Soviet Union of the late 1980s was characterized by fiscal deficits, price controls, and an allocation of resources disproportionately to national defense and producer-good output. As Nordhaus (1990) reports, this led to shortages of consumer goods, repressed inflation, and an undesired buildup in private holdings of liquid assets. McKinnon (1991) also notes the positive correlation of the liquid-asset buildup with the Soviet budget deficit. His figures are provided in Table 7.3. Prior to 1986 private bank deposits rose at a roughly one-for-one rate with the government budget deficit. Subsequent to that time the budget deficit totaled much more than the increase in deposits, with the balance being made up through excess growth in both currency and credit stocks.

The inflation dynamic described in (7.7) was stifled during this period by a system of price controls. As Tables 7.3 and 7.4 illustrate for the period 1987 to 1989, despite a 33 percent annual growth on average in the budget deficit and cash emission that averaged over 13 percent growth per annum, retail inflation rates averaged under three percent per annum. Figure 7.3 illustrates the consequent buildup of private-sector holdings of financial assets.

Fiscal policy choices have left the economies of the former Soviet Union along a continuum of budgetary deficit that ranges from the incredibly large to budgetary balance. As Figure 7.4 illustrates, the budget surplus as a share of GDP in seven former Soviet republics observed in mid-1993 ranges from very negative to zero. The Baltic economies of Estonia and Lithuania have implemented fiscal reforms leading to budgetary balance. The non-Baltic economies have opted for large (by Western standards) budget deficits, with those of Georgia and Ukraine taking on pathological dimensions.

Table 7.3. Financial statistics for the Soviet economy.

		Government Budget Deficit		*Government Debt*		
	Deposits: Billions of Rubles	*Percent of GNP*	*Billions of Rubles*	*Percent of GNP*	*Billions of Rubles*	*Household Saving: Percent of Retail Sales*
1979	n.a.	n.a.	64	n.a.	146.2	57.6
1980	12	1.9%	76	12.2%	156.5	57.9%
1981	9	1.4	85	13.1	165.7	57.9
1982	15	2.2	100	14.4	174.3	58.9
1983	10	1.4	110	15.1	186.9	61.1
1984	9	1.2	119	15.7	202.1	64.9
1985	14	1.8	133	17.1	220.8	68.0
1986	46	5.8	179	22.4	242.8	73.1
1987	52	6.3	231	28.0	266.9	78.2
1988	81	9.3	312	35.7	296.7	81.0
1989	92	6.9	404	43.4	337.7	83.7

Source: McKinnon (1991, Table 11.1).

Table 7.4. Growth of currency in circulation, 1987 to 1990.

	1987	*1988*	*1989*	*1990*
Growth of currency in circulation	7.7	13.6	19.5	24.3
Real growth in net material product	0.7	4.6	1.9	−3.6
Retail price inflation	2.0	0.0	6.0	5.6

Sources: World Bank (1992, p. 8); Goskomstat-USSR (1991, p. 28).

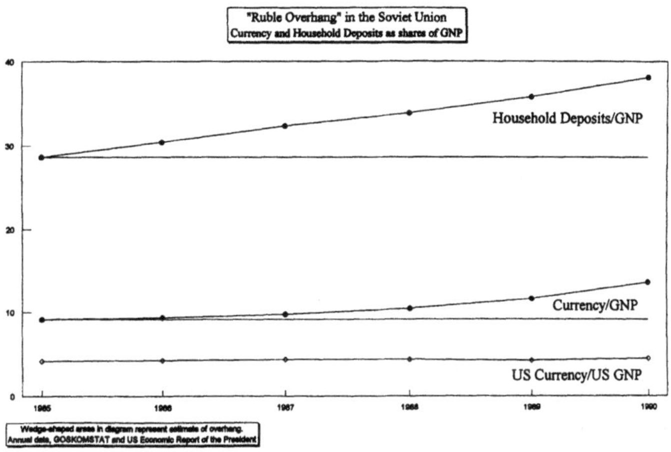

Figure 7.3. "Ruble overhang" in the Soviet Union

Private saving was inadequate to finance these deficits. The result was a continuing episode of extreme inflation that is also illustrated in Figure 7.4. Nonbudgetary factors certainly played a role in price increases, but the continuing inflation can be attributed to the excess demand driven by budgetary deficits.

Decomposing the Supply-Mix versus Portfolio-Demand Sources of Cash Shortage

The explanations of supply-mix and portfolio imbalance that are summarized in equation (7.11) are not mutually exclusive. Further, there are no independent observations of h^s and h^d or of a^s and a^d: there are only observed stocks h_o and a_o at any point in time. I set up the hypothesis test as

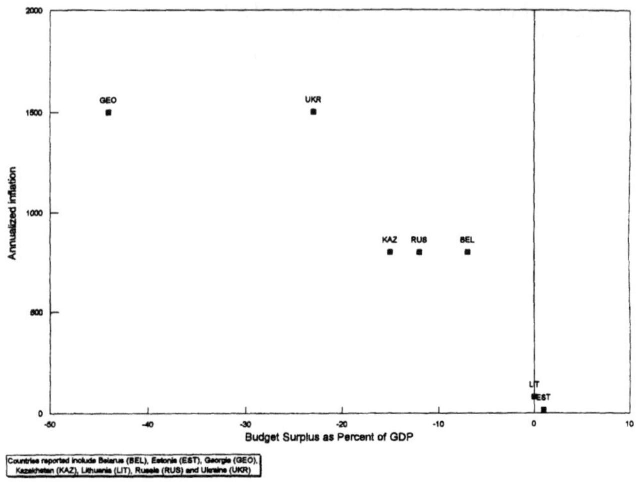

Figure 7.4. Budget surpluses and inflation rates for various formerly Soviet economies

follows. The inequality of (7.11) can be decomposed into two parts. For the supply-based explanation, set the right side equal to zero. This assumes no change in desired portfolio shares; for the inequality to hold, the ratio h_o/a_o observed over time should fall. For the portfolio-balance hypothesis, set the left side of the inequality to zero (no change in relative mix of instruments supplied). If the portfolio-balance explanation holds, then the observed ratio h_o/a_o should rise over time.

Table 7.1 indicates those economies facing cash shortage serving in the sample: they can be separated into three groups. First is the group for which shortages were observed throughout the period January 1992 to June 1993: these are Belarus, Kazakhstan, and Ukraine. Second is the group for which cash shortages continued through 1992 but not up to June 1993: this includes only Georgia. In the third group, cash shortages were endemic only in the first half of 1992: these countries were Lithuania and Russia. The top panel of Table 7.5 provides figures on these observed ratios for the six economies under consideration. The ratios observed at the end of 1991 are taken as initial ratios.[18] Growth in the ratio from the end of 1991 is then reported for each of the following six-month periods.

Support for the supply-based hypothesis will be provided by negative growth in the ratio, while for the portfolio-balance hypothesis by positive growth in the ratio. Consider the first group: in Belarus, Kazakhstan, and Ukraine there is consistent growth in the ratio through all three six-month observations, and the cumulative growth rate for the eighteen-month period is highest in those countries. Georgia is the second group; it exhibits the same characteristics as the first group, but has a lower cumulative growth rate than the previous three by mid-1993, when cash shortages were no longer observed. In the third group, Lithuania provides evidence of portfolio-imbalance cash shortage for the first six-month period, which was the only one characterized by cash shortage. Russia's behavior is an anomaly: the movement in its asset ratio is quite similar to that of Georgia, but it has no observed cash shortages past mid-1992.

One possible explanation for the Russian anomaly is provided in the bottom panel of Table 7.5 in the evolution of the ratio of currency to the stock of domestic credit issued by the banking system (Ω). In Belarus, Kazakhstan, and Lithuania this ratio is declining throughout the period in question. In Georgia decline continued until the first half of 1993; with Georgia's introduction of a ruble supplement the decline was reversed. In Ukraine the existence of a ruble supplement from January 1992 allowed a rise in this ratio until the first half of 1993; at that time the

Table 7.5. Credit, currency, and deposit creation in selected republics.

		Ratio, End of 1991	*Percent Increase over End of 1991*		
			Mid-1992	*End of 1992*	*Mid-1993*
Belarus	(h/a)[a]	0.098	118	253	2451
Georgia	(h/a)	0.412	42	106	1139
Kazakhstan	(h/a)	0.200	97	339	1839
Lithuania	(h/a)	0.376	51	–262	–222
Russia	(h/a)	0.161	38	106	1108
Ukraine	(h/a)	0.147	233	1026	2345
Belarus	(h/Ω)[b]	0.096	–10	–137	–713
Georgia	(h/Ω)	0.223	–20	–427	315
Kazakhstan	(h/Ω)	0.205	–165	–364	–759
Lithuania[c]	(h/Ω)	0.704	–169	–439	–629
Russia	(h/Ω)	0.186	16	185	1096
Ukraine	(h/Ω)	0.134	13	144	–247

Source: International Monetary Fund (1993), Supplement on Countries of former Soviet Union.

a *h/a* is calculated with the ratio of currency to deposits. Domestic credit refers to "net claims on government" plus "claims on rest of economy" from the Banking Survey section of that source.

b h/Ω is approximated with the ratio of currency to domestic credit.

c Mid-1993 evaluated at end-May.

public-sector borrowing requirement jumped sharply. Finally, in Russia the ratio was rising throughout the period. Russia's control over emission of the ruble certainly contributed to its ability to avert cash shortages by increasing h^s to match and exceed the public-sector borrowing requirements.

Support of the portfolio-balance explanation of cash shortage implies a changing incentive to the holding of various financial assets. In the transition economies of the former Soviet Union, this changing incentive was the real interest rate on banking deposits. The banking system of the former Soviet Union was unprepared to raise nominal interest rates with the onset of inflation. Historically, saving deposits held with Gosbank were characterized by quite low interest rates of two percent in nominal terms per annum, but price inflation was insignificant until the last years of the Soviet Union. Nominal interest rates were largely unchanged in the non-Baltic economies in the months after independence. Inflation reduced the willingness to hold financial deposits by reducing the real interest rate offered on saving deposits and certificates (certificates of deposit) to sharply negative values. Table 7.6 provides profiles of interest rates on credits and deposits in a number of transition economies in mid-1993, two years after the first observance of extreme inflation, and indicates the inability (or unwillingness) of banks to raise interest rates to positive real levels.[19]

Restrictions on convertibility also discouraged holdings of bank credit because saving and time deposits were much less liquid than cash. Withdrawal rights were limited in the Soviet Union during the indexation of April 1991 and were limited in Ukraine, Kazakhstan, and Georgia at various times after independence. The rationing scheme in Georgia was illustrative: the National Bank of Georgia regulation of June 1, 1992, stated three rules for withdrawals. There were no limits on withdrawals in cash by state enterprises. The ministries policed those withdrawals themselves. Cooperatives and nongovernmental enterprises were allowed to withdraw in cash only that component of their accounts deposited in cash after April 1. Citizens with accounts at the Saving Bank could withdraw from their accounts only the portion due to current wage and pension payments entered directly at the bank by the employer. In practice, even these latter withdrawals were rationed when cash was scarce. Firms faced an additional disincentive to depositing cash in formal intermediaries: the government uses the formal banking system for the collection of value-added and other production taxes.

Thus, despite the urgent need for additional private saving to offset government deficits, controls on interest rates and withdrawals at the formal financial intermediaries in the former Soviet Union made them

Table 7.6. Interest rates on saving and lending (nominal annual rates in 1993, domestic currency accounts).

	Belarus	*Georgia*	*Kazakhstan*	*Lithuania*	*Russia*	*Ukraine*
	July 17	*July 1*	*July 1*	*June 10*	*June 14*	*July 1*
Saving bank deposits:						
Sight	20	5	15		140	80
Less than 1 year				60–75		220
1 to 3 years	40	15	30			
Loans:						
Refinance credits	140	20?	25		140	240
1 year commercial loan	200	65	200	60–160	200	280
Auction rate	200		163–177	160–175	161–168	
Memo:						
Monthly inflation rate	30.5	40.0	30–40	12.7–0.9	19	21.3

Sources: Saving Bank-successor agencies in each republic, reports from correspondents, news reports.

Notes: (1) Sberbank deposits in Russia were recorded in Saratov. Commercial bank was Promstroi Bank for Belarus and Georgia, Kazcommercebank for Kazakhstan, Electronbank of Lvov for Ukraine, and Sberbank of Saratov for Russia. (2) In Lithuania, deposit rates vary by number of months of obligation and size of deposit. Lending rates differ by source: 60.5 percent for central bank credits, 60 to 90 percent for household credits, 160 percent for enterprise credits. (3) Monthly inflation rates are taken for the last available month before the observed interest rate. That is May in Georgia, Lithuania, Russia, and Ukraine, and June for Belarus. In Lithuania I also report the much lower rate for August, expectations of which may have been incorporated in the deposit and loan rates.

unattractive depositories. This break in the cash flow accelerated the cash shortages observed in these countries.

Implications for Policy

The three competing explanations for cash shortage have quite different recommendations for removing the shortage in a noninflationary way. The first explanation (with exogenous price increases) suggests that cash emission does not affect inflation; thus, emit currency sufficient to remove the shortage. The supply-mix explanation suggests that a stock-swap of cash for bank deposits will be noninflationary and will remove the cash shortage. The portfolio-balance explanation suggests that the most effective removal of cash shortages will come through financial-market liberalization or budget balance.

Given that the evidence supports the portfolio-balance explanation, consider the implications of the recommendations based on the other theories. First, emission of cash will alleviate the cash shortage but only temporarily. The underlying cause of inflation is the public-sector borrowing requirement, and this will continue. Cash emission will in fact cause a jump in inflation and will cause further shifts of portfolio demand toward cash and foreign-exchange holdings. The dynamic result is increased inflation, recurring cash shortage, and dollarization. As noted below, this was the impact in Georgia of introducing its ruble supplement (or coupon). Second, a stock swap of cash for bank deposits in an attempt to eliminate the cash shortage will not necessarily achieve the desired goal. Such a swap replaces the less liquid bank credit with the more liquid cash; due to the rationing feature of bank credit represented by the premium ρ, this swap will have an inflationary consequence. This is illustrated in equation (7.12) below. It is also evident in the differentiation of the inflation generation process provided in equation (7.7). Since $d(h/a)/dt = (1/a)[\dot{h}^s - (h/a)\dot{a}^s]$, the inflation dynamic can be expressed as in (7.12) for constant nominal interest rate and constant budget deficit (i.e., $\dot{h}^s = -\dot{a}^s$):[20]

$$d(i-\pi) = -(\pi/(b-s))\left[(1-\rho)(a^s)^2/(a^s+h^s) + (\beta/\alpha)(\dot{a}^s - \dot{a}^d)\right] d(h^s/a^s). \tag{7.12}$$

This describes the evolution of the real interest rate from a rationing position (as at point A in Figure 7.1) as the swap of cash for bank credit is implemented. Note that the impact on the real interest rate is negative due to the inflationary pressure. The inflationary pressure is larger for smaller ρ. Thus, the farther from stock equilibrium is the beginning point, the greater the inflationary pressure in swapping cash into the financial markets. There is also an inflationary effect in the increase in ρ due to the cash swap activity in the second term in brackets. This effect is also larger for greater initial disequilibrium.

The convergence of the supply and demand ratios through this cash omission (that is, even at unchanging budget deficit) depends on the relative slopes of the curves (7.5) and (7.12). If the real interest rate in (7.12) is declining faster from the cash swap than does the demand ratio equilibrium condition, then an equilibrium will not be achieved. If by contrast the real interest rate declines more slowly with the cash swap than does the equilibrium condition in (7.5), then there will be convergence. As the effect in (7.12) is increasing with the degree of cash shortage, there is some watershed real interest rate above which the cash swap will be effective and below which the consequences will be continuing cash shortage and inflation. Thus, for extreme cash shortage at least partial liberalization of nominal interest rates is necessary for a convergent outcome. Note, however, that even in the convergent case this cash swap also worsens the inflation of the economy as it reduces the goods market rationing of the private sector implicit in the cash shortage. The inflationary effects of this strategy too may eliminate cash shortage only at the cost of widespread dollarization of the economy.

There are alternatives to currency emission or stock swaps to deal with cash shortage, as the portfolio-balance approach makes clear. The first possibility is to allow the nominal interest rate on bank deposits to rise to an equilibrium value. This policy of financial liberalization is illustrated in Figure 7.1 by a shift from *A* to *E*. If this policy is followed, then there will be attainment of *E* in the present. However, in future periods this higher nominal interest rate will be incorporated in debt service of the government and will thus raise the budget deficit. There will be a growth in the public-sector borrowing requirement that if unmatched by growth in real saving will cause increasing inflation. If the supply ratio h^s/a^s remains constant, then cash shortages will reappear or the nominal rate must be increased. Continual increase in the nominal interest rate could lead to continual increase in budget deficit and an inflationary spiral. This is the scenario examined by Giovannini and de Melo (1993) in their defense of financial repression.[21]

The least complicated but most difficult solution to cash shortage is found in inflation reduction. Excess demand can be reduced so that the existing nominal interest rate combines with a reduced inflation rate to yield the real interest rate at equilibrium *E*. Stock equilibrium is attained. Reduction in noninterest expenditures of the budget to offset the increase in interest expenditures will eliminate the problem of an inflationary spiral.

Case Studies from the Former Soviet Union

The examples of Estonia, Georgia, and Ukraine provide case studies in dealing with cash shortages. Estonia addressed the budget deficit-financial disintermediation linkage and provides a success story.[22] Georgia was successful at eliminating cash shortages but has in the process discouraged citizens from holding their currency, the menati. Ukraine was unable to avoid cash shortages despite rapid emission of their own currency, the karbovanets.

Estonia was initially a member of the ruble zone but suffered though cash shortages in early 1992 as reported in Table 7.1. For this, as well as for nationalist political reasons, Estonia on June 20–22, 1992, introduced the kroon as its national currency. The kroon was established with a fixed exchange rate compared to the German deutsche mark (DM) of 8 kroon per DM.[23] At that rate the initial official reserve holdings of the central bank (mostly monetary gold held in the West since 1939) more than equaled the money stock broadly defined (that is, M2).

The central bank established itself as a currency board. Its monetary policy was simply to ensure convertibility of the kroon for current account transactions. In particular, the central bank was forbidden to provide credits to finance the budget and is confined to foreign-exchange transactions at the fixed exchange rate. This required large fiscal adjustments: reductions in expenditures and tax revenue increases. The results of the postconversion period were positive. The kroon has been stable and convertible while the ruble continued to depreciate against the DM. Cash shortages also disappeared, despite the strict rules on money creation imposed by the case board.

Georgia's cash shortages were extreme throughout most of 1992 and the beginning of 1993. By April of that year wages and pensions of the government and wages of state-owned enterprises were four months in arrears: they were credited to the individuals' banking system accounts but could not be drawn down. The menati (Georgian for coupon) was introduced on April 5, 1993, to circulate as a supplement to the ruble and was established with value at par with the ruble. In the two weeks after introduction, 31 billion menati were placed in circulation, while 19 billion were drawn down by firms and the government to make payments in arrears.[24] The introduction of a large additional mass of cash led to food price increases of approximately 20 percent in the first two weeks. Although the pricing at par with rubles was maintained by the government, the menati quickly sold at a 20 percent discount in private shops. State shops simply would not sell many goods for menati.

With the beginning of June 1993 the situation for the menati grew precarious. They were accepted for few goods, and the price in rubles was inflated 2.5 to 3 times for sale in menati. State shops continued to sell rationed goods (bread, sugar, macaroni, butter) for menati at par with rubles, but these goods were in short supply. State shops were rapidly transforming into commercial shops, as well, to sell in foreign currencies so these rationed goods became harder and harder to find. Remaining state shops had few goods on the shelves for those wishing to spend menati.

Georgia was successful at eliminating cash shortages, but only through a complete validation of demands arising from excess credit creation. There were sufficient menati in circulation, but they were supplanted as a store of value and medium of exchange by U.S. dollars or rubles. Financial repression remained extreme.

The karbovanets (KBV) was issued by the National Bank of the Ukraine (NBU) on January 10, 1992, in response to growing cash shortages and was introduced as legal tender in state stores. The karbovanets was initially seen as a ruble supplement and was designed to exchange one for one with rubles. However, the cash KBV bills were not evaluated by the private sector as equal in value to the ruble. The NBU was unsuccessful at establishing free conversion of ruble bills for KBV bills, and conversion took place at a discount on the bazaar market

On November 15, 1992, the karbovanets became the sole legal tender in the Ukraine. Despite rapid emission of KBV, cash shortages developed in June to August 1993. These took the specific form noted above: shortages of cash in formal financial institutions for use by state enterprises and the government in paying wages and pensions. Financial repression continued in Ukraine (although less so than in Georgia, due to higher nominal interest rates), and public-sector borrowing requirements remained extremely large.

Cash shortages occurred in earlier high-inflation economies and at times took on a persistent nature. Bresciani-Turroni (1937, p. 80), for example, provides a description of persistent cash shortages in Germany before the Dawes Plan that is strikingly similar to the one presented above:

> Private banks, besieged by their clients, found it practically impossible to meet the demand for money. They had to ration the cashing of cheques presented to them. On some days they declared that they were obliged to suspend payments or open their offices for a few hours only. Panic seized the industrial and commercial classes, who were no longer in a position to fulfil their contracts. Private cheques were refused because it was known that the banks would be unable to cash them.... The panic spread to the working classes when they learned that their employers had not the cash with which to pay their wages.

These shortages were attributed at the time to the inability (or unwillingness) of the German Reichsbank to issue currency quickly enough to offset the rise in consumer prices. The cash shortages were viewed by contemporaries as only the beginning of difficulties; as Helfferich put the argument, if the demand for cash were not validated, "In a few weeks, besides the printing of notes, . . . all national and economic life would be stopped."[25] Later analysts of the German experience (including Bresciani-Turroni, 1937; Graham, 1967; and Sargent, 1986) dispute Helfferich's reasoning on the relation between inflation and cash issuance and note the existence of both deficit spending and financial repression. They do not, however, relate these conditions to the cash shortages.[26]

Conclusions

Cash shortage poses a difficult policy dilemma for economies in transition. As first noted in the German hyperinflation, and more recently in the former Soviet economies, the shortage of cash was a symptom of the fundamental financial-market distortion associated with financial repression. As the cases of Georgia and Ukraine indicate, attempts to treat the symptom rather than the fundamental distortion led to continued inflation, recurrent cash shortage, and a progressive substitution away from the domestic currency. Estonia provided an example of effective treatment through financial-market reform.

The insights drawn from these episodes about financial repression are important but are only a part of the total contribution of financial-market reform. The gains from raising the real interest rate in this economy are those of portfolio reallocation. In addition to these stock reasons for reform, there is as well the flow rationale of encouraging private saving. Movement toward a positive real interest rate is an effective means of attacking both stock and flow aspects of the shortage: an increased real interest rate increases the relative demand for bank credit, while also encouraging private saving in a noninflationary environment. There is as yet no consensus on the elasticity of private saving with respect to the real interest rate, with some research (for example, Fry, 1988; Ostry and Reinhardt, 1992) indicating significant positive elasticities and other (such as Giovannini, 1985) indicating no significant covariation. The evidence for the transition economies (as summarized in Conway, 1995b) remains inconclusive.

A number of authors have made similar recommendations for financial-sector reform. Sachs and Lipton (1992) do not present their argument in terms of alleviating cash shortages, but their recommendations on banking system and monetary reform in Russia are consistent with the present analysis. Their recommendations for improving the attractiveness of financial-sector deposits, including the raising of interest rates on these deposits to positive real rates, are squarely in the spirit of these recommendations.[27] Pleskovic (1993) provides a stantement of the needed reforms in the former Soviet Union that stresses the opportunities for Western aid in this process.

McKinnon (1991) speaks of monetary reform in the former Soviet Union, but his recommendations would also alleviate the problem of financial repression.

The role of membership in the ruble currency area in causing financial-sector dislocation is an interesting further direction for research. Conway (1995a) provides an in-depth look at the entwined issues of budgetary deficit, financial repression, and the introduction of new currencies.

Acknowledgments

The author received financial support from World Bank Research Support Budget RPO 678-08, but all conclusions in this chapter are his alone. Thanks to Wafik Grais, Daniela Gressani, Ricardo Martin, Michael Michaely, Kent Osband, and Chandrashekar Pant for comments on a previous draft and to Anders Åslund for useful conversations on the Russian perspective to the ruble union. Special thanks are due to my collaborators from former Soviet republics: Alla Suvorova of Belarus, Lali Kikalishvili and David Onoprishvili of Georgia, Zhanar Abdildina and colleagues of Kazakhstan, and Alexander Bazarov and colleagues of the Ukraine.

Notes

1. The use of directed credits in the former Soviet economies could be construed as the banking sector running a net deficit. The impact of such activity is no different in this model from that of a public sector borrowing requirement financed by the banking system, and thus I subsume that case within the one considered explicitly here.

2. This is a Fisherian view of the quantity theory (Fisher, 1922). Friedman's reformulation would have the velocity a function of nominal interest rates on alternative financial assets, and the transactions variable a function of permanent income (Friedman, 1956). The latter is consistent with the expanded model exploited in the next section.

3. This stands the Fisherian argument on its head and is more closely related to a structuralist view of price determination (see Taylor, 1983).

4. As will become clear, foreign exchange represents any asset that serves as a hedge against inflation.

5. The seminal presentation of this type of model is Tobin (1969). Branson and Henderson (1985) provide a review of its uses in open-economy modeling. As noted in the earlier section, the opportunity costs of cash holdings are the nominal domestic interest rate (for deposits in home currency) and the interest rate of foreign-currency deposits plus the inflation rate (assuming foreign inflation is zero). These are restated in the current discussion by subtracting the inflation rate from each, yielding the real interest rate and the nominal interest rate on foreign currency deposits (or currency holdings). Real income is composed of payments from the public sector ω and from the banking sector ia.

6. Superscripts s and d indicate supply and desired demand, respectively. Dots over the variable indicates the change in the variable per unit of time. I follow the convention of describing real variables with lowercase letters. Thus, $h = (H/P)$ is the real stock of cash at a given point in time. The real value of cash emission H/P has two components: the change in real cash stock plus the reduction in the value of carried-over stocks due to inflation. In symbols, $H/P = h + h\pi$. The net claims on foreign economies is defined in foreign currency and is defined as $f = P^f F/P$. The product ef, with e the nominal exchange rate, thus represents the real value of claims on foreigners.

7. This is contingent as well on the exchange rate because the net shortage in these two assets must just offset the surplus in the foreign asset. If the exchange rate is assumed flexible, then supply and demand for that asset will be balanced, and I can speak of a shortage in cash offset by a surplus in bank credit.

8. The equilibrium with desired demands equal to supplies of financial assets has the form (for constant inflation)

$$\begin{aligned} hs &= \alpha(i^* - \pi, y)\theta \\ a^s &= \beta(i^* - \pi, i^f, y)\theta \\ ef^s &= \gamma(i^* - \pi, i^f, y)\theta \\ \alpha + \beta &+ \gamma = 1. \end{aligned}$$

The endogenous variables are θ, i^*, e, and a^s.

9. The disequilibrium with cash shortage takes the form (for constant inflation)

$$\begin{aligned} \rho^h h^s &= \alpha(i^o - \pi, y)\theta \\ \rho^a a^s &= \beta(i^o - \pi, i^f, y)\theta \\ ef^s &= \gamma(i^o - \pi, i^f, y)\theta \\ \alpha + \beta &+ \gamma = 1. \end{aligned}$$

The endogenous variables are θ, ρ^h, ρ^a, and e. The discount on bank deposits in the text is defined

$$\rho = \rho^a / \rho^h .$$

10. See, for example, Drazen (1980) on fix-price equilibria. McKinnon (1973) put forward this rule for the loanable funds market under financial repression: if the supply of loanable funds is less than demand, then the effective demand will be equal to available supply.

11. Weitzman (1991) derives an analogous shadow price of disequilibrium in his modeling of commodity rationing.

12. This is the mechanism modeled in Dornbusch, Sturzenegger, and Wolf (1990), although that paper provided less detail on the components of the money supply. In the stylized version of the banking sector described here, the only asset of the banking system is the government liability represented by ω. The only liabilities are the currency emitted and the accounting credits (or deposits) extended to the private sector. Introduction of foreign-exchange holdings or additional liabilities will make the story more complex while retaining the features of the present discussion.

13. In addition to the equalities (7.2), I use the facts that $(h^s - h^d) = -(a^s - a^d)$ and that the private-sector portfolio includes only cash, bank credit, and foreign exchange. The market for foreign exchange is assumed always in balance, as well, so that $ef^s = ef^d$.

14. Ex post the differential between supply and demand for financial instruments is erased through inflation's effect on the real supply of the instrument as well as through any effect on demand for real balances.

15. Conway (1994) provides a theoretical analysis of this and related propositions. It can be derived generally from Walras' Law: an excess demand in one market must be offset by excess supply in at least one other.

16. *Minsk Economic News*, July 1993.

17. Ukase of N. Nazarbayev, February 13, 1992; Resolution #483 of the Cabinet of the Republic of Kazakhstan, June 8, 1993.

18. The quantities of financial assets observed at the end of 1991 were not equilibrium levels, as the preceding discussion of ruble overhangs indicated. However, there is little reason to believe that the ratio of cash holdings to bank deposits was out of line.

19. Competition for funds could be expected to drive up these negative real interest rates, but there was little evidence of such competition. Due to the proclivity of the government to refinance lending at negative real interest rates, there was little incentive for the banking system to go further in attracting private deposits. The lack of competition among formal financial intermediaries for deposits is illustrated by the disparities in interest rates on similar deposits in the Ukraine in mid-1993: they ranged from 70 percent (at Prominvestbank) to 220 percent (at Electronbank) per annum. The annualized inflation rate in Ukraine at that time was about 1,000 percent.

20. This uses a substitution from equation (7.6) for the derivative of ρ.

21. It does ignore, as I do, the possibility of real saving growth in response to the increase in the real interest rate.

22. Pleskovic and Sachs (1993) describe a similar success story in Slovenia. The details of money creation and exchange-rate regime differ somewhat, but the prescriptions for budget balance and financial reform are quite similar.

23. The market exchange rate of rubles to DM at that time was about 75:1, so the fixed rate represented a slight depreciation.

24. In contrast, only 17 billion rubles in cash had been drawn down during the entire first quarter of the year.

25. Helfferich attributed the rise in consumer prices to the depreciation of the exchange rate, and that in turn he attributed to the need to pay reparations. As translated in Bresciani-Turroni (1937, p. 81).

26. Sargent (1986) and Graham (1967) remark on the phenomenon of falling *desired* real cash balances during an inflationary process but not to the inability to obtain desired nominal balances.

27. They emphasize bringing the cash and deposit components of money supply into balance by issuing more cash; I disagree with that recommendation, as outlined above.

References

Branson, W., and D. Henderson. (1985). "The Specification and Influence of Asset Markets." In R. Jones and P. Kenen (eds.), *Handbook of International Economics* (ch. 15). Amsterdam: North-Holland.

Bresciani-Turroni, C. (1937). *The Economics of Inflation*. Northampton, UK: Augustus Kelly.

Bruno, M., G. di Tella, R. Dornbusch, and S. Fischer (eds.). (1988). *Inflation Stabi-*

lization: The Experience of Israel, Argentina, Brazil, Bolivia and Mexico. Cambridge, MA: MIT Press.

Conway, P. (1994). "The Economics of Cash Shortages." World Bank Policy Research Working Paper 1367, October.

Conway, P. (1995a). *Currency Proliferation: The Economic Legacy of the Soviet Union.* Princeton, NJ: Princeton Essays in International Finance 197, Princeton University.

Conway, P. (1995b). "Saving in Transition Economies: The Summary Report." World Bank Research Working Paper 1509, September.

Conway, P. (1995c). "Saving Mobilization in Transition Economies." World Bank Policy Research Working Paper.

Conway, P. (1997) "Ruble Overhang and Ruble Shortage: Were they the Same Thing?", *Journal of Comparative Economics* (forthcoming).

Cottarelli, C., and M. Blejer. (1992). "Forced Saving and Repressed Inflation in the Soviet Union, 1986–90." *IMF Staff Papers* 39(2): 256–286.

Dornbusch, R. (1992). "Lessons from Experiences with High Inflation." *World Bank Economic Review* 6: 13–32.

Dornbusch, R., F. Sturzenegger, and H. Wolf. (1990). "Extreme Inflation: Dynamics and Stabilization." *Brookings Papers on Economic Activity* 2: 1–64.

Drazen, A. (1980). "Recent Developments in Macroeconomic Disequilibrium Theory." *Econometrica* 48: 283–306.

Easterly, W., and P. Vieira da Cunha. (1993). "Financing the Storm: Macroeconomic Crisis in Russia, 1992–1993." Processed.

Fisher, I. (1922). *The Purchasing Power of Money.* New York: Macmillan.

Friedman, M. (1956). "The Quantity Theory of Money: A Restatement." In M. Friedman (ed.), *Studies in the Quantity Theory of Money.* Chicago: University of Chicago.

Fry, M. (1988). *Money, Interest and Banking in Economic Development.* Baltimore, MD: Johns Hopkins Press.

Giovannini, A. (1985). "Saving and the Real Interest Rate in LDCs." *Journal of Development Economics* 18: 197–217.

Giovannini, A., and M. de Melo. (1993). "Government Revenue from Financial Repression." *American Economic Review* 83: 953–963.

Goskomstat-USSR. (1991). *Narodnoe Khoziaistvo SSSR v 1990 g.* Moscow: GOSKOMSTAT.

Graham, F. (1967). *Exchange, Prices and Production in Hyper-Inflation: Germany, 1920–1923.* New York: Russell and Russell.

Gros, D. (1995). "The Disintegration of the Soviet Union." CEPS Working Document 90.

Hansson, A. (1992). "Transforming an Economy While Building a Nation: The Case of Estonia." Processed.

Hansson, A., and J. Sachs. (1992). "Crowning the Estonian Kroon." *Transition* (October): 1–2.

Hardy, D., and A. Lahiri. (1992). "Bank Insolvency and Stabilization in Eastern

Europe." IMF Staff Papers 39(4): 778–800.
Ickes, B., and R. Ryterman. (1994). "Financial Underdevelopment and Macroeconomic Stabilization in Russia." In G. Caprio, D. Folkerts-Landau, and T. Lane (eds.), *Building Sound Finance in Emerging Market Economies.* Washington, DC: IMF.
International Monetary Fund. (Various issues). *International Financial Statistics.* Washington, DC: IMF.
Kornai, J. (1980). *The Economics of Shortage.* Amsterdam: North-Holland.
Lin, S. (1993). "A Monetary Model of a Shortage Economy." *IMF Staff Papers* 40(2): 369–394.
Lipton, D., and J. Sachs. (1992). "Prospects for Russia's Economic Reform." *Brookings Papers on Economic Activity* 2: 213–265.
McKinnon, R. (1973). *Money and Capital in Economic Development.* Washington, DC: Brookings Institution.
McKinnon, R. (1991). *The Order of Economic Liberalization: Financial Control in the Transition to a Market Economy.* Baltimore, MD: Johns Hopkins University Press.
Minsk Economic News. (Various issues).
Nordhaus, W. (1990). "Soviet Economic Reform: The Longest Road." *Brookings Papers in Economic Activity* 1: 287–308.
Ostry, J., and C. Reinhart. (1992). "Private Saving and Terms of Trade Shocks." *IMF Staff Papers* 39: 495–515.
Pleskovic, B. (1993). "Regional Development and Transition in the Former Soviet Union: A Comment." *International Regional Science Review* 15: 297–305.
Pleskovic, B., and J. Sachs. (1993). "Political Independence and Economic Reform in Slovenia." In O. Blanchard, K. Froot, and J. Sachs (eds.), *Economic Transition in Eastern Europe* (pp. 191–230). Chicago: University of Chicago and NBER.
Sachs, J. (1994). "Russia's Struggle with Stabilization: Conceptual Issues and Evidence." In *Proceedings of the World Bank Annual Conference on Development Economics 1994*, Supplement to the *World Bank Economic Review*, pp. 57–92.
Sachs, J., and D. Lipton. (1992). "Remaining Steps to a Market-Based Monetary System in Russia." Working Paper 54, Stockholm Institute of Soviet and East European Economics.
Sargent, T. (1986). *Rational Expectations and Inflation.* New York: Harper & Row.
Taylor, L. (1983). *Structuralist Macroeconomics.* New York: Basic Books.
Tobin, J. (1969). "A General Equilibrium Approach to Monetary Theory." *Journal of Money, Credit and Banking* 1: 15–29.
Weitzman, M. (1991). "Price Distortion and Shortage Deformation, or What Happened to the Soap?" *American Economic Review* 81(3): 401–414.
World Bank. (1992). "Russian Economic Reform: Crossing the Threshold of Structural Change." Processed.

8 FINANCIAL SYSTEMS IN TRANSITION

The Role of Banks in Corporate Governance

Irena Grosfeld

Introduction

It is widely recognized that putting in place appropriate financial institutions is a crucial element of any transformation strategy in Central and East European countries (CEECs). The importance of financial systems is documented in a number of empirical studies that have shown the positive impact of financial development on economic growth (see King and Levine, 1993; Pagano, 1993). Also, the lack of a full-fledged financial system has often been identified as one of the main weaknesses of centrally planned economies. However, looking for an appropriate model of a financial system, the managers of transition are inevitably confronted with the diversity of contemporary institutional arrangements in this domain. In particular, various countries differ as far as the nature of the relationship between banks and industrial enterprises is concerned. Arm's-length finance, characterized by weak links between investors and borrowers, is often opposed to relational investment, which allows investors to closely monitor the firm's investment decisions.[1]

Several authors have argued that the countries in transition should adopt the German model with strong universal banks exercising directly control on management (Tirole, 1990; Corbett and Mayer, 1992; Mayhew and Seabright, 1993; Frydman et al., 1993; van Wijnbergen, 1994; Aoki, 1994). Such claim is based either on a mixture of theoretical and empirical arguments in favor of close bank-firm relationships or on a purely pragmatic view according to which there is nobody else to do the job.

The actual evolution of the financial systems in CEECs shows that banks are indeed playing an increasingly important role and that very close links are developing between the banking and the industrial sectors. I would like to discuss the arguments pro and con of such involvement, not in terms of an optimal model, the shape of which remains obscure, but from the viewpoint of the medium-term objectives of transformation.

According to my understanding, the crucial issue in transforming CEECs is enterprise restructuring and the necessity for a profound redeployment of assets. Those economies differ from developing countries: their state sector is much bigger, and they are not in the process of industrialization with capital-intensive sectors becoming increasingly important. They rather have to improve the quality of industrialization (or, in some cases, to deindustrialize): to channel resources from one industrial branch to another, from industrial sector to services, and within a given branch from one firm to another. They have to deconcentrate their industrial structure and to disbundle irrationally bundled assets. In other words, an unusually large amount of resources should be liberated from their entrenched uses and moved to their highest-value use. In order to identify the directions of such reorientation, we need good restructuring ideas. Generating such information appears critical for enterprise restructuring.

The main point of this chapter is that introducing (or not breaking up) early in the process close links between banks and industry will hinder rather than facilitate enterprise restructuring. A bank-dominated system does not create appropriate incentives for the generation of information about different investment opportunities.

In this chapter I look at theoretical arguments and empirical evidence about costs and benefits of banks' involvement in corporate governance as owners, analyze the particular needs of CEECs, and consider the potential role of a financial system in assisting the necessary restructuring. Then I present the evolving relationships between the financial and industrial sectors in CEECs (mainly in the Czech Republic and Poland) and notably the role of banks. Finally, the critical assessment of banks as agents of restructuring is confronted with the actual constraints of transition and the feasible alternatives.

Costs and Benefits of Banks' Involvement in Corporate Governance of Firms

Advantages of Bank Monitoring

Recent economic theory provides several arguments in favor of close relationships between financial intermediaries (mainly banks) and industrial firms. Banks can play a role in corporate governance of firms through holding enterprise debt or through ownership rights. Whether banks hold shares or not, they actually have control over firms, but the pattern of effective control is different in the two cases. As creditors, banks exercise control over firms using the threat of withdrawing credits; in the case of long-term loans, such intervention is obviously less frequent than in the case of short-term loans. Banks also intervene if a firm cannot face its promised payment: during periods of poor financial performance the right to control is transferred from shareholders to creditors (Aghion and Bolton, 1992; Dewatripont and Tirole, 1994). Providers of debt decide in the case of bankruptcy whether the firm should be liquidated or reorganized under new management. As owners, banks may have their representatives on the company board and can influence the selection and the dismissal of management. The efficiency of banks' role in corporate governance obviously depends on the degree of concentration of debt (the size of loans) and of equity claims (the voting rights). It also depends on banks' specific skills as monitors.

The most common argument in favor of banks having concentrated stakes (debt and equity) in firms is based on the economies of scale in monitoring managers. A concentrated stake overcomes the public-good problem of monitoring: banks act as delegate monitors (Diamond, 1984) for a large number of small savers. In the world of informational asymmetry between financiers and managers, dispersed security holders contracting directly with borrowers would either free ride on monitoring (because their share of the benefit is small) or would have to repeat monitoring individually, which is costly and useless. Both solutions are inefficient. Consequently, it is argued, delegating monitoring to financial intermediaries contributes to the lowering of the fixed cost of information collection.

According to Edwards and Fischer (1994) banks have an additional advantage over other financial intermediaries (such as pension funds or insurance companies) because they have direct access to important information: firms usually hold their accounts with the banks, and thus the latter can directly observe all withdrawals and deposits, which allows the firms' financial situation to be assessed.

Another theoretical argument in favor of bank intermediation underlines the advantages of commitment to long-term relationships (Shleifer and Summers, 1988; Mayer, 1988). They argue that in the situation of incomplete contracts (that is, when it is impossible to specify all future actions and payments because these are too complex to be described or because managerial decisions are not verifiable) banks help reduce moral hazard between financiers, managers, and employees through the creation of the mechanism for long-term commitment. Without such commitment, implicit contracts between investor, manager, and employees may be unsustainable (Franks and Mayer, 1990). Employees, for instance, may be unwilling to invest in firm-specific training, and managers may be unwilling to invest in long-term R&D projects; if firms are listed on the stock exchange, takeovers and the resulting change in ownership may breach an implicit contract. A relational investor as a long-term stakeholder in the firm introduces an element of trust and long-term commitment.

Finally, it is argued, in the case of firms with cash-flow problems, concentrating firms' financial obligations may facilitate coordination and may allow for the reduction of reorganization or liquidation costs (Hoshi, Kashyap, and Loveman, 1994).

Empirical Evidence

Empirical evidence about the benefits of banks having concentrated stakes in firms is rather ambiguous. For Germany, Cable (1985) provides some evidence that banks actively monitor their customers. But generally it is admitted that the efficiency of German corporate governance mechanism may be mainly due to the high concentration of ownership stakes among large firms and not so much to banks equity holdings (cf. Franks and Mayer, 1992; Edwards and Fischer, 1994; Dittus and Prowse, 1994). Edwards and Fischer (1994) provide a lot of arguments showing that the role of German banks in controlling and monitoring management boards is limited: the representatives of the three big banks intervene on the supervisory boards of firms, but they account for a relatively small part of the banking system. For Japan, Hoshi, Kashyap, and Scharfstein (1990) have found that the investments of firms having a main bank are less sensitive to fluctuations of firms' cash flows than independent firms. Aoki (1994) views the Japanese system of corporate governance and finance as an appropriate solution for developing countries at the catching up stage: when advanced technologies are known and have simply to be imitated and the skills for external monitoring are scarce, the quasi-centralized system of monitoring appears the most efficient. But Weinstein and Yafeh (1994) suggest that firms with close ties to a bank did not grow faster or perform better than other firms. They interpret the low growth rate of main bank firms as the consequence of bank pressure to avoid some risky investment projects with positive net present value to shareholders. They argue that when capital markets are underdeveloped, a system of close ties between firms and financial institutions is likely to lead to a redistribution of rents away from the manufacturing sector to the financial sector.

In general, there is a growing awareness that neither the Anglo-Saxon nor the German-Japanese systems are working well and the process of adaptation in those countries clearly shows signs of convergence. On the one hand, in the United States and in the United Kingdom (Cadbury Commission), it has been proposed to increase the accountability of managers to the boards and that of boards to shareholders by following the continental tradition: by introducing a two-tier internal system of corporate governance and/or by creating a special class of professional outside directors independent from managers and maintaining close links with institutional shareholders. In the same spirit it was suggested that external discipline exercised through takeovers and bringing about short-termism, should be supplemented by internal discipline exercised by investors committed to holding significant blocks of a corporation's stocks.

On the other hand, what was considered as the strength of the German or Japanese economies, and notably the strong ties between banks and industry, is now often viewed as an obstacle to rapid adjustment in a changing economic environment. In Germany the relationship between finance and industry is becoming less close, with several companies deciding to open up their until recently strongly interlocked capital structures and control systems. The German firms seem to be discovering the virtues of public quoting. The long-term relationships established between firms and banks are considered to be beneficial in terms of providing commitment and trust but less so in imposing pressure on managers.

So comparing the performance of countries characterized by close relationships between the banking and the industrial sectors with those where finance is more arm's-length does not give clear-cut conclusions about the superiority of one financial system over another. The obvious problem with the empirical argument is that a particular shape of the financial system alone can hardly explain national economic growth, during some period of time. There are so many other intervening factors—macroeconomic policy, legal framework and regulatory history,[2] path of economic development, social structure and political forces, cultural specificity—that we are unable to extract the influence of institutional arrangements concerning the financial system. It is clear, however, that the potential benefits of close links between banks and firms (due to better incentives to monitor and to better access to information) should be confronted with the cost of such involvement.

Costs of a Bank-Oriented Corporate Governance

If banks are not only creditors but also hold shares of a firm, the conflict of interests between the two classes of financiers may be reduced, which eases an agreement in and lowers the cost of bankruptcy; however, from the ex ante perspective this may weaken the credibility of the threat of nonrefinancing (Hellwig, 1990). A strong bank-firm link creates a commitment that can be detrimental for the bank and for the firm. Banks' objective as creditors is to assure a low probability of bankruptcy: debt does not give appropriate incentives to exploit the upside potential. Consequently, banks are interested in gathering a very specific type of information, and the objective of their monitoring is obviously very different from that of shareholders: to minimize losses and to ensure a low probability of bankruptcy , on the one hand; and to maximize the overall return to capital, on the other. If banks also have ownership stakes in the firm, they can reap some benefits from a riskier strategy. In such a case, however, the risk of stopping a particular investment project will be smaller than if creditors do not own shares.[3]

If the bank performs badly, the firm may have difficulty switching to another creditor (unless there is competition among banks, in which case in the long run depositors will quit). If the firm performs badly, the bank may have difficulty ending the relationship with the firm, which may increase the risk of bank failure. In the countries trying to separate the until recently closely interlinked political and economic spheres, creating a bank-based financial system and an interlocking ownership structure may lead to strong pressures for financing based on political connections. In order to avoid cartelization, collusion, and monopoly abuses, strong government regulation would be necessary. But if regulation fails—because of the lack of experience or because the government proves to be unable to resist a great number of conflicting claims and pressures—then the whole system will be in jeopardy.[4] Moreover, from the economywide perspective strong bank-firm ties may have an anticompetitive effect because they hinder the exit of firms and make it difficult for competitors to enter the market:

banks may have incentives to lend unsoundly to firms in their portfolio, which will restrict credit to competing firms. There is the risk that existing borrowers would be favored to the detriment of new clients, the latter having difficulty in raising funds from banks: instead of demanding the liquidation of hopeless cases, banks have a tendency to roll over bad debt.

Dittus and Prowse (1994) carefully analyze the cost and benefits of a bank-based system and its relevance for the CEECs. They conclude that a system based on ownership and governance by banks may have important advantages, but they warn against introducing it in economies in transition when banks are not adequately supervised, there is not enough competition among them, and the state strongly intervenes in their operation.

From the viewpoint of enterprise restructuring in the CEECs there is, however, another important argument against intimate relationships between banks and enterprises: it can be traced back to the work of Sah and Stiglitz (1986, 1991) and Sah (1991). They (realistically) assume that people are fallible in their judgments, which means, for instance, that some bad investment projects get accepted, and some good projects get rejected. The decision-making structure influences the type of errors committed and, consequently, the performance of the economic system. Sah and Stiglitz show in particular that the performance of a centralized system is more volatile than the performance of a decentralized system. This difference is larger if the abilities and the quality of decision makers greatly differ. In such a case, decentralized screening devices have an advantage over centralized arrangements because they allow for greater diversification of performance and consequently higher expected profit. So in terms of Sah and Stiglitz, centralized monitoring by banks may be costly because it increases the probability of rejection of good projects. Such a cost will be large if there is considerable variability in the quality of projects.

The Sah and Stiglitz analysis has been developed in the context of the optimal structure of financial institutions by Allen (1993). Allen explicitly challenges the main argument in favor of monitoring by banks—namely, the uselessness of duplicated monitoring. He admits that in the case of competitive industries with well-established technologies where the opinions of a great number of producers about the production technology are confronted and give rise to a common view of how the firm should be run, repeated monitoring may not be useful. In such a case, the issue is to check whether standard production technologies are effectively implemented, and for that centralized screening by banks may be efficient.[5] But in monopolistic and oligopolistic industries or in sectors characterized by rapid technological change there are big differences in the quality of projects, and there is no widely shared consensus about the optimal policies a firm should pursue. In such cases, duplicating monitoring may be desirable.[6] The question is what is the nature of enterprise restructuring in CEECs and what kind of information and monitoring it requires.

Enterprise Restructuring in CEECS: The Need for the Generation of Information

In transition economies any restructuring strategy of the industrial sector must deal with the problem of irrationally bundled assets. This is the legacy of the investment process in centrally planned economies. Property rights were untradeable, and the state was actually the owner of the firms: it exercised political control over the economy by imposing its preferences but also by rescuing firms from financial difficulties. Central planners disposed themselves of capital: they used to decide what part of the GDP should be devoted to investment, how the investment funds should be allocated between sectors and individual enterprises, and which enterprises should be created, enlarged, or contracted. As has been fully shown in the literature these decisions were taken in the process of permanent negotiations and bargaining with enterprises, industrial associations, and ministries, who manipulated information and used overbidding as their main investment strategy. Central planners provided themselves some checks on firms' decisions through a baroque and contradictory system of permanently changing success indicators and incentive schemes for managers.[7] State intervention in the everyday functioning of firms created an institutional environment that was basically unstable and discouraged the firms' effort, while the lack of the risk of bankruptcy created a feeling of security. Both gave the firms an incentive to formulate very ambitious investment demands. The final allocation of investment funds, resulting from a complicated bargaining process between enterprises and various layers of economic bureaucracy, was highly inefficient.

The break with the old regime implies a change in the paradigm: no central institution is supposed to know the comparative advantage of a particular firm, industry, or sector. This uncertainty about what should be produced and how is magnified by the need for a profound redeployment of assets of previously state-owned enterprises. What this really implies is not simply reorganizing firms in order to improve their productive efficiency or restating balance sheets and writing off debts, but also transforming the enterprise product mix, withdrawing capital from some lines of production and from particular enterprises and sectors, and investing it in new ventures. This process inevitably takes place in the situation where it is extremely difficult to find guidance for the necessary recombining of assets and to assess the prospects of a firm. Several factors explain this unusually high uncertainty:

- Rapid changes in relative prices and demand for the firm's products due to price and trade liberalization, the breakup of CMEA trade, and uncertainties of macroeconomic policy (inflation, taxes);
- The lack of a reliable historical track record of firms: accounting under central planning was a kind of arithmetical exercise and was not supposed to be an information system; a modern accounting system is slowly being put in place;
- High indebtedness of enterprises makes the sorting out of the hopeless cases from the potentially promising ones hazardous; it is difficult to tell whether poor performance of a firm should be attributed to managerial inefficiency or to unfavorable conditions external to the firm;
- Young and unexperienced democratic institutions, uncertainties of the legal system *in statu nascendi*, and high costs of market-oriented transformation put a permanent stress on the reform process and amplify political uncertainty.

The difficulty of assessing the value of and the prospects for a firm makes the *generation* of information about various investment opportunities the critical issue in enterprise restructuring in CEECs. It is important to work out imaginative business plans, introduce new product lines, and propose new ideas, processes, products. After years of the lack of contestability there is a great need for external evaluation of the potential of the companies. This view might be surprising, as the usual discussion of enterprise restructuring in CEECs focuses on the problem of the lack of capital as the main impediment to successful adjustment. It is obviously important to raise finance externally: Table 8.1 shows indeed that firms in CEECs mainly finance their investment through retained earnings and that bank credit is used to a very limited extent.[8] A number of improvements can be, however, carried out without large new outside finance.

Buchtiková and Capek (1994) suggest that in 1992 the enterprise sector in the Czech Republic "more than covered its investment needs." Several fund managers in Poland and in the Czech Republic stress the fact that the bottleneck of enterprise restructuring is not the lack of capital but the scarcity of good ideas with reasonable prospects for success (Nowotarski, 1994; Lipinski and Dunin-Wasowicz, 1993; Anderson, 1994). It is often emphasized that the most valuable element that is lacking is good judgment

Table 8.1. Sources of investment finance.

	Poland		*Hungary*	*Czech Republic*
	1992	*1993*	*1993*	*1st half 1993*
Internal sources	58.1	63.3	54.2	72.7
Subsidies	5.6	4.7	26.1	4.8
Bank credit	10.8	8.7	3.4	16.8
Other[a]	25.5	23.3	16.3	5.7

Source: *Rocznik Statystyczny*, GUS, 1994; Magyar Statisztikai Evkönyv, Budapest, 1994; Buchtikova and Capek (1994).

Note: Data for Poland exclude housing cooperatives.

a Includes, for Poland: incompleted investment, investment from abroad (9.8 percent in 1993), etc.; for Hungary: credit from international financial institutions; for the Czech Republic: investment from abroad (2.0 percent).

about strategic goals for restructuring (Wendelova, 1993). In Poland the difficulty of working out a credible restructuring program has been identified by banks as the key obstacle in the implementation of Bank Conciliatory Agreements (Pawlowicz, 1994).[9] Also, in the case of Germany, Carlin and Richthoven (1995) report that even bankers view capital infusion as less important for successful restructuring than knowledge, skills, and adequate expertise. In many enterprises profitability and growth can often be regained very quickly if competent managers can implement good restructuring projects (for example, the spectacularly successful case of Szczecin Shipyard, as compared with the failure of Gdansk Shipyard).

From the viewpoint of enterprise restructuring, the critical issue seems to be the improvement of the quality of restructuring projects and the selection of the most competent managers. What can be the role of banks in this process?

The quality of restructuring projects is obviously strongly correlated with the quality of managers. Various surveys and case studies of enterprise restructuring in CEECs show a great heterogeneity in the behavior of firms operating in the same sector and in principle subject to similar demand shocks. We can find enterprises doing very well and doing very poorly, expanding and contracting, burdened with debt and financially very sane, passively waiting for rescue proposals or implementing for themselves imaginative restructuring solutions (Carlin et al., 1994). Some of the incumbent managers proved to be successful in the new environment, capable of independent judgment and initiative, but others are clearly unable to offer their firms any prospects of survival: they lack a fresh view of the company's potential in a completely different environment and are unable to work out innovative programs.[10] Such managers should clearly be replaced.

The usual argument in favor of leaving incumbent managers in place refers to the informational asymmetry between insiders and outsiders: it is supposed that firms' managers have superior, intimate knowledge of their enterprise and that they know better than outsiders do the value of the firm's assets and its opportunities. It also is argued that in transition economies incumbent managers should not be considered the main responsible for the sickness of the company, as its failure may have a number of reasons external to the firm (various transformation shocks, government policy, unresolved problem of indebtedness, and so on). Thus, it is argued, incumbent managers should retain control of the firm.

Managers should obviously be given the right to make mistakes, and the penalty for failure should not discourage risk taking. It is also true that managers have privileged access to some kinds of information: they have some historical knowledge of the firm and know the pattern of previous activities. Such information is valuable in a routine situation, when it is well known what should be produced and how. However, this informational asymmetry should not be overestimated in economies in transition. Choosing restructuring projects in CEECs is not a routine decision. The firms have to redefine their production profile, search for organizational innovations, and discover their production possibilities. This makes them rather like startup firms or companies with innovative projects: the expected returns may be much more dispersed than in the case of routine projects. Some of them may prove to be extremely profitable; others may appear as entirely inefficient. Different managers and investors may have different ideas about the possible future performance of the firms and may differ in assessing the firms' production functions. They should be induced to spend time and resources on searching improvements relative to the plans of incumbent managers.[11]

Banks know well enterprises with which they have been linked for a long time. This knowledge, however, which is often considered to be the main argument for making banks play an active role in the restructuring of the enterprise sector, does not seem to be adequate for enhancing the efficiency of resource allocation. To some extent banks can also be considered as insiders having privileged access to a specific type of information, notably that helping to alleviate moral hazard: they may facilitate *gathering* existing information on managerial slack and actual return. But they are unable to provide a fresh view of the company's potential or to make various ideas about the production function enter in competition one with another.

If we distinguish, following Aoki (1994) ex ante, interim, and ex post monitoring[12] it seems that banks are much less good in ex ante screening: they are excessively careful in accepting new projects. In the situation of great uncertainty banks behave indeed in a risk-averse manner and require, for instance, very high collateral before loans are granted. They also prefer conservative ideas ensuring the repayment of loans rather than riskier but potentially more profitable programs. This tightness of bank screening suggests that the analysis of Sah and Stiglitz (1986) applies. They show that if the screening function is tight, the performance of the decentralized system is better than that of a centralized system: in such a case, it is more important to avoid the rejection of good projects than to avoid the acceptance of bad projects. The probability of finding value-increasing investment opportunities will be higher if a great number of various assessment are encouraged to compete. Hierarchical choice may hinder innovation. Moreover, the level of resources and effort spent on the research of good ideas will be influenced by the likelihood of acceptance for projects.[13]

So the problem with banks as agents of restructuring is not only that banks do not have adequate skills to assess the company's potential and to provide help in working out a restructuring plan. The problem is that a bank-based financial system increases the probability of rejection of good projects and may fail to create incentives for the generation of information about different investment opportunities. If confronting diverse views about how the firm should be run is important when industries are uncompetitive or when technology is evolving quickly, mobilizing all the dispersed and idiosyncratic knowledge and stimulating the search for new ideas may also be particularly valuable if an economy is in the process of profound restructuring.

The Evolution of the Relationships Between the Industrial and the Financial Sectors in CEECS

The Central and East European countries came a long way from the previous banking arrangements. In most of the transforming economies major decisions were made early in the process to create a full-fledged banking sector and a capital market. The monobank system characteristic for the centrally planned economies has been dismantled and transformed into a two-tier system based on the separation of the central bank and commercial banks. Competition between banks has been enhanced by the liberalization of the conditions for entry of new banks. Privatization of the state-owned banks has started.

Table 8.2. Cross-ownership in Czech and Slovak banking sector.

	CS	*IB*	*KB*	*VUB*	*SIB*
Ceská Sporitelna	—	0.5	4.9	?	?
Investicní Banka	8.8	17.0	10.8	?	0.4
Komercní Banka	3.9	—	3.4	4.2	?
Vseobecná Uverová Banka	1.6	3.5	4.3	10.8	4.1
Slovenská Investicni Banka	0.8	6.9	1.1	18.8	18.8

Source: Based on Mejstrik (1994).

Careful description of the progress with financial reforms is provided in Dittus (1994). In this section I focus only on those elements of financial reform that have influenced the equity links between the banking and the industrial sectors for the last few years.

New prudential regulation has been imposed on the banking system, although each country has chosen its own rules and regulatory framework. As far as the involvement of financial institutions in nonfinancial companies is concerned, the banking law in Poland imposes no limits on the maximum equity share any financial institution can acquire in a (financial or nonfinancial) company, but the prudential regulation requires that investment in shares and bonds of companies not exceed 25 percent of the capital of the bank and that the maximum loan to one company not exceed 15 percent (unless the president of the National Bank of Poland agrees to raise any of those limits to 50 percent). In the Czech Republic a financial institution cannot own more than 20 percent of the capital of any company, and the maximum share of the overall assets of one financial intermediary invested in one company cannot exceed 10 percent. In Hungary, bank ownership of shares is restricted to 60 percent of own capital; universal banks cannot invest more than 15 percent of capital in one company, while investment banks can go up to 40 percent (Dittus and Prowse, 1994). In the Czech Republic and in Hungary restrictions on bank ownership of shares do not apply to shareholdings arising in the course of classical banking business, leading to debt/equity swaps. In the Czech Republic such shareholdings have to be reduced, however, within two years and in Hungary within six months. Poland stands apart in treating indiscriminately two kinds of bank shareholdings. Even in the United States, where other form of bank shareholdings are forbidden, banks may acquire shares if a borrower is in financial distress, but they have to sell such shares within five years (Baums, 1992).[14]

Because of the burden of bad debts, mostly inherited from the past but also accumulated during the first stage of transition, several countries have adopted various programs of financial restructuring and consolidation. In Hungary and the Czech Republic recapitalization of banks was unconditional, and in Hungary it even seemed to punish banks that had been trying to restructure their loan portfolio: recapitalization was indeed the highest in banks having the worst loan portfolio. In Poland the rationale for the law on financial restructuring of enterprises and banks, which enables banks to initiate bankruptcy proceedings without court participation, was that the consolidation of the financial system would not succeed if the enterprise sector were not restructured at the same time. The ex ante recapitalization was linked with the imposition on banks of the obligation to take a decision about debts qualified as bad.

Beyond the initial deliberate decisions setting up the stage for the development of the financial sector, its evolution has been responding, often in an unexpected way, to the process of privatization.

The development of the Warsaw, Budapest, and Prague stock exchanges has been stimulated by different privatization strategies. In the Czech Republic the development of the capital market was directly influenced by voucher privatization, which created over 6 million individual shareholders holding equity in about 1,700 firms. Czech citizens could bid for shares of companies privatized by the voucher method or entrust their investment points to one of hundreds of investment privatization funds (IPF) that emerged spontaneously. The reallocation of assets and the concentration of ownership was supposed to occur through the exchanges on the stock market. Two parallel structures for trading shares have been created: Prague Stock Exchange and RM over-the-counter system designed for retail investors. For the time being, the market remains, however, very illiquid (only about 100 companies are more or less regularly traded). Some observers forecast that because many manufacturing companies privatized in "mass privatization" are not viable economic units, the number of companies listed on the PSE will have shrunk from 1,700 to 200 within four to five years (see Jenkins, 1995). An important impediment to trading is the lack of transparency of the market: the existing securities law does not ensure public availability of accurate information about Czech companies, which is instead often used in off-market trades (investment funds trade with each other getting prices many times over those quoted on the Prague Stock Exchange).

In Poland and in Hungary privatization strategies were more traditional (IPOs, trade sales, buyouts) and until 1995 did not include the quasi-free distribution of property to the population. Consequently, the number of firms listed on the Warsaw and Budapest Stock Exchanges is rather limited: seventy firms in Warsaw[15] and over thirty firms in Budapest. The development of markets for corporate securities strongly depends on the disclosure requirements imposed on firms. In Poland firms issuing shares to the public are submitted to strong disclosure requirements, and shareholder rights are well protected; buyers must disclose their equity holdings exceeding 5 percent of a company stock, and if they intend to buy over 33 percent of shares, they must offer the same bid to all shareholders. Such regulation is appreciated by investors and encourages nonintermediated finance. The Warsaw Stock Exchange may be fueled by the implementation of the Polish mass privatization program, which eventually got off the ground in 1995 and which may result in the listing of an important number of firms and investment funds.

The shares of 512 Polish enterprises were distributed to 15 National Investment Funds (NIF), the citizens getting a perfectly diversified portfolio: a share in each fund. The NIFs are managed by consortia established by foreign universal and investment banks, venture capital, and consulting firms in cooperation with Polish banks and consulting firms. Taking into account the agency problem of publicly and largely held corporations the allocation of enterprises to funds was organized to allow an individual fund

Table 8.3. Top ten Czech funds, first wave, by market capitalization.

Fund	*Fund Management Company*	*Market Capitalization ($ million)*
1. Sporitelni Privatizacni	Sporitelni Investicni Spolecnost (Bank)	296
2. Harvard Dividend	Harvard Capital & Consulting a.s. (Private)	159
3. Komercni Banka IF	IKS Komercni Banky (Bank)	148
4. RIF	Prvni Investicni a.s. (Bank)	147
5. PIF IPF	KIS Ceska Pojistovna (Insurance Company)	96
6. Harvard Growth	Harvard Capital and Consulting (Private)	91
7. Fond Rychleho Vynosu	Prvni Investicni a.s. (Bank)	74
8. Creditanstalt IPF	Creditanstalt Investment Co. (Bank)	66
9. Rentiersky	Prvni Investicni a.s. (Bank)	63
10. Zivnobanka IF	Zivnobanka Trust a.s. (Bank)	57

Source: King (1995), based on Wood & Co. Securities.

to acquire a large block of shares (33 percent) that gives it sufficient control to initiate restructuring.[16] A complex remuneration scheme for the managers of NIFs has been designed in order to make them maximize the value of the firms in their portfolios.[17]

Initially, it seemed that the Czech voucher scheme and the Polish mass privatization program have been inspired by two different models of financial system: the voucher scheme was expected to bring about the development of capital market and could be interpreted as motivated more by the Anglo-Saxon model with widely held equity and an active stock exchange; the Polish program could be viewed as influenced by the German-type system, with a stable core of equity owners exercising direct control on management.

These contrasting initial inspiration notwithstanding actual developments suggest that in the Czech Republic banks came to strongly dominate the enterprise sector. In both financial systems emerging in the Czech Republic and in Poland, financial intermediaries and notably banks play an increasingly important role, although each country is characterized by a specific mixture of market and intermediated systems.

In the Czech Republic major commercial banks have acquired a great power in the privatization process. In the first wave of voucher privatization, the four biggest bank-affiliated funds have attracted more than 40 percent of all investment points (calculations based on Mejstrik, Marcincin, and Lastoviska, 1995).

Indirectly, banks not only became owners of a large part of nonfinancial companies, but also, regulatory restrictions notwithstanding, they came to own each other (see Table 8.2).

Regulation intended to limit banks' involvement in nonfinancial companies was introduced after the funds started operating and has not been respected. The rules forbidding a fund to own more than 20 percent of the capital of any company and setting the maximum share of the overall assets of one investment privatization fund invested in one company to 10 percent were flouted: the government apparently has been captured by funds claiming that if they had to sell shares they own in excess of the limit, the stock prices would abruptly go down. In order to circumvent the provision forbidding bank funds to own shares in their founders or in other banks, major commercial banks acquired shares in each other through the intermediary of their daughter investment companies. In some cases banks indirectly became even owners of their own shares: this is notably the case of the Czech Investicní Banka, which owns 17 percent of its own shares and of Slovak Investicní Banka, which owns 19 percent of its own shares (Mejstrik, 1994).

The fact that banks emerged as key equity holders has been an unexpected consequence of the weakly regulated privatization process. However, the rationale for accepting such development was probably provided by the concern that the dispersed ownership structure of the firms privatized through the voucher scheme might be inefficient. Eventually, this initial concern was replaced by the fear that strong industrial equity holdings of large financial intermediaries may be harmful for the performance of the Czech economy.

All investment privatization funds (IPFs) are not affiliated with banks: some of them are independent and emerged spontaneously (see Table 8.3). The difference in the behavior of these two types of funds is striking: they adopted different strategies in bidding for shares and in portfolio selection. As Coffee (1994) shows, the large bank-affiliated funds proved to be risk averse and invested heavily in the early rounds; they also chose to create broad portfolios, often acquiring shares in several hundred companies (the fund owned by the largest saving bank Ceska Sporitelna acquired shares in more than 500 companies). Privately owned funds chose a riskier strategy and waited for final rounds to bid for shares with lower prices; they also chose to create much narrower portfolios (the largest private fund, Harvard Capital and Consulting, has about fifty companies in its portfolio). Coffee (1994) suggests that the contrast between private investment funds and bank-affiliated funds may be explained by the fact that IPFs established by banks were used to promote their banking parents' interests and to get many firms into banking business. Consequently, independent funds are more likely to behave as active monitors: as venture capital funds, having a concentrated portfolio, rather than as pursuing risk-diversification strategy mutual funds.[18]

Only after the two waves of the voucher scheme had ended did the debate about the regulatory system constraining the IPFs start: should they be encouraged to become active owners or rather forced to remain portfolio-oriented intermediaries; should the current 20 percent ownership limit be scrapped altogether, which would allow more control-oriented funds to become like venture capital companies, or should some ownership ceiling be maintained (for instance at the 30 to 35 percent level), which would create a system of cross-monitoring between large shareholders?[19] By the end of 1995 these questions had not been settled. In the legislative void a dynamic process of reallocation of control started and is sometimes called the third wave of privatization ("Third Wave," 1996). The most spectacular takeovers have been led by an American firm (Stratton) and by a Czech investment firm (Motoinvest). Their takeover strategy was aimed at firms and investment funds. Even funds run by large established banks such as Komercni Banka, Zivnostenska Banka, or Creditanstalt are threatened (see Vojtech, 1995). The activism of private independent funds and of foreign investors injects contestability in the Czech system, which may menace the peculiar web of close relationships between the financial and industrial sectors in the Czech Republic.

In Poland, banks participate in privatization by acquiring shares of enterprises privatized through initial public offerings or investing in the shares of companies listed on the stock exchange.[20] They sometimes provide equity capital to companies bought out by the employees[21] or sold to domestic investors. Since 1994 banks have been also involved in underwriting issues, which has often led them to take shares in underwritten companies. Finally, banks may convert debt into equity in the case of bankrupt firms and in the framework of the Conciliation Proceedings Act of 1934.[22] Several interviews with managers of major commercial banks show that banks are rather reluctant to invest in the equity of industrial firms. Most of banks' equity investment was concentrated in ventures promoting financial infrastructure (financial institutions, telecommunication services, schools of banking, agencies for promoting regional development). If banks have a controlling stake in a firm, this is the result of debt/equity swaps.

However, several mechanisms have been designed in Poland to make banks actively participate in the privatization and restructuring of the enterprise sector. Converting debt into equity was considered as the key mechanism for solving the problem of bad debts in the framework of the law on financial restructuring of enterprises and banks: the law enables banks to initiate bankruptcy proceedings without court participation. State-owned banks were capitalized with treasury bonds, and an effort has been made to provide banks with correct incentives to collect relevant information about the performance and the prospects of firms. However, banks still remain reluctant to swap debt into equity and to take control of enterprises. According to preliminary assessment, in 96 cases out of the total of 152 conciliatory agreements debts have been converted into equity (*Rzeczpospolita*, January 2, 1996). Bank managers argue that they do not feel competent enough to play the role of strategic investors and controll the management of enterprises.[23] In the state-owned commercial banks managers also blame contradictory expectations of various stakeholders in the case of debt/equity conversion: "The managers of the firm ask for new credits, the crew call us communists. If we speak about economic interests, there is a telephone call from the office of the prime minister reminding us that as a state bank we should think about 'national interests'" (see Rabiej, 1995). Another reason that banks resist playing the role of strategic investors is fiscal disincentives: after the conversion of bad debts into equity, banks do not have to build reserves against bad loans, which could reduce the tax base.

There are exceptions, however, to this general reluctance of banks to acquire shares of firms. Some of the banks show less resistance to taking over shares of defaulting firms: Powszechny Bank Gospodarczy in Lodz and Bank Depozytowo-Kredytowy created special investment funds to manage the shares in their portfolios. Powszechny Bank Gospodarczy has taken over 10 to 60 percent of shares in twenty-five companies. The conversion of debt into equity gives the bank control over implementation of the restructuring programs. As an owner, the bank has the right to influence the appointment of manager, the right it obviously does not have as creditor. Another bank, Bank Rozwoju Eksportu, which was not designed for capitalization, also proved to be more keen to become strategic investor in a number of firms in the result of debt/equity swaps. But still bank managers viewed these decisions as a lesser evil. It is plausible that differences in bank attitudes toward debt/equity swaps are largely due to the different availability of appropriate skills and management expertise.

Since 1995, when the Polish mass privatization program eventually started, banks have become involved in the process of restructuring and privatization of the industrial sector through the participation in the consortia managing the NIFs. Nine Polish banks (six of which are still state-controlled) appear as significant shareholders (holding between 20 and 51 percent of shares) in nine out of fourteen management groups, having signed management contracts with the NIFs (Table 8.4).

A NIF can be seen as a mixture of a venture capital fund (from the viewpoint of the managerial and financial expertise, they are supposed to bring together with the provision of capital) and a mutual fund (allowing its shareholders to diversify risk). At the time of writing it is obviously too early to assess the actual behavior of NIFs: the allocation of the 512 companies ended in December 1995. Before the process of allocation started, the funds had only a very approximate knowledge of the firms based on the information provided by the Ministry for Ownership Transformation and on casual contacts with some firms. Once each fund became a strategic investor in about thirty-four firms, they started to carefully analyze the specific problems and prospects of individual firms. However, it is interesting to note that already at the preliminary stage of the selection of the companies the fifteen funds used very different strategies in choosing enterprises: some of them were looking for sales or assets maximization, other carefully analyzed financial results, some stressed the importance of the quality of firm managers, other aimed at sectoral concentration or diversification, or else considered potential interest of foreign investors; some

Table 8.4. Bank participation in the Consortia Managing National Investment Funds (NIF) in Poland (December 12, 1995).

NIF	*Bank*	*Bank Share Ownership in the Consortia Managing NIFs (%)*	*Direct and Indirect State Ownership in the Capital of the Bank*
I	Bank Rozwoju Eksportu	51	9.3
II	Bank Gdanski	25	40
III	PKO SA	33.33	100
V	Polski Bank Rozwoju	49.9	79
VI	Wielkopolski Bank Kredytowy	40	25.5
VII	Bank Gospodarstwa Krajowego	33.33	100
VIII	Bank Handlowy	20	100
X	BISE	4	48.5
XII	Polski Bank Inwestycyjny	20	100
XIV	Bank Zachodni	33.66	100

Source: Anusz and Bielecki (1995), *Gazeta Bankowa*, 39, 1995, and 8, 1996.

funds relied in their selection decisions on special algorithms, other were using more qualitative criteria (cf. *Zycie Gospodarcze*, Nos. 33, 34, 35, 1995).

So both in Poland and in the Czech Republic, intermediaries created in the process of privatization use very different strategies in dealing with the firms in their portfolios. These differences are important despite the fact that the Polish funds have been set up by the state and the Czech funds emerged spontaneously, and that the deliberate effort of the Polish founders of the mass privatization program to create strong financial intermediaries capable of taking the responsibility for the restructuring of the privatized firms contrasts with the initially more laissez-faire attitude in the Czech Republic. Such heterogeneity in behavior suggests, in my view, that the regulatory framework for intermediaries should be flexible enough to allow various funds to find their own comparative advantage: some of them may be more efficient as portfolio managers; others may have skills making them successful as venture capitalists.

Overall it appears that despite the banks' reluctance to hold shares in industrial firms,[24] banks emerge from the process of privatization and bad debt treatment in Poland and in the Czech Republic with strong industrial equity holdings. In the light of the analysis presented in previous sections it appears, however, that such bank domination is not favorable to enterprise restructuring and should not, therefore, be encouraged.

Is There an Alternative to a Bank-Based System?

Is there, however, an alternative to banks? Even if one agrees that it is desirable to have a system stimulating external assessment of the potential of firms, is it a realistic option given the existing conditions and constraints? Capital market is illiquid, there are few rating agencies, investment banks, or specialists analyzing information about firms, and so on. Should not we follow therefore van Wijnbergen (1994) when he argues that although banks may not be good in judging the potential of firms in transition, they are "better than anyone else" and in particular better than the government? How can an external assessment by third-party bidders be provided?

The stock exchange may initially be a poor alternative to the banks as an agent of restructuring. Its capacities to fully exercise information and control functions are certainly limited. But the development of the stock markets emerging in Central Europe will largely depend on the understanding of the relative merits of various financial institutions. Even if financial markets will probably play a limited role for some time to come, they should not be considered as a byproduct of the childish fascination of East European reformers with "capitalism," and their development should be stimulated. Although at the beginning stock markets may not properly reflect the value of firms, the quality of information they generate improves with time: Nivet (1994) shows, for instance, that profit plays an increasingly important role in the valuation of firms listed on the Warsaw Stock Exchange.

An advantage of mass privatization programs from the point of view of generating and transmitting information necessary for the improvement of resource allocation is that they bring an important number of firms to the stock exchanges. The development of financial intermediaries is obviously necessary in order to strengthen corporate governance in firms with largely dispersed shareholders. But as far as these programs lead to the emergence of strong financial intermediaries, from the information-generation point of view, it is not indifferent whether those intermediaries will be German-type banks maintaining close links with enterprises or investment funds listed themselves on the stock exchange and having in their portfolio listed firms.

However, the stock market is only one of the mechanisms capable of injecting contestability in the process of enterprise restructuring. It also would be important to stimulate the development of the secondary market for debt. Banks obviously have their role to play in the case of defaulting firms. But if we agree that banks do not have a comparative advantage in being at the same time creditors and shareholders, they should not be encouraged to become owners. Instead of making banks swap debt into firm equity, banks should rather be encouraged to sell the debt on the market and let the buyer convert debt into equity. It would be a more efficient privatization method, leaving the responsibility of reorganization or liquidation to those who give the highest value to the debt of the firm. The recent experience in Poland shows a dynamic development of the secondary market for debt, which has been fueled by the implementation of the law on financial restructuring of banks and enterprises. Some nonbank debt bought on the secondary market and equity swaps have already occurred and appear as a promising privatization route.

A natural alternative to banks as agents of restructuring could be venture capital funds (Grosfeld and Roland, 1995). In venture capital firms the provision of capital (through the purchase of stocks, options, or convertible securities) is correlated with managerial expertise, monitoring, and selection functions. This is notably the case of independent venture capital companies that are not owned by banks or other financial intermediaries (as opposed to "captive funds" being usually a bank subsidiary (Beecroft, 1994). The managers of such funds usually have skills that go beyond purely financial analysis: they provide strategic guidance, business expertise, and experience in industrial management, marketing, and so on. Given the needs of the firms in transition, the emergence of venture capital funds should clearly be encouraged.

Conclusions

The form of financial institutions that will prevail in CEECs may prove to be crucial for the quality of restructuring and adjustment of the industrial sector. It is difficult, however, to find clear guidelines for building the institutions of financial system. Empirical evidence is, not surprisingly, rather ambiguous as far as the performance of different financial systems is concerned. Economic theory provides, at best, some clues about the tradeoffs that might exist between information and the control functions that any financial system should perform. It suggests that we can only speak about *relative* advantages of various institutional arrangements: their costs and benefits can be properly examined if we distinguish notably between, on the one hand, their capacity to *generate* information about the value of firms, reducing adverse selection, and on the other hand, their capacity to *collect* information about managers' behavior alleviating moral hazard. Close links between banks and firms may be appropriate for dealing with the latter; an open contest with a great number of evaluations by third-party bidders may have an advantage in the former cases.

A particular form of financial system may be appropriate at some stage of economic development or in some specific industries. The main point of this chapter is that for the countries in transition, where large amounts of resources should be liberated from their entrenched uses and moved to their highest-value use, the priority should be given to stimulating information generation about various investment opportunities. Even if such institutions as the stock exchange develop progressively, there are other mechanisms providing competitive assessment of firms' expected future performance, and banks should not be allowed to have a firm grip on enterprises.

The establishment of universal banking in CEE countries has occurred and anyway conforms to the spirit of European financial institutions. However, within the universal banking regulation there are important differences between, for instance, Germany, France, and the United Kingdom. Commercial and investment banks can certainly play an important role in Central and East European countries, but it would be important to retain some of the benefits of bank involvement (mitigating moral hazard) without the concentration of ownership and interlocking relationship that characterize the German system. Given the starting point of the reforms—high concentration, lack of information about the value of capital stock, lack of competition and of managerial competence—a pure insider model, in which a bank is not only a privileged creditor but also a shareholder of a firm, may not contribute to a dynamic adjustment of enterprises. The information needed for an efficient restructuring may become the victim of an excessive commitment.

Appendix

The German System

In Germany, the financial system is dominated by a few universal banks involved in both commercial and investment banking and maintains close links with industry. Banks provide typically long-term loans but also the whole range of financial services, including the issuing of securities. Banks have extensive relationships with corporate customers: their executives sit on supervisory boards, hold concentrated blocks of stocks, act as stock brokers, and serve as underwriters. Banks control large blocks of equity voting rights (mainly through proxy votes). The company law based on the two-tier system makes the management board accountable to the supervisory board. A member of the management board cannot sit on the supervisory board. There are almost no hostile takeovers. Little information on the value of securities is publicly available: information can be obtained through close relationship. Most firms are privately owned. A small number of shares are listed on the stock exchange (about 600 in Germany), in many of which banks own big stakes (more than 25 percent of equity). Banks have a privileged access to information. Accounting information is limited. In Germany only 200 firms are covered by financial analysts (Allen, 1993).

The Anglosaxon System

In the United States and United Kingdom financial institutions have been either deliberately fragmented (as in the United States, where the Glass-Steagall Act of 1934 imposed the separation of commercial banking and investment banking) or remained specialized even in the absence of special legal barriers (as in the United Kingdom). Corporate ownership is split between nonbank financial institutions and a minority shareholders. The power of individuals is negligible and that of institutional investors is rarely exercised: they use *exit* rather than *voice*. Having diversified across a wide range of shares (because of various laws and regulations), they change constantly their portfolio in order to maximize returns to their own shareholders. Boards of directors are dominated by management (and nonexecutive officers appointed by management), which remains weakly accountable to shareholders. Because shareholders rarely act to change the management, the latter is dismissed if there is change in ownership: takeovers, buyouts, buyins. Financial markets are very liquid, which creates incentives for information analysts to permanently estimate the firms' value and to discover potential synergies (in the United Kingdom 1,200 firms are covered by financial analysts). The information about investment prospects is rapidly incorporated into stock prices.

Notes

1. The usual reference is to the German type and U.S. type financial systems, which are schematically presented in the annex. Clearly, the systems actually existing in most developed

countries are very complex and can at best be described as a mixture of ideal types. For comparisons of various financial systems, see, for instance, Franks and Mayer (1990) and Allen and Gale (1995).

2. Laws and regulations do not predetermine unambiguously the effective operation of financial systems: in the United Kingdom, where there was no law against universal banking, commercial banks spontaneously specialized in deposit banking; in Japan, where after World War II a law imposed a separation of deposit activities and of investment banking, in practice creditors have been playing a role similar to that of shareholders.

3. Several authors stress the advantage of specialization among monitoring agents: they show that it is efficient to have different intermediaries performing control in default and nondefault states (see Bergloff, 1994, and Dewatripont and Tirole, 1994).

4. Dittus and Prowse (1994) consider, however, that giving banks the possibility of holding shares in firms offers them an opportunity of diversification that lowers overall bank risk. So it is not clear what will be the net effect of bank equity holdings on bank risk.

5. A similar argument is formulated by Aoki (1994) when he explains the advantage of the Japanese main bank system at the catching-up stage.

6. Allen (1993) focuses on the stock market as an alternative to bank monitoring: he views stock markets as performing better in checking the managers' views of their firms' production functions. Investors and managers have constant incentive to check how the firm quoted on the stock exchange is managed. They express their opinions on the stock market, which, due to the spillover and aggregation of this information, improve the allocation of capital.

7. At the macro level, planners reacted to various disequilibrium signals but only after the imbalances went beyond some threshold (cf. Grosfeld, 1987).

8. If in developed countries retentions strongly dominate all other sources of finance (Mayer and Alexander, 1990), in developing countries the pattern of financing is quite different. Singh and Hamid (1992) show that in such countries as Korea, Mexico, Thailand, or Turkey corporations financed over 80 percent of their investment from external sources. Moreover, in most of the countries studied new equity issues dominated in the 1980s other sources of external finance: for instance, the top corporations in Jordan financed over 50 percent of their growth from equity issues, the biggest Turkish firms over 60 percent, and the Korean firms over 40 percent.

9. Typically, the quality of reorganization programs submitted by the debtor was rather poor, and about one-third of the programs that have been agreed on are actually not being implemented (Pawlowicz, 1995).

10. Economic journals in different countries provide us with a lot of anecdotic evidence and complaints about the weakness of reorganization proposals submitted by incumbent managers. Even in developed countries, where the allocation of managerial talent may be supposed to be more efficient, there is evidence that the continued involvement of original management in the restructuring process is strongly associated with poor postbankruptcy performance (see Schwalb Hotchkiss, 1995).

11. The importance of stimulating competition among potential investors and managers has apparently been well understood by the architects of the Czech large-scale privatization program: outsiders were encouraged to submit privatization projects. Unfortunately, probably because of conflicting objectives the program was supposed to realize, privatization projects actually accepted were rarely those submitted by outsiders: 85 percent of the privatization projects approved by the Ministry of Privatization in the first wave of the voucher scheme were submitted by incumbent managers.

12. Aoki (1994) defines ex ante monitoring as screening of projects, interim monitoring as

checking whether managers are acting in the interest of investors, and ex post monitoring as verifying the results of managers' action and taking decisions sanctioning this action.

13. As Sah and Stiglitz (1986) put it: "The architecture of the system may influence the mix of available projects because the likelihood of acceptance for projects of various types may well affect research incentives."

14. According to the Banking Directive of the European Union a single bank holding must not exceed 15 percent, and all holdings together must not exceed 60 percent of the capital of the bank (cf. Baums, 1992).

15. Most of them have been privatized, previously state-owned enterprises, but some newly created private firms are also present.

16. About 27 percent of shares were distributed among other funds, 15 percent were given to the employees, initially 25 percent of shares kept by the state.

17. The remuneration structure is composed of a flat fee and a performance-related element. Giving the difficulty to determine the "basic value" of the firm, a solution chosen consists in supplementing the constant part of the remuneration with the value of 1 percent of stocks every year plus 5 percent at the end of the ten-year period.

18. Also in the case of venture capital funds in developed economies Beecroft (1994) shows that bank-affiliated funds behave differently from independent venture capital funds.

19. See Coffee (1994) for an excellent analysis of these issues.

20. For instance, PKO BP owns 24 percent of Wolczanka, Bank Handlowy owns 30 percent of Bytom, Bank Slaski owns 16 percent of Polifarb Cieszyn, and Bank Handlowo-Kredytowy owns 9 percent of Wolczanka and 7 percent of Zywiec (*Gazeta Bankowa*, January 28, 1996). Banks also acquire shares of other banks: for example, BIG Bank, one of the banks listed on the stock exchange, has bought 24 percent of shares of the recently privatized Bank Gdanski (*Gazeta Bankowa*, December 11, 1995).

21. For example, Polski Bank Rozwoju invested in Budokor.

22. For instance, Bank Zachodni has acquired 66 percent of porcelain factory "Ksiaz," and Polski Bank Rozwoju has bought the debt of Bank Gdanski and converted it into 10 percent of equity of Szczecin Shipyard.

23. As was expressed by one banker: "Banks are looking for secure investments. It is easier to deal with bad credits than with bad shares. The best situation for banks is when large foreign investor comes in and banks take minority shares. Banks do not want to become dominant shareholder and creditor at the same time" (quoted in Boguszewski, 1993).

24. Banks' attitudes about sharing ownership and control is well presented in Dittus and Prowse (1994).

References

Aghion, Philippe, and Patrick Bolton. (1992). "An Incomplete-Contract Approach to Financial Contracting." *Review of Economic Studies* 59: 473–494. (October).

Allen, Franklin. (1993). "Stock Markets and Resource Allocation." In C. Mayer and X. Vives (eds.), *Capital Markets and Financial Intermediation*. Cambridge: CEPR and Cambridge University Press.

Allen, Franklin, and Douglas Gale. (1995). "A Welfare Comparison of Intermediaries and Financial Markets in Germany and the US." *European Economic Review* 39: 179–209.

Anderson, Robert. (1994). "Voucher Funds in the Transition Economies: The Czech and Slovak Examples." The World Bank. *Technical Department ECA/ MNA Regions.*

Anusz, Jan, and Jerzy Bielecki. (1995). *Gramy w NFI.* Warsaw: Wydawnictwo Inago.

Aoki, Masashiko. (1994). "Monitoring Characteristics of the Main Bank System: An Analytical and Developmental View." In M. Aoki and H. Patrick (eds.), *The Japanese Main Bank System: Its Relevance for Developing and Transforming Economies.* Oxford: Oxford University Press.

Baums, Theodor. (1992). "Should Banks Own Industrial Firms? Remarks from the German Perspective." *Revue de la Banque* 5: 249–255.

Beecroft, Adrian. (1994). "The Role of Venture Capital." In N. Dimsdale and M. Prevezer (eds.), *Capital Markets and Corporate Governance.* Oxford: Clarendon Press.

Bergloff, Erik. (1994). "Corporate Governance in Transition Economies: The Theory and Its Policy Implications." World Bank EDI Working Paper. Washington.

Boguszewski, P., et al. (1993). "Banki a Przedsiebiorstwa." Instytut Badan and Gospodarka Rynkowa, September.

Buchtiková, Alena, and Capek, Ales. (1994). "Financial Structure, Performance and the Banks." Working Paper 18, Ceská Národni Banka.

Cable, John. (1985). "Capital Market, Information and Industrial Performance: The Role of West German Banks." *Economic Journal* 95 (March): 118–132.

Carlin, Wendy, et al. (1994). "Enterprise Restructuring in the Transition: An Analytical Survey of the Case Study Evidence from Central and Eastern Europe." EBRD Working Paper 14. London.

Carlin, Wendy, and Peter Richthofen. (1995). "Finance, Economic Development and the Transition: The East German Case." *Economics of Transition* 3(2): 169–195.

Coffee, John C. (1994). "Investment Privatization Funds: The Czech Experience." Paper presented at a joint conference of the World Bank and the Central European University Privatization Project, December 15–16, Washington, DC.

Corbett, Jenny, and Colin Mayer. (1992). "Financial Reform in Eastern Europe: Progress with the Wrong Model." *Oxford Review of Economic Policy* 7(4): 57–76.

Dewatripont, Mathias, and Jean Tirole. (1994). "A Theory of Debt and Equity: Diversity of Securities and Managements-Shareholder Congruence." *Quarterly Journal of Economics* 109(4): 1027–1054.

Diamond, D.W. (1984). "Financial Intermediation and Delegated Monitoring." *Review of Economic Studies* 51: 393–414.

Dittus, Peter. (1994). "Bank Reform and Behavior in Central Europe." *Journal of Comparative Economics* 19: 335–361.

Dittus, Peter, and Stephen Prowse. (1994). "Corporate Control in Central Europe and Russia: Should Banks Own Shares?" Paper presented at a joint conference of the World Bank and the Central European University Privatization Project, December 15–16, Washington, DC.

Edwards, Jeremy, and Fischer Klaus. (1994). *Banks, Finance and Investment in Germany*. Cambridge: Cambridge University Press and CEPR.

Franks, Julian, and Colin Mayer. (1990). "Capital Markets and Corporate Control: A Study of France, Germany and the UK." *Economic Policy* (April) 5(1): 189–231.

Franks, Julian, and Colin Mayer. (1992). "Corporate Control: A Synthesis of the International Evidence." IFA Working Paper 165–92, London Business School, London.

Frydman, Roman, et al. (1993). "Corporate Governance and Finance." *Economics of Transition* 1(2): 171–207.

Grosfeld, Irena. (1987). "Modelling Planners' Investment Behaviour: Poland, 1956–1981." *Journal of Comparative Economics* 11: 180–191.

Grosfeld, Irena, and Gérard Roland. (1995). "Defensive and Strategic Restructuring in Central European Enterprises." CEPR Discussion Paper 1135. London.

Hellwig, M. (1990). "Banking, Financial Intermediation and Corporate Finance." In A. Giovannini and C. Mayer (eds.), *European Financial Integration*. Cambridge: CEPR and Cambridge University Press.

Hoshi, Takeo, Anil Kashyap, and Gary Loveman. (1994). "Financial System Reform in Poland: Lessons from Japan's Main Bank System." In M. Aoki and H. Patrick (eds.), *The Japanese Main Bank System: Its Relevance for Developing and Transforming Economics*. Oxford: Oxford University Press.

Hoshi, Takeo, Anil Kashyap, and David Scharfstein. (1990). "The Role fo Banks in Reducing the Costs of Financial Distress in Japan." *Journal of Financial Economics* 27(1): 67–88.

Jenkins, Iain. (1995). "Best Bets in the Czech Republic May Lie Off the Beaten Path." *International Herald Tribune*, June, 3–4.

King, Neil Jr. (1995). "Can Anything Tame the Fund Monsters?" *Central European Economic Review* (June).

King, R.G., and R. Levine. (1993). "Finance and Growth: Schumpeter Might Be Right." *Quarterly Journal of Economics* 58 (August): 717–737.

Lipinski, S., and M. Dunin-Wasowicz. (1993). "Przybysze z misja." *Gazeta Bankowa* 45.

Mayer, C. (1988). "New Issues in Corporate Finance." *European Economic Review* 32: 1167–1188.

Mayer, Colin, and Ian Alexander. (1990). "Banks and Securities Markets: Corporate Financing in Germany and the UK." CEPR Discussion Paper 433. London.

Mayer, Colin, and Xavier Vives (eds.). (1993). *Capital Markets and Financial Intermediation*. Cambridge: CEPR and Cambridge University Press.

Mayhew, Ken, and Paul Seabright. (1993). "Incentives and the Management of Enterprises in Economic Transition: Capital Markets Are Not Enough." *Oxford Review of Economic Policy* 8(1): 1050–1129.

Mejstrik, Michal. (1994). "Czech Investment Funds as a Part of the Financial Sector and Their Role in the Privatization of the Economy." Mimeo, April.

Mejstrik, Michal, Anton Marcincin, and Radek Lastovicka. (1995). "Voucher Privatization, Ownership Structures and Emerging Capital Market in the Czech Republic." Paper presented at the European Association Congress in Prague, September.

Nivet, J.-F. (1994). "Privatisation et Restructuration dans les Economies en Transitions. L'Expérience de la Pologne." Ph.D. Dissertation, Ecole des Hautes Etudes en Sciences Sociales, Paris.

Nowotarski, A. (1994). "Restrukturyzacja Przedsiebiorstwa na Przykladzie Zakladow Chemicznych 'Vicoplast' S.A. we Wroclawiu." *Spolki Skarbu Panstwa*, Marzec.

Pagano, Marco. (1993). "Financial Markets and Growth: An Overview." *European Economic Review* 37: 613–622.

Pawlowicz, L. (ed.). (1994). *Restrukturyzacja Finansowa Przedsiebiorstw i Bankow. Pierwszy Raport z Badan*. Gdansk: Instytut Badan and Gospodarka Rynkowa.

Pawlowicz, L. (ed.). (1995). *Restrukturyzacja Finansowa Przedsiebiorstw i Bankow. Drugi Raport z Badan*. Gdansk: Instytut Badan and Gospodarka Rynkowa.

Rabiej, P. (1995). "Wierzytelnosci pod mlotkiem." *Gazeta Bankowa* 53 (December 31).

Sah, Raaj K. (1991). "Fallibility in Human Organizations and Political Systems." *Journal of Economic Perspectives* 5(2): 67–88.

Sah, Raaj K., and Joseph Stiglitz. (1986). "The Architecture of Economic Systems: Hierarchies and Polyarchies." *American Economic Review* 76: 716–727.

Sah, Raaj K., and Joseph Stiglitz. (1991). "The Quality of Managers in Centralized Versus Decentralized Organizations." *Quarterly Journal of Economics* (February) 106: 289–296.

Schwalb Hotchkiss, E. (1995). "Postbankruptcy Performance and Management Turnover." *Journal of Finance* 50(1): 3–21.

Shleifer, A., and L. Summers. (1988). "Breach of Trust in Hostile Takeovers." In A.J. Auerbach (ed.), *Mergers and Acquisitions*. NBER, University of Chicago Press.

Singh, A., and J. Hamid. (1992). "Corporate Financial Structures in Developing Countries." International Finance Corporation Technical Paper 1.

"Third Wave." (1996). *Business Central Europe* (February).

Tirole, Jean. (1991). "Privatization in Eastern Europe: Incentives and the Economics of Transition." *NBER Macroeconomic Annuals*, pp. 221–259.

van Wijnbergen, S. (1994). "On the Role of Banks in Enterprise Restructuring: The Polish Example." CEPR Discussion Paper. London.

Vojtech, Ondrej. (1995). "Droga do Imperium." *Gazeta Bankowa* 53.

Weinstein, D.E., and Y. Yafeh. (1994). "On the Costs of Universal Banking: Evidence from the Changing Main Bank Relations in Japan." Mimeo, Harvard University.

Wendelova, P. (1993). "Investment Privatization Funds as New Owners of Privatised Enterprises." CERGE Lecture, April 19.

9 FINANCIAL REFORMS AND COMMERCIAL BANK BEHAVIOR IN POLAND

Kanhaya L. Gupta and Robert Lensink

Introduction

In 1990 Poland launched a policy reform by means of a new economic program developed with the help of the International Monetary Fund and the World Bank. This program aims at stabilizing the Polish economy and transforming it in the direction of a true market economy. An important component of the Polish policy package relates to the financial sector in general and to the control of money supply, interest rates, and exchange rates, in particular. The main components of the Polish monetary policy were formulated on February 23, 1990, by the Act of the Seym of the Republic of Poland. This act states that the monetary policy of the Narodowy Bank Polski (NBP), the central bank of Poland, should be focused on a reduction of inflation, a restoration of the overall monetary balance, and the internal convertibility of the zloty (NBP, 1990, p. 10). Important instruments in this respect are interest-rate policies, policies with respect to the obligatory reserves, the elimination of preferential credits, the cessation of automatically financing of the government budget deficit, and the maintenance of a fixed exchange rate compared to the dollar

(NBP, 1990, p. 10). In general, strong financial and monetary restrictions are imposed.

The financial liberalization policies introduced in Poland are described in many studies (see, for example, Ebrill et al., 1994). However, a formal analysis of these policies is lacking. But studies in which models suitable for analyzing financial liberalization policies in Poland are developed and estimated seem to be of utmost importance. This chapter forms part of a larger project in which we try to develop and estimate a macroeconometric model for Poland, in which ample emphasis is given to the financial sector in general and the financial relations between different sectors in Poland in particular. The ultimate model will be used to assess effects of financial liberalization policies on, for example, private investment, private consumption, financing of government deficits, and external relations.

This chapter presents the model and the estimation results for the commercial banking sector, being one sector of the macroeconometric simulation model to be developed. In addition, we also present some simulations with the model. These simulations are meant to give more insights into the effects of changes in different yield indicators and some other independent variables on the commercial banking behavior in Poland. Although this submodel for the commercial banking sector is an incomplete model in some important ways, the results obtained are, in our opinion, of sufficient interest as to be worth reporting, particularly in view of the fact that such estimates are not available elsewhere. The formal submodel presented in this chapter is based on the Brainard-Tobin (1968) model of portfolio behavior. A special feature of the model is that the commercial banks' portfolio behavior is assumed to differ with respect to domestic-currency- and foreign-currency-denominated deposits, which is an important aspect of the Polish financial system. Further, the banks' portfolio behavior takes default rates for firms into account. Finally, the model is estimated using monthly data for Poland.

The chapter is organized as follows. It starts with a short description of the main regulatory changes with respect to the Polish financial sector in the 1980s and the 1990s. It then presents the theoretical model, describes the estimation results, and presents some simulation results. The final, section summarizes the chapter and outlines some areas for further research.

Reforms of the Polish Banking Sector

The Polish financial sector consists of a central bank (the NBP), state-owned commercial banks, state-owned specialized banks, private banks, and cooperative banks. The most important institutional change leading to the current system is a privatization program introduced in 1989. This program has had far-reaching consequences for the ownership structure of the Polish banking system. Until 1989 the NBP had a monopoly position with respect to central bank and commercial bank activities. The financial sector until 1989 can be described by a monobank system, in which the central bank, complemented by some state-owned specialized banks, were most important. Financial-sector policies at that time were totally determined by credit demands of the state plans: the financial sector was passive. The state determined how much and to which enterprises credit was to be allocated, which implied that interest rates had no allocative role, indirect monetary policy instruments were nonexistent, and financial flows to enterprises and households were segmented (Calvo, Kumar, Borensztein, and Mason, 1993, p. 7). At the beginning of the privatization process the asset portfolio of banks mainly consisted of loans of enterprises. But since budgetary targets have been very soft, and because of the enormous decline in profitability of many of the enterprises after the liberalizations, a substantial part of bank assets became of a poor quality. Thus, it has been estimated that at the end of 1991, 20 to 30 percent of Polish bank assets were substandard (Calvo et al., 1993, p. 13). Another feature of the "old" system was that there was no competition among banks and capital markets did not exist.

In 1989 in Poland a privatization program with respect to nine former branches of the NBP was introduced. The program established a two-tier banking system in which financial intermediation and monetary control functions were separated. The first step in this process was the transformation of nine former branches of the NBP into nine state treasury companies (NBP, 1991, p. 22). The nine former branches of the NBP were transformed into nine state-owned commercial banks, which are responsible for the commercial bank operations of the NBP. Two of these state-owned commercial banks—the Wielkopolski Bank Kredytowy of Poznan and the Bank Slaski of Katowice—were privatized in 1993. Another bank, the Bank Przemyslowo-Hanlowy SA, is currently under a process of privatization. An important implication of the privatization program is that the NBP becomes responsible only for the monetary control functions. The current NBP's main activity is the strengthening of the Polish currency, the zloty. With respect to the restructuring of the state-owned banks, it should be noted that in March 1993 a new plan to restructure loan portfolios and to deal with bad debts came to the fore. For further information on this plan, sponsored by the World Bank in the form of a Financial Sector Adjustment Loan, see Ebrill et al. (1994, p. 36).

Besides the current and former state-owned commercial banks, the Polish financial system entails four state-owned specialized banks: the Bank Handlowy, dealing with foreign traded, the PKO-SA, dealing with consumer foreign currency deposits and transactions, the Bank for Food Economy (the BGZ), dealing with agro-industry lending and local cooperative banks, and the PKO-BP, dealing with consumer deposits and housing construction loans (Ebrill et al., 1994, p. 37). For the specialized banks no reform programs are yet developed. The state-owned specialized banks and the nine (formerly) state-owned commercial banks are still responsible for the overwhelming proportion of financial intermediation of the Polish financial sector. Together they account for about 75 percent of total banking-sector assets (Ebrill et al., 1994, p. 37).

The 1989 privatization program allowed the opening of new private banks. In 1990 the NBP, together with the Minister of Finance, issued forty-nine new licenses for the establishment of new banks, increasing the total amount of private banks to seventy-four (NBP, 1990, p. 46). Banks had to fulfill three requirements to qualify for a license: an appropriate banking experience of the managerial staff, sufficient physical facilities, and a minimum initial capital (NBP, 1991, p. 22). In 1991, eighteen new licenses were issued. Although the program has led to an increase in the amount of private banks, they are still relatively unimportant as regards financial intermediation in the Polish economy. In 1993 there were about eighty-five private banks, accounting for about 10 percent of the banking-sector assets (Ebrill et al., 1994, p. 38).

The organizational changes also affected the cooperative banks. At the end of 1991 the cooperative banks were forced to be amalgamated into four associating banks: the Bank for Food Economy, the Wielkoposlski Economic Bank, the Bank for Economic Union SA, and the Lower-Silesian Economic Bank SA. Of these banks the Bank for Food Economy was most important; about 95 percent of the cooperative banks were associated with this bank (NBP, 1991, p. 23). The NBP became the de facto supervisor of the cooperative banks. The credit decisions of the cooperative banks ceased to be autonomous; they have to be taken by a committee in which somebody of the associated bank participates (Ebrill et al., 1994, p. 39). Poland has more than 1,600 cooperative banks, but they hold only some 6 percent of the total banking sector assets (Ebrill et al., 1994, p. 39) and hence are relatively unimportant for financial intermediation.

Despite the liberalization attempts in the Polish financial sector as started in 1989 and despite some satisfactory progress, the current situation is not yet encouraging. For instance, the problem of bad loans and inadequate capital and insolvency is still enormous, both for the state-owned banks and the private banks. The NBP (1995, p. 7) states that at the end of June 16, 1995, 9 percent of total bank lending to enterprises consisted of lending to enterprises in a bad financial standing. One of the important problems in this respect is that, despite many regulatory reforms (see, e.g., Ebrill et al., 1994, p. 34), the regulatory framework is still inadequate. In addition, it appears that intermediation of banks has only marginally improved, mainly due to the lack of banks' experience in assessing the creditworthiness of firms and the lack of confidence in firms accounts. In other words, banks keep on specializing. Moreover, despite the increase in private banks, competition between private banks is limited, mainly because of uncertainties with respect to the macroeconomic environment and again due to an insufficiently transparent regulatory framework (Calvo et al., 1993, p. 16). Finally, the financial sector is still dominated by the banking sector. Although the Warsaw Stock Exchange (WSE) was re-opened in July 1991 and has grown rapidly, capital markets are not yet important with regard to financial intermediation.

The Theoretical Model

The commercial banking sector in our model is a consolidated banking sector, consisting of the state-owned commercial banks, specialized banks, cooperative banks, and private banks. The balance sheet is modeled as follows:

$$\Delta NW = \Delta NFA + \Delta S + \Delta L_h + \Delta L_f + \Delta ER + \Delta RR - \Delta D - \Delta FCD, \quad (9.1)$$

where NW = net wealth, NFA = real net stock of foreign assets, S = real stock of government securities, L_h = real stock of loans to households, L_f = real stock of loans to firms, RR = real stock of required reserves held at the central bank, ER = (net) real stock of excess reserves held at the central bank, D = real stock of zloty deposits, FCD = real stock of foreign currency deposits, and Δ = a change in a variable

The balance sheet of the commercial banks needs some clarification. First, the balance sheet of the commercial banking sector explicitly distinguishes between loans to firms and to households. Second, the model considers foreign asset holdings of commercial banks. They appear to be a very important component of the commercial bank assets. Third, an important feature of the Polish financial sector is the importance of foreign-currency denominated assets held at commercial banks. Polish citizens are, since 1967, allowed to hold foreign currency deposits, which mainly serve as an inflation hedge (Nijsse and Sterken, 1995, p. 8). The Polish authorities even encouraged the holdings of foreign assets since they needed foreign exchange to pay for international debt services. The importance of foreign-currency denominated assets can be indicated by considering their share in total deposits (zloty and foreign currency deposits), which is currently above 30 percent. There even seems to be an intensification of the process of currency substitution, or in other words the dollarization, of the economy during the 1980s. Zloty and foreign-currency deposits have became important substitutes, which has important different implications for monetary and fiscal policy of the Polish government. Since the government only partly controls the domestic money stock, the existence of foreign-currency-denominated deposits complicates monetary policy. Moreover, the possibility of using the inflation tax measure is reduced as households may substitute foreign-currency-denominated assets. In order to be able to consider the implications of the existence of a substantial stock of foreign-currency-denominated assets, our model explicitly distinguishes between zloty and foreign-currency deposit holdings at commercial banks. Fourth is the important role that the commercial banks play in lending to the government sector. Calvo and Kumar (1994, p. 337) state that "a key feature of the banking sector in the former socialist economies is that the state banks, which dominate the banking sector, are undercapitalized, and their asset portfolios contain a large proportion of nonperforming loans." This has induced commercial banks to concentrate on government securities. Government securities are seen as a high-quality asset, currently resulting in a high share of government securities in the portfolio of commercial banks (see Ebrill et al., 1994, p. 25, for Poland). Therefore, our model explicitly considers government securities as one of the assets of the consolidated commercial banking sector. Finally, the model explicitly distinguishes between required and excess reserves since Polish banks appeared to hold large excess reserves mainly caused by their substantial portfolios of nonperforming loans.

The asset-demand equations of the commercial banks are determined by a multiasset partial adjustment process (see, e.g., Owen, 1981). This implies that the change in the different assets can be written as

$$\Delta a_i = \sum_{j=1}^{n} a_{ij}\left[a_j^* - a_{j,-1}\right]; \quad \text{for } i = 1, \ldots n, \tag{9.2}$$

where $a_{j,-1}$ is the beginning-of-period holdings of the *i*th asset and a_j^* is the desired holding of the *i*th asset. The desired stock is assumed to be of the following form:

$$a_j^* = \beta_{j,1} i_s + \beta_{j,2}\left(\left(1-d_h\right)i_h - d_h\right)$$
$$+\beta_{j,3}\left(\left(1-d_f\right)i_f - d_f\right) + \beta_{j,4}e^e + \beta_{j,5}\pi \;;$$
$$+\beta_{j,6}\left(D - RR + NW\right) + \beta_{j,7}FCD \qquad \text{for } j = 1, \dots \text{n}, \qquad (9.3)$$

where i_f = nominal rate of return on loans to firms, i_h = nominal rate of return on loans to households, i_s = nominal rate of return on government securities, π = rate of inflation, e^e = rate of depreciation of the home currency, d_f = default rate for firms, and d_h = default rate for households.

In (9.3) it is assumed that the desired asset-demand equations depend on the nominal interest rates on the various assets, taking into account the default rate on loans to the private sector and the inflation rate. It should be noted that in (9.3) it is assumed that commercial banks lack control over the level of zloty and foreign-currency demand deposits and the required reserves, which are determined by the private sector and the central bank, sectors to be developed in the ultimate model. This implies that the portfolio decision of commercial banks with respect to S, L_h, L_f, NFA, and ER is constrained by zloty and foreign-currency deposits minus required reserves plus net worth. Further, instead of using real interest rates, we have included the nominal rates and the inflation rates as separate arguments. The reason is that empirically it is not clear at all that effects of a 1 percent increase in nominal rates are identical to effects of a 1 percent decline in inflation rates. At the very least, this should be treated as a testable hypothesis. As can be seen in (9.3) we do not assume that the demand for assets is homogeneous of degree one in $(D - RR + NW)$. Moreover, we explicitly allow for the possibility that an increase in foreign-currency deposits and zloty deposits may have different implications for commercial banks' lending policy.

By substituting (9.3) into (9.2) the following real asset-demand equations can be derived:

$$\Delta S = \alpha_{10} i_s + \alpha_{11}\left(\left(1-d_h\right)i_h - d_h\right) + \alpha_{12}\left(\left(1-d_f\right)i_f - d_f\right)$$
$$+\alpha_{13}e^e + \alpha_{14}\pi + \alpha_{15}\left(D - RR + NW\right) + \alpha_{16}FCD$$
$$-\gamma_{11}S_{-1} - \gamma_{12}L_{h,-1} - \gamma_{13}L_{f,-1} - \gamma_{14}ER_{-1} - \gamma_{15}NFA_{-1} \qquad (9.4)$$

$$\Delta L_h = \alpha_{20} i_s + \alpha_{21}\left(\left(1-d_h\right)i_h - d_h\right) + \alpha_{22}\left(\left(1-d_f\right)i_f - d_h\right)$$
$$+\alpha_{23}e^e + \alpha_{24}\pi + \alpha_{25}\left(D - RR + NW\right) + \alpha_{26}FCD$$
$$-\gamma_{21}S_{-1} - \gamma_{22}L_{h,-1} - \gamma_{23}L_{f,-1} - \gamma_{24}ER_{-1} - \gamma_{25}NFA_{-1} \qquad (9.5)$$

$$\Delta L_f = \alpha_{30} i_s + \alpha_{31}\left(\left(1-d_h\right)i_h - d_h\right) + \alpha_{32}\left(\left(1-d_f\right)i_f - d_f\right) + \alpha_{33} e^e + \alpha_{34}\pi + \alpha_{35}\left(D - RR + NW\right) + \alpha_{36} FCD - \gamma_{31} S_{-1} - \gamma_{32} L_{h,-1} - \gamma_{33} L_{f,-1} - \gamma_{34} ER_{-1} - \gamma_{35} NFA_{-1} \tag{9.6}$$

$$\Delta ER = \alpha_{40} i_s + \alpha_{41}\left(\left(1-d_h\right)i_h - d_h\right) + \alpha_{42}\left(\left(1-d_f\right)i_f - d_f\right) + \alpha_{43} e^e + \alpha_{44}\pi + \alpha_{45}\left(D - RR + NW\right) + \alpha_{46} FCD - \gamma_{41} S_{-1} - \gamma_{42} L_{h,-1} - \gamma_{43} L_{f,-1} - \gamma_{44} ER_{-1} - \gamma_{45} NFA_{-1} \tag{9.7}$$

$$\Delta NFA = \alpha_{50} i_s + \alpha_{51}\left(\left(1-d_h\right)i_h - d_h\right) + \alpha_{52}\left(\left(1-d_f\right)i_f - d_f\right) + \alpha_{53} e^e + \alpha_{54}\pi + \alpha_{55}\left(D - RR + NW\right) + \alpha_{56} FCD - \gamma_{51} S_{-1} - \gamma_{52} L_{h,-1} - \gamma_{53} L_{f,-1} - \gamma_{54} ER_{-1} - \gamma_{55} NFA_{-1} \tag{9.8}$$

It can be easily shown that the adding up restrictions are

$$\sum_{j=1}^{5} \alpha_{j,k} = 0; \quad \text{for } k = 0, \ldots 4 \tag{9.9a}$$

$$\sum_{j=1}^{5} \alpha_{j,k} = 1; \quad \text{for } k = 5, 6 \tag{9.9b}$$

$$\sum_{j=1}^{5} \gamma_{j,k} = 1; \quad \text{for } k = 1, \ldots 5. \tag{9.9c}$$

Estimation Results

It should be noted at the outset that the econometric exercise, given the limited data reliability and data availability, should be taken with some caution. For instance, it appeared to be virtually impossible to use time-series data for a long period—say, starting in the 1980s or the 1970s. First, the collapse of the communist system probably caused a serious structural break, which may have affected behavior of the different agents in our model. Second, even if this is not considered to be a major problem, using data for the 1980s and the 1970s is troublesome since data for these periods are extremely unreliable and often not available. Moreover, during 1991 the system of accounts for most monetary variables has been changed, so that data series on monetary variables before and after 1991 are not comparable. Therefore, we were forced to use data for the period beginning in December 1991 until December 1995. However, this would imply that the number of observations would be very small when annual or even when quarterly data are used. For this reason, we decided to use monthly data.

With respect to the estimation method, Zellner's seemingly unrelated regression (iterative SUR) method is used. To circumvent the problem of the singular variance-covariance matrix of disturbances when all equations are estimated simultaneously, one of the equations is deleted from the system. The coefficients for this equation are obtained by using the adding-up restrictions. We present the derived results for the variable not taken into account in the estimation procedure in order to assess whether the implied effects on the deleted variable are reasonable as well. Finally, we converted nominal values to real values by using the consumer price index (Information Bulletin of the NBP: INBP). December 1991 is normalized at one. The data construction and the data sources are described in detail in Appendix 9.1. All data refer to billions of so-called old zloty. The current new value of the zloty equals 0.0001 times the old value of the zloty.

The estimation results for the full model are presented in Table 9.A3 in Appendix 9.2. Due to lack of data we could not differentiate between i_h and i_f and d_h and d_f, so that in the estimations we have assumed an equal (after default) lending rate for firms and households. Table 9.A3 shows that i_s and e^e are always insignificant at the usual significance levels. Moreover, from alternative estimates it appeared that i_s and i_f are highly correlated. Therefore, i_s and e_e are deleted from the list of explanatory variables. After reestimating the model, and omitting the highly insignificant and wrongly signed coefficients, the final result is presented in Table 9.1 and Figures 9.1 to 9.5.

Figure 9.5 is obtained by simulating the model, using the coefficients for ΔNFA found by the adding-up restrictions. For reasons of clarity we have only presented the residuals in Figure 9.5.

The estimation results are self-explanatory. However, some remarks are in order. In general, the estimates, including the results for the deleted variable, seem to be reasonable. The fit of all equations, except for the demand for government securities, is quite good. Moreover, the signs of the coefficients are in line with theory. Inflation appears to negatively affect loans to households and firms. One remark is necessary: we had some problems in finding significant effects of the different yield indicators. The after-default loan rate seems to positively affect loan supply to firms, implying a negative effect of firm default rates on loan supply. But, as already stated above, we were not successful in finding a significant influence of the relative change in the exchange rate and the nominal rate of return on government securities. Moreover, and except for the inflation rate, the

Table 9.1. Estimates for the commercial banking sector.

	ΔL_f	ΔL_h	ΔS	ΔER	ΔNFA
$D-RR + NW$	0.2007 (5.35)	0.0145 (4.59)	0.1056 (3.17)	0.5005 (7.95)	0.1787
FCD	0.1711 (2.71)		0.4520 (4.21)	0.1144 (1.68)	0.2625
$((1 - d_f)i_f - d_f)$	31389.37 (2.08)				−31389.37
π	−110885 (−6.39)	−8845 (−4.17)			119730
$L_{f,-1}$	−0.1920 (−4.47)	−0.0069 (−2.53)		−0.6351 (−9.16)	−0.166
$L_{h,-1}$	−0.5403(−1.32)	−0.0457 (−2.53)			−0.414
S_{-1}	−0.1506 (−3.23)	−0.0085 (−2.80)	−0.3137 (−3.93)	−0.3358 (−4.09)	−0.1914
ER_{-1}	−0.1447 (−2.62)			−0.7001 (−9.57)	−0.1552
NFA_{-1}		−0.0075 (−1.98)	−0.5419 (−5.03)		−0.4506
R^2	0.72	0.66	0.18	0.50	
DW	2.4	1.5	2.0	2.0	

Note: The last column is calculated by using the adding-up restrictions. The number of observations is forty-eight for all equations. t-values are given in parentheses.

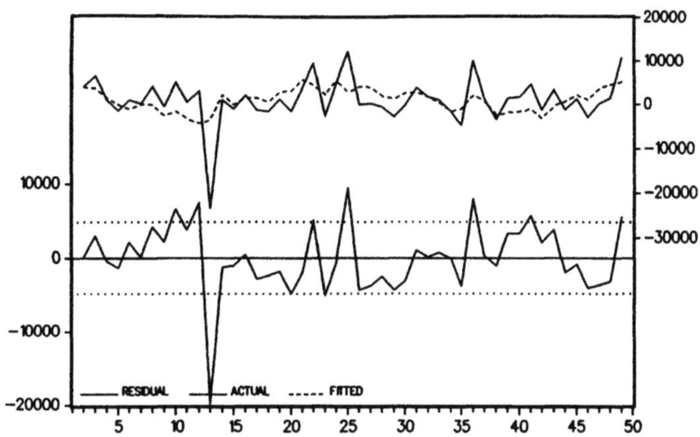

Figure 9.1. Estimation results ΔS

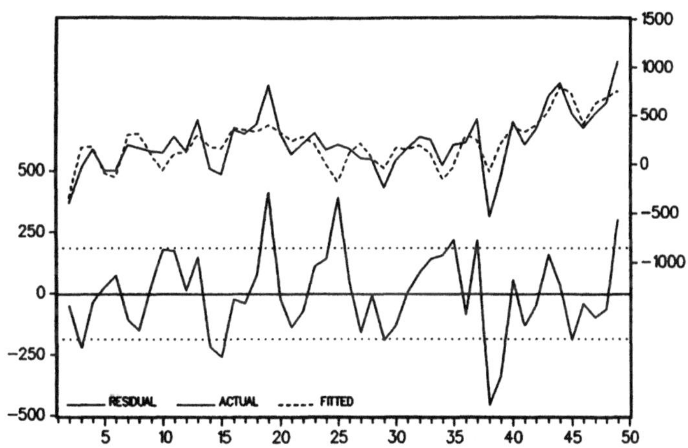

Figure 9.2. Estimation results ΔL_h

supply of loans to households appears not to be affected by any yield indicator. One interesting result is worth mentioning. The foreign-currency deposits and zloty deposits appear to be differently distributed over commercial bank assets, which may not be surprising given the problems banks otherwise would have with respect to exchange-rate risk. A much larger part of foreign-currency deposits, as compared to zloty deposits, is used for government securities and foreign assets. This may be a reflection of the

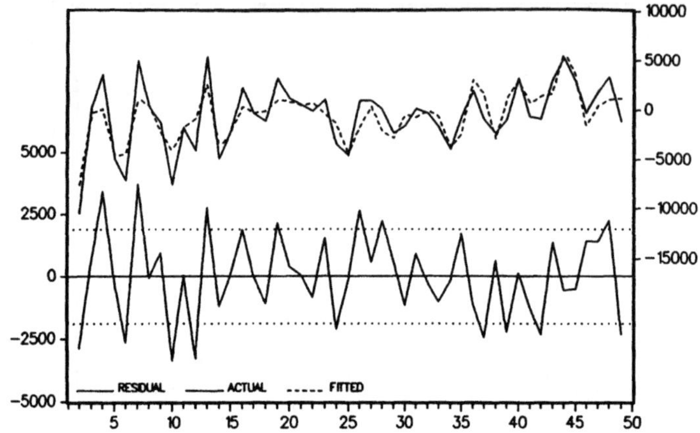

Figure 9.3. Estimation results ΔL_f

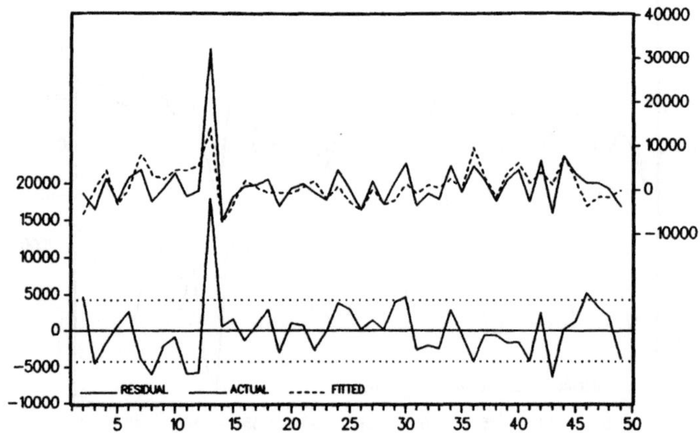

Figure 9.4. Estimation results ΔER

fact that it was the government sector that stimulated the private sector to hold foreign "currency" denominated deposits, since the government needs foreign exchange to pay its foreign debt obligations. An increase in foreign-currency deposits does not have a significant effect on commercial bank lending to households. The outcome with respect to both types of deposits confirms the relevance of our distinction.

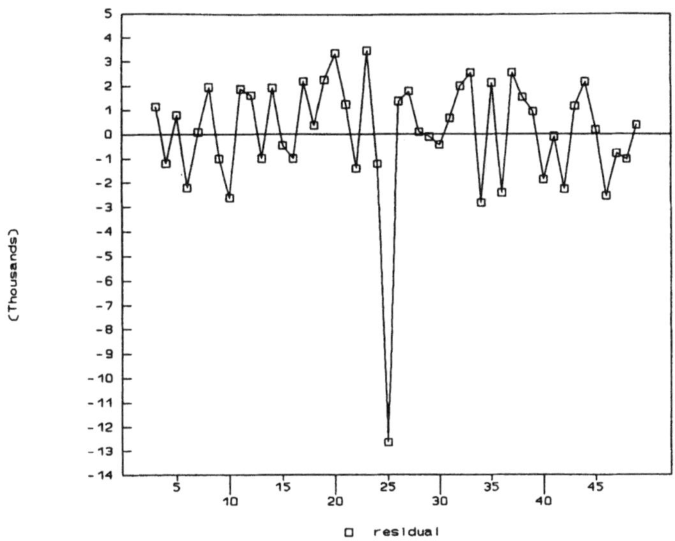

Figure 9.5. Estimation results ΔNFA

Simulation Results

In order to test the behavior of our commercial banking-sector model, this section presents some ex ante simulation results—that is, simulations outside the estimation period. The simulations refer to the so-called dynamic, or endogenous simulations, in which the lagged endogenous variables are computed by the model. The model presented above is, therefore, extended by the following equations, determining the evolution of the real stocks:

$$S = \Delta S + S_{-1}$$

$$L_h = \Delta L_h + L_{h,-1}$$

$$L_f = \Delta L_f + L_{f,-1}$$

$$NFA = \Delta NFA + NFA_{-1}$$

$$ER = \Delta ER + ER_{-1}.$$

The starting simulation period is January 1996, so that the December 1995 values for the lagged endogenous variables (see Table 9.A2) are used to get the simulations started. In the simulations we have used the coefficients presented in Table 9.1.

Our simulation strategy is as follows. We start with a base simulation in which all exogenous variables needed to run the model (i_f, d_f, π, D, RR, NW, and FCD) are set at their December 1995 value (see Tables 9.A1 and 9.A2 and the discussion below these tables) during the whole simulation period. Next, we simulate the model by increasing the value of one of the exogenous variables at a time. In the figures we plot the deviations from the base simulation. The meaning of the figures is straightforward. If the figures are positive, then it implies that the variable under consideration is positively affected by the change in the exogenous variable. We present the time path of the real stocks of all endogenous variables of our commercial banking sector model (that is, S, ER, L_f, L_h, and NFA) in one figure. Hence per alternative simulation we present one figure.

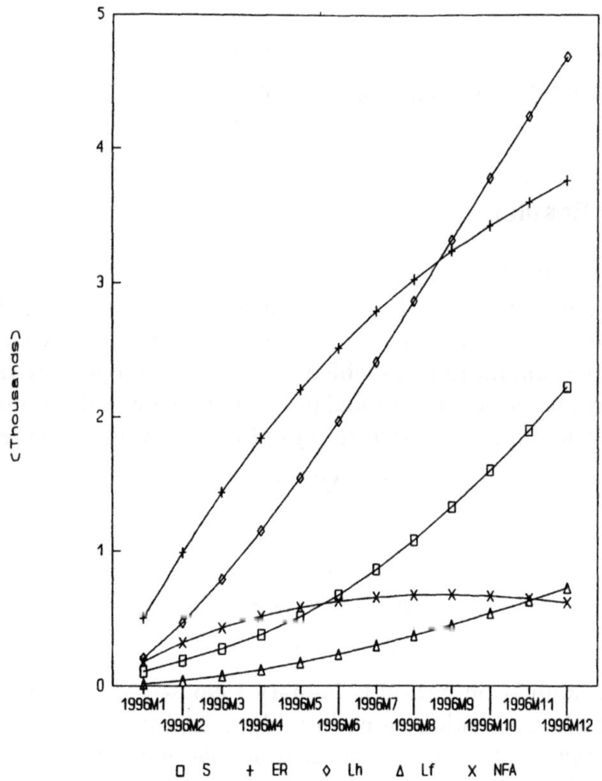

Figure 9.6. Increase zloty deposits

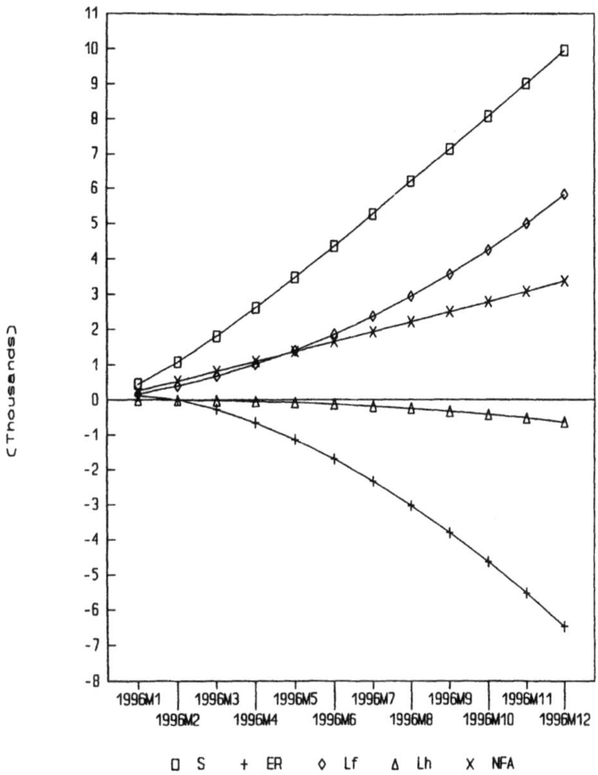

Figure 9.7. Increase foreign-currency deposits

In principle we are able to present alternative simulations related to the seven exogenous variables. For reasons of space we concentrate on the effects of changes in only five of them: increases in D, FDC, d_f, i_f, and π.

Figures 9.6 and 9.7 present the effects of an increase in zloty deposits (D) and an increase in foreign-currency-denominated deposits (FCD) with 1,000 zloty per month, respectively. The time path of the endogenous variables appears to be very different, implying that Polish commercial banks react differently to an increase in zloty or foreign-currency-denominated deposits. While an increase in zloty deposits positively affects all endogenous variables during the whole simulation period, with the largest positive effect being on loans to households and excess reserves, the increase in foreign-currency-denominated deposits has, after some simulation periods, even a negative effect on loans to households and excess reserves. These negative effects cannot only be explained by the direct effects of an increase of *D* or *FCD* on these variables, since these direct effects were positive or insignificant. The negative time path of these variables stems mainly from the coefficients for the lagged dependent variables, which determines the dynamic behavior of the model. For example, our equation for excess reserves suggests that the adjustment coefficient of excess reserves with respect to loans to households and loans to the government are relatively high, which implies that if loans to firms or loans to the government increase, this will have a negative effect on excess reserves in the next period.

The Figures 9.8 and 9.9 percent the effects of a doubling of the default rate of firms (from 0.196 to 0.392) and a doubling of the loan rate for firms (from 0.018 to 0.036) during the whole simulation period, respectively. Not

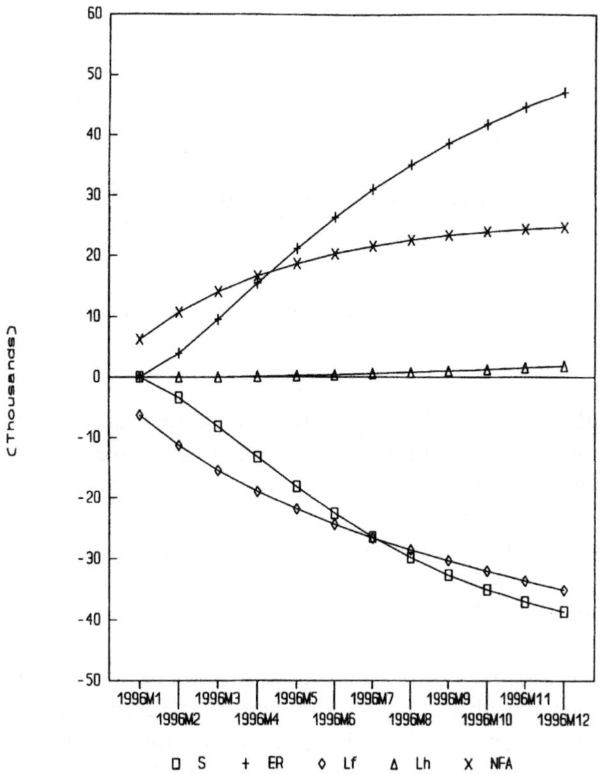

Figure 9.8. Increase default rate

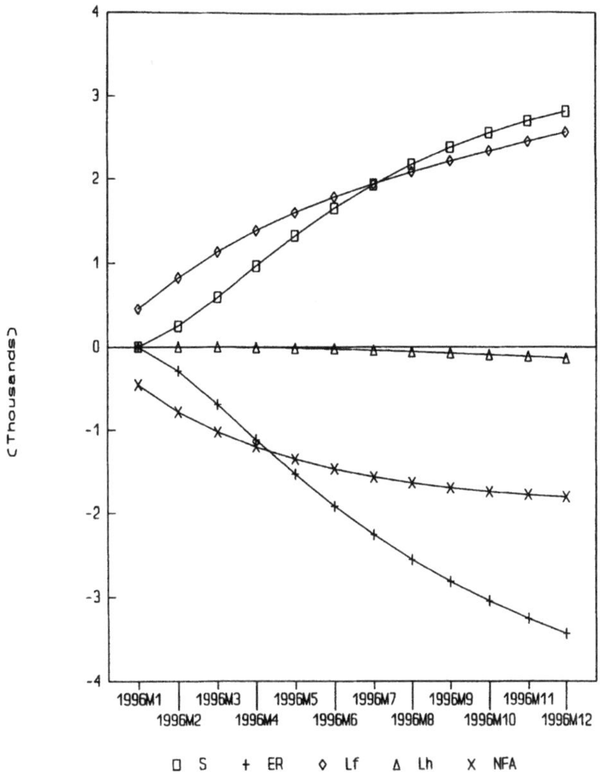

Figure 9.9. Increase rate of return on loans to firms

surprisingly, the effects of these two shocks are opposite to each other. In line with the positive coefficient for the after-default loan rate, determining the direct effect, an increase in the default rate negatively affects loans to firms, while an increase in the loan rate stimulates loans to firms. What may come as a surprise is that the increase in the default rate has a strong positive effect on excess reserves of commercial banks in Poland. This positive effect is totally determined by the behavior of the lagged dependent variables, since the direct effect of an increase in the default rate on excess reserves is insignificant. Excess reserves are positively affected by an increase in the default rate since an increase (decrease) in loans to firms has a strong negative (positive) effect on excess reserves in the next period. Hence, although our estimation results suggest that changes in the default rate do not directly affect excess reserves, our simulation shows that, indirectly via the effect on loans to firms, an increase in the default rate stimulate excess reserves, which is in line with practice in Poland. Figure 9.9 shows that, although most variables are interest-rate inelastic, which suggests that they are irrelevant for commercial-banking-sector behavior, the dynamic effects of an increase in the loan rate may be substantial. This again confirms the importance of taking into account total effects of a change in an exogenous variables rather than considering their direct effects only.

Finally, Figure 9.10 presents the effect of a doubling of the inflation rate. In this simulation the inflation rate is increased from 0.015 to 0.030 during the whole simulation period. The figure shows that an increase in inflation has a strong negative effect on loans to firms and loans to the government. On the other hand, an increase in inflation stimulates the demand for foreign assets (capital flight) and the demand for excess reserves.

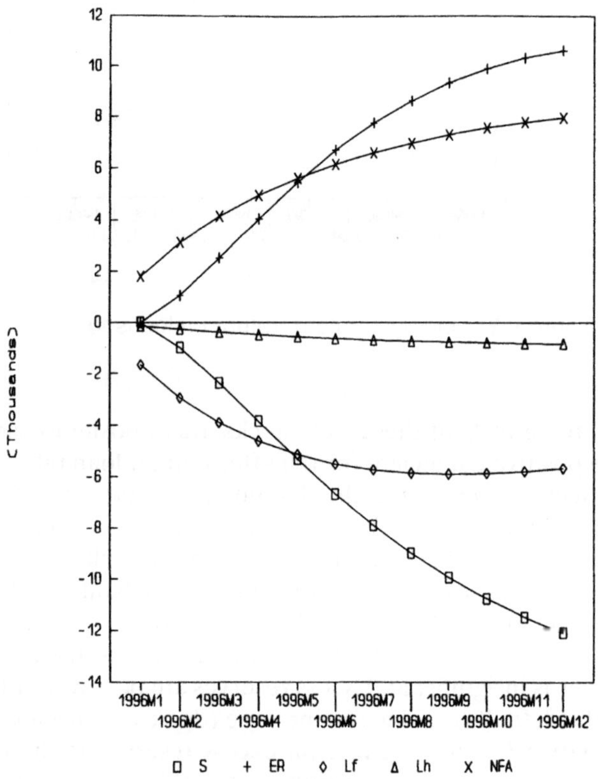

Figure 9.10. Increase in inflation

Conclusions

This chapter specifies, estimates, and simulates a portfolio model for the commercial banking sector in Poland. To our knowledge this has not been done before. A special feature of the model is that we have explicitly distinguished the funds distributed by commercial banks into domestic and foreign-currency-denominated deposits. Further, we have tried to assess the relevance of firm default rates in loan behavior of commercial banks.

The estimation results suggest that domestic and foreign-currency-denominated deposits are distributed differently over the different assets of commercial banks. A substantial part of foreign-currency-denominated assets appears to be distributed to the government and appears to be held in foreign assets. Otherwise, domestic-currency-denominated deposits are mainly used for loans to firms and, to a large extent, excess reserves held at the central bank. This clearly shows the relevance of distinguishing foreign-currency-denominated deposits and zloty deposits if one tries to explain commercial banking behavior in Poland. Our estimation results also point at significant negative effects of firm default rates and of higher inflation rates on the supply of loans to firms.

The simulation experiments in this chapter are related to the effects of increases in zloty deposits, foreign-currency-denominated deposit rates, default rates, loan rates for firms, and inflation rates. The simulation results clearly indicate the importance of considering the dynamic behavior of the model: direct effects appear to differ fundamentally from the total effects. The simulations again show the relevance of distinguishing zloty and foreign-currency-denominated deposits. An increase in zloty deposits has a positive effect on all endogenous variables in our model, while an increase in foreign-currency-denominated deposits has a negative effect on loans to households and excess reserves. One of the other interesting results worth mentioning is that an increase in the default rate or the inflation rate has no direct effect on commercial banks demand for excess reserves but has a strong positive total effect on excess reserves. The simulations also show that an increase in the inflation rate and a decrease in the default rate have negative effects on loans to firms, which implies that a restructuring of private firms, leading to lower default rates, and a macroeconomic policy leading to lower inflation rates may appear to be very important for increasing the amount of funds that become available for firms.

An obvious extension of the work presented in this chapter is to combine the portfolio model for the commercial banking sector with a model explaining demand for domestic and foreign-currency-denominated deposits by households and firms. A further fruitful extension would be to take into account the effects of bank loans on firms' investment behavior and to include a model that explicitly considers government behavior with respect to the financial sector. This will be the task of the larger project currently under preparation.

Appendix 1: Data Set, Construction, and Sources

All data used in this paper are derived from the *Information Bulletins of the Narodowy Bank Polski* (*INBP*), Table 1, Table 2, or Table 3. We have used issues of the *INBP* between November 1992 and December 1995.

Table 9.A1. Exchange rate, prices, interest rates, and default rates.

Month and Year	*ER*	*P*	$i_{h,y} = i_{f,y}$	$i_{s,y}$	d_f
12/91	11564	1	0.4		0.15211
1/92	11387	1.075	0.4	0.429	0.16373
2/92	13051	1.094	0.4	0.435	0.208465
3/92	13627	1.116	0.4	0.441	0.21887
4/92	13598	1.157	0.4	0.437	0.224891
5/92	13805	1.204	0.4	0.437	0.228007
6/92	13523	1.224	0.4	0.431	0.231757
7/92	13484	1.24	0.38	0.407	0.235023
8/92	13620	1.274	0.38	0.404	0.236299
9/92	13823	1.341	0.38	0.403	0.237514
10/92	14964	1.381	0.38	0.42	0.240313
11/92	15564	1.412	0.38	0.405	0.240102
12/92	15879	1.443	0.39	0.414	0.234926
1/93	15726	1.502163	0.39	0.393	0.241
2/93	16213	1.552668	0.39	0.336	0.238
3/93	16707	1.585857	0.35	0.279	0.25
4/93	16471	1.621932	0.35	0.311	0.247
5/93	16792	1.652235	0.35	0.327	0.2395
6/93	17713	1.67388	0.35	0.33	0.233
7/93	18121	1.692639	0.35	0.332	0.23
8/93	19439	1.7316	0.35	0.333	0.2365
9/93	19495	1.77489	0.35	0.334	0.243
10/93	20197	1.808079	0.35	0.334	0.243
11/93	20558	1.881672	0.35	0.333	0.2495
12/93	21308	1.985568	0.35	0.336	0.256
1/94	21362	2.021308	0.35	0.336	0.257
2/94	21599	2.043149	0.35	0.306	0.264

Table 9.A1. *Continued*

3/94	21734	2.084846	0.35	0.298	0.271
4/94	22088	2.144413	0.35	0.3	0.259
5/94	22238	2.182139	0.33	0.296	0.272
6/94	22233	2.231778	0.32	0.289	0.258
7/94	22472	2.265533	0.31	0.287	0.273
8/94	22789	2.303259	0.31	0.274	0.274
9/94	22972	2.408494	0.31	0.268	0.274
10/94	22931	2.477989	0.31	0.269	0.269
11/94	24513	2.523657	0.31	0.27	0.261
12/94	24261	2.571311	0.31	0.27	0.252
1/95	23977	2.676734	0.28	0.27	0.2435
2/95	23959	2.733303	0.28	0.27	0.2435
3/95	23509	2.777015	0.28	0.28	0.235
4/95	23312	2.841298	0.28	0.27	0.232
5/95	23113	2.892724	0.28	0.25	0.220238
6/95	23260	2.921009	0.26	0.25	0.222
7/95	23457	2.892724	0.26	0.25	0.215
8/95	24179	2.90301	0.26	0.25	0.21
9/95	24467	2.990434	0.24	0.25	0.202188
10/95	24252	3.04186	0.24	0.24	0.203
11/95	24550	3.08043	0.24	0.24	0.196
12/95	24942	3.126714	0.24	0.24	0.196

Notes: *ER* is the free-market average exchange rate (zloty per dollars). e^e in the estimates is calculated as.

$(ER - ER(-1))/ER$.

P is the consumer price index. π in the estimates is calculated as $(P - P(-1))/P(-1)$.

$i_{h,y} = i_{f,y}$ is the lowest-risk principal zloty lending rates for commercial banks.

$i_{s,y}$ is the yields on thirteen-week treasury bills.

It should be noted that we have recalculated all above given early interest rates on a monthly basis by using the following formula: $i_s = (i_{s,y} + 1)^{(1/12)} - 1$.

d_f is approximated by the percentage of bank claims on business in had financial standing of total corporate outstanding debt to fifteen or sixteen most important banks.

Table 9.A2. Assets and liabilities of commercial banks.

Month and Year	L_f	L_h	*D*	*FCD*	*S*	*NFA*	*RR*	*ER*
12/91	186280.5	7138.9	139835.8	54218.5	55751.5	40820.2	29229.9	–45550.8
1/92	189054.2	7258.5	147178.2	56587.5	64272.9	47099.4	30578	–49750.9
2/92	192797.1	7333.8	149605.5	64292.8	72642.7	49745.3	31714.8	–55497.1
3/92	200676.8	7651.3	159089.4	65679.8	75239.5	50611.7	30901.8	–53674.2
4/92	202415.5	7863	164250.8	66334.3	76348.3	54081.3	32697.9	–58545.2
5/92	202098.8	8106.8	168434	68320	80748.8	55061.5	29938.2	–57596.6
6/92	211559	8487.7	178083.4	68433.2	82309.8	57892.8	30660	–52885.1
7/92	214818.8	8806.2	187215	70688.9	88465.2	60498.9	31626.2	–56795.4
8/92	219139.1	9216.2	192960.5	71934.4	90208.5	60312.9	33163	–58077.1
9/92	220550.5	9858.8	199545.5	75425.1	101805.9	65262.2	32101.6	–56071.5
10/92	224808.7	10545	207412.2	79936.4	105621.2	70514.7	33035.4	–59764.2
11/92	224109.5	10971.1	213029.9	83598.9	112367.3	72683.3	33772.6	–61546.2
12/92	236770	11872	230492.8	87323.4	81159.9	74537.2	34878.1	–16816.5
1/93	239043.1	12295.2	234231.7	89001.3	86212.6	81035.6	38620.1	–28077.8
2/93	243570.1	12553.1	237014.5	91633.5	87590.6	81303.3	37892.6	–31490.9
3/93	252396.4	13381.1	243859.7	93886.9	92925.3	81921.3	37554.6	–31080.5
4/93	257667.2	14190	246351.1	95582.2	93020	87301.6	38855.5	–30058.2
5/93	260653.9	15146.5	250717.2	98091.4	92139.9	86219.5	39101.2	–26923.6
6/93	269421.7	16708.8	252004	102545.6	95482.2	88380.9	40183.5	–33610
7/93	274496	17420.7	259619.7	107786.4	93904.2	91086.7	40235.7	–33593.3
8/93	281788	17999.2	265238.4	119731.5	102917.4	96273.3	41653.3	–32409.5
9/93	288714.3	18833.2	266083.5	122426.8	122368.4	97143	42712.4	–34430.4
10/93	296092.5	19758	271346.3	127976.3	119763.9	102013.1	43140.4	–39321.6
11/93	301695.2	20840.9	276707.6	146768.6	134077.7	109213.4	43951.8	–32507
12/93	309304.8	22384.5	298413.3	154271.9	165721.6	95103	46732	–34250.2
1/94	316747.6	23117.6	296755.6	156722.3	168693.9	101039.1	49837.2	–44093.8
2/94	322138.1	23496	303924.2	159936.5	171063.1	107224.2	50101	–40768.7
3/94	328817.7	24085.5	306184.9	162283.3	173624.9	109015.3	51244.2	–48415.6
4/94	333251.3	24262.7	309614.4	164383.1	172508.1	112362.1	51089.7	–46244.9
5/94	335729.6	24775.5	318808.8	167357.2	175143	115382.8	51149.4	–33981.3
6/94	343814	25697	328283	171856	187919.1	120830.2	53682.4	–42727.8
7/94	348505	26725	342321	177457	195131	127177	54463	–45322
8/94	350457	27748	357121	183291	201126	132757	56126	–51023
9/94	356990	29000	363488	187089	206467	135871	59466	–50355
10/94	365737	30335	367006	191441	200937	143478	63323	–42796
11/94	377451	31457	380016	200284	229840	143185	56973	–30044
12/94	382144	33242	429687	209064	237135	151082	56968	–24557
1/95	391461	33168	412117	211243	237678	157578	62707	–32336
2/95	396905	33543	424479	210197	246542	157757	63055	–26622
3/95	411968	35294	447556	209120	255126	149740	61516	–14277
4/95	419751	36675	464162	206322	274233	148922	61494	–22316
5/95	424872	38398	487155	196211	275657	137779	65209	–3209
6/95	437871	40819	500083	197254	288414	136929	69740	–18863
7/95	448916	42850	524759	198339	282193	134788	71148	3704
8/95	459005	44527	549083	200934	287168	130517	73418	14298
9/95	471947	46970	557869	197836	286883	124571	73413	19269

Table 9.A2. *Continued*

10/95	485626	49372	580913	198171	292219	124062	77971	24396
11/95	502079	51941	595800	199712	300359	120783	80424	25378
12/95	506112	56027	634297	197122	338046	125468	80418	13485

Notes: L_f is assets due from corporate sector.

L_h is assets due from personal sector.

D is zloty deposits of nonfinancial sector.

FCD is foreign-currency deposits of nonfinancial sector minus firms' holdings of foreign-currency-denominated deposits.

S is assets due from general government plus treasury bills plus treasury bonds minus liabilities due to general government.

NFA is assets due from abroad minus foreign liabilities.

ER is from assets due from financial institutions the rules vault cash and NBP (the central bank) plus NBP bills plus NBP bonds minus liabilities to NBP minus required reserves (RR).

RR is total required reserves held.

In the estimates the above nominal values are converted in real values by using the consumer price index (see Table 9.A1). The first differences are also calculated from these variables. Moreover *NW* is calculated as $NFA + L_f + L_h + S_b + RR + ER - D - FCD$.

Table 9.A3. Estimates for the commercial banking sector.

	ΔL_f	ΔL_h	ΔS	ΔER
$D - RR + NW$	0.1834 (3.42)	0.0197 (3.56)	0.1922 (1.28)	0.6041 (4.79)
FCD	0.1959 (1.98)	−0.0065 (−0.64)	0.5389 (1.95)	0.1129 (0.55)
$((1 - d_f)i_f - d_f)$	10085.27 (0.50)	−4325.65 (−2.07)	21682.99 (0.39)	−6791.23 (−0.14)
i_s	213225.62 (0.98)	14156.6 (0.63)	−731487.4 (−1.21)	501582.68 (0.98)
e^e	194.06 (0.02)	432.55 (0.28)	39819.12 (1.65)	−28559.36 (−1.40)
π	−155215 (−6.55)	−5071 (−2.06)	102735 (1.55)	99113.58 (1.78)
$L_{f,-1}$	−0.1876 (−2.96)	−0.0179 (−2.72)	0.0378 (0.213)	−0.876 (−5.87)
$L_{h,-1}$	−0.5879 (−1.37)	0.0203 (0.30)	−1.698 (−0.95)	1.552 (1.03)
S_{-1}	−0.1454 (−2.58)	−0.0169 (−2.90)	−0.246 (−1.57)	−0.541 (−4.09)
ER_{-1}	−0.0863 (−1.37)	−0.0097 (−1.48)	0.0023 (0.01)	−0.9040 (−6.10)
NFA_{-1}	−0.1178 (−1.14)	−0.0183 (−1.71)	−0.5119 (−1.78)	−0.092 (−0.38)
R^2	0.77	0.70	0.27	0.58
DW	2.7	1.9	2.0	1.9

Acknowledgments

The authors would like to thank Tadeusz Kowalski, Erwin Nijsse, and Elmer Sterken for helping us find necessary data.

References

Brainard, W.C., and J. Tobin. (1968). "Pitfalls in Financial Model Building." *American Economic Review* 58: 99–122.

Calvo, G.A., and M.S. Kumar. (1994). "Money Demand, Bank Credit, and Economic Performance in Former Socialist Economies." *IMF Staff Papers* 41: 314–349.

Calvo, G.A., M.S. Kumar, E. Borensztein, and P.R. Mason. (1993). *Financial Sector Reforms and Exchange Arrangements in Eastern Europe*. Occasional Paper 103. Washington, DC: IMF.

Ebrill, L.P., A. Chopra, C. Christofides, P. Mylonas, I. Otker, and G. Schwartz. (1994). *Poland: The Path to a Market Economy*. Occasional Paper 113. Washington, DC: IMF.

Narodowy Bank Polski (NBP) (Various issues, 1992–1995). *Information Bulletin*.

Nijsse, E., and E. Sterken. (1995). *Shortages, Interest Rates, and Money Demand in Poland, 1969–1994*. Department of Economics, Groningen, July.

Owen, P.D. (1981). "Dynamic Models of Portfolio Behavior: A General Integrated Model of Incorporating Sequential Effects." *American Economic Review* 71: 231–238.

IV THE MIDDLE EAST EXPERIENCE

10 FINANCIAL LIBERALIZATION UNDER EXTERNAL DEBT CONSTRAINTS

The Case of Turkey

Nazim Kadri Ekinci

Introduction

Development planning constituted the main focus of economic policy making in Turkey from the 1960s until the mid-1970s. The external resource requirements of the plans were financed essentially through state-to-state loans or project credits from other governments or supranational institutions. Domestically, the financial structure involved the allocation of credit and foreign exchange according to the priorities of the plans. In this setting, finance is repressed in the sense of Shaw-McKinnon—that is, the allocation of financial resources is based on nonprice criteria, so that the prices, usually implying negative or insignificant yields for financial assets, are not indicative of the true scarcity of financial resources. Moreover, the financial-repression hypothesis implied that because finance was repressed, financial resources would be scarce. The idea of financial repression rested on the belief that repressed finance and planning, on the one hand, and liberal finance and allocation of resources through the market, on the other, form two mutually exclusive resource allocation mechanisms. Thus, financial reform has almost invariably been implemented as part of a wider project involving a market-oriented structural adjustment program. In the market-oriented scheme, the economy is to borrow from international financial markets through the mediation of domestic financial institutions, and domestic credit allocation is to be based on price criteria. The expectation (and this was the aspect most emphasized by the early literature) was that as a result of market-determined prices that fully reflect the scarcity of resources, savings and investment would increase both in quality and quantity, thereby enhancing the sustainable-growth prospects of the reforming economies.

The growth of literature both on the financial-reform experiences of various countries and the theoretical reconsideration of the financial-repression hypothesis has been impressive.[1] It is now generally recognized that the process of liberalization has not been as smooth as originally expected and that the evidence on the growth record of reforming economies is not conclusive. Country experiences indicate that reform may result in a financial crash, and the problems of capital inflows and real exchange-rate misalignments may be overwhelming. Hence, fiscal discipline and setting up the necessary institutional framework, especially an adequate prudential supervision and regulation of financial institutions, are now considered to be sine qua nons in any reform process. All of these points are more or less verified in the case of Turkey, as will be shown.

The plan of the chapter is as follows. The rest of the introduction outlines the conditions under which the financial reform was initiated together with a description of the stabilization measures during the 1980 to 1983 period. The next section evaluates the phases of the liberalization process, starting with domestic financial liberalization—that is, the removal of controls on domestic interest rates, especially those offered by the banking system. The next phase is external financial liberalization—that is, the deregulation of restrictions pertaining to financial transactions and debtor-creditor relationships between residents and nonresidents, as well as those among residents, denominated in foreign currency.[2] In the third section a review of post-1989 developments and the problems faced by policy makers in a financially open economy in which the public sector runs sizeable deficits is provided, followed by conclusion.

The process of financial liberalization in Turkey began after a major debt crisis, which came much earlier than the world debt crisis that manifested itself in 1982. After the first oil shock of 1973 to 1974, the external financing requirements increased sharply. The authorities considered the problem as temporary and sought to achieve the ambitious investment and growth targets of the third five-year plan that was in force, relying essentially on short-term borrowing from private creditors. Turkey started experiencing balance-of-payments difficulties in 1977 and became unable to service foreign debt, which had become increasingly short-term in nature. Once the suppliers of short-term credit withdrew, a severe shortage of foreign exchange ensued, resulting in rapidly deteriorating macro balances during 1978 to 1980. There were two unsuccessful stand-by agreements with the IMF during the same period. The major area of dispute between the Turkish authorities and the IMF was that while the authorities demanded the resumption of external financing to continue with plan implementation, the IMF had in mind a completely different scenario involving the abandonment of the planning process in favor of a market-based process. In the end, the famous January 24 policy package was announced in 1980, which initiated changes that meant a radical break with the past and resulted in developments that have pervaded the whole period since then.[3] In retrospect, it is unavoidable to conclude that the reform process was initiated once it became clear that the Western sources were determined not to finance a planned development process as they had done in the previous decades.

The January 24, 1980, package had two aspects; a stabilization aspect as well as a market-oriented outward-looking structural adjustment aspect that envisaged a series of liberalization measures. As the latter aspect is the subject of the rest of the chapter, only the stabilization aspect that was more or less conventional is considered here. It involved a steep devaluation, measures to reduce the public-sector deficit, limits on domestic credit creation, reduction or removal of subsidies, and lifting of price controls, in particular those on public enterprises. These measures were implemented with rigor, especially by the governments appointed by the military, following the coup in September 1980. The initial results were impressive enough for Turkey to be cited as a success case of the IMF-World Bank-sponsored stabilization attempts. The extent of the success is immediately visible from Table 10.1. By 1981, the public-sector deficit per GNP ratio was halved, inflation was sharply reduced, growth recovered sharply from negative figures, and the share of exports in GNP more than doubled within two years.

The reasons for this initial success are varied, and only a few major ones are mentioned in this brief review. First, the January 24 package was heavily backed by the IMF and the World Bank. Turkey became the first country to conclude a three-year stand-by agreement with the Fund in June 1980. Turkey was also the first country, together with Kenya, to receive a World Bank Structural Adjustment Loan in 1980. Generous credit lines were made available through an OECD consortium. Finally, a massive debt rescheduling covering the 1980 to 1985 period was concluded with the creditors. All these helped postpone net resource transfers abroad, so that

Table 10.1. Macroeconomic indicators.

	Billions of U.S. $		*GNP Growth*	*Exports/ GNP*	*PSBR/ GNP*	*Inflation*	*Real Depreciation*
	GNP	*CAB*	*(%)*	*(%)*	*(%)*	*(%)*	*(%)*
1980	68.39	–3.4	–2.8	4.2	–8.8	89.6	–28.4
1981	71.50	–1.9	4.8	6.6	–4.7	44.3	–5.6
1982	64.21	–1.0	3.1	8.8	–3.5	28.3	–13.0
1983	60.49	–1.9	4.2	9.3	–4.9	26.0	–5.1
1984	59.10	–1.4	7.1	11.8	–5.4	48.5	–5.3
1985	66.89	–1.0	4.3	11.7	–3.6	52.9	1.8
1986	75.17	–1.5	6.8	9.8	–3.7	35.6	–10.0
1987	85.98	–0.8	9.8	11.8	–6.1	33.5	–2.7
1988	90.46	1.6	1.5	13.0	–4.8	69.7	–1.3
1989	107.55	1.0	1.6	10.8	–5.3	75.5	9.5
1990	150.76	–2.6	9.4	8.6	–7.4	57.6	18.7
1991	150.17	0.3	0.3	9.0	–10.2	59.2	–1.7
1992	158.13	–1.0	6.4	9.2	–10.6	63.5	–4.0
1993	178.77	–6.4	8.1	8.4	–12.2	67.4	–1.2
1994	128.70	2.6	–6.1	13.8	–8.1	107.2	–19.1

Source: State Planning Organization.

increased exports earnings could be used to augment import capacity, which was necessary for growth. Furthermore, the burden of domestic demand contraction fell on wage earners, including government employees and the agricultural sector, in which more than 50 percent of the population finds some sort of employment. There was no serious opposition from these groups until 1989. Massive relative price changes, in the form of real devaluations, real wage cuts, and domestic terms of trade shifts against the agricultural sector, took place initially and were maintained until 1989. These relative price shifts were instrumental in reducing the public-sector deficit and increasing exports. As for the latter, the role of a generous subsidy scheme in the form of tax rebates to exporters must also be mentioned.[4]

A glance at Table 10.1 reveals that the initial success of the stabilization measures could not be maintained. Chronically high fiscal deficits, fluctuating growth rates, a stagnating share of exports in GNP, an increase in the core rate of inflation, and a deterioration current account balance are the main features after 1986. These problems culminated in a major crisis in 1994, when the economy came to face external payment difficulties once again.

An Overview of the Process of Liberalization

The first phase of financial liberalization in Turkey was initiated in June 1980, amid a rigorous stabilization process, when the interest rates on bank deposits were deregulated and the banks were allowed to issue negotiable certificates of deposits (CDs). The banks, especially the larger ones, responded with forming a cartel, in the form of a so-called gentlemen's agreement, and the rate on one year deposits was set at 30 percent, just ten points above the preliberalization period at a time when the inflation rate was approaching three-digit levels. Smaller banks evaded the agreement by charging higher rates, and the agreement was renewed at the beginning of 1981, this time setting the rate for one-year deposits at 50 percent, but most banks were offering much higher rates through CDs. By then the inflation rates had started falling as a result of the stabilization measures, so that ex post the real rates of interest were to turn significantly positive.[5] Obviously, the banks were passing the higher costs of funds to borrowers in the form of higher loan rates. And this was happening at a time when the firms were under stress due to demand contraction accompanying the stabilization measures.

The result, as expected, was an increase in the nonperforming loans of the banks. Sharp reductions in inflation rate and demand contraction reduced the debt-servicing potential of firms as revenues turned out to be much lower than expected, while higher loan rates increased the amount of debt servicing. At such a time, banks would be expected to be reluctant to lend more because of the increased riskiness of the average borrower or lack the necessary funds because they are not paid back. However, it now appears that the banks, perhaps excepting a few, did try to lend more, and they initiated a competition for new deposits to be able to continue lending.[6] The main tool of competition was the CDs, as they were not subject to the gentlemen's agreement or even if they were, it was much easier to circumvent the limits imposed. In the mean time, distress borrowing by some firms was being met by private brokers ("bankers" as they came to be called in Turkey) who were, in turn, offering extremely high, eventually as high as 10 percent a month, interest rates to the public to fund their lending. It should come as no surprise that the operations of the "bankers" soon turned into a classic case of Ponzi finance. To complicate the matters further, some banks, which were experiencing a severe shortage of liquidity, started to market their CDs through larger "bankers", thereby effectively being drawn into the Ponzi scheme. The system exploded in mid-1982 when the largest "banker" collapsed.

The authorities came to realize by mid-1981 that the crisis was escalating, but they had no means of knowing the amount of CDs marketed by the banks, let alone the means of intervening. In July 1981, the Capital Market Law (CML) was enacted. The law envisaged the establishment of a Capital Market Board, which was to regulate the issuance of securities and supervise all institutions in the securities market. This was an early reaction to the mounting "banker" crisis, and the Board became operational at the beginning of 1982. Later in November 1981, banks were forbidden to market CDs through third parties and were instructed to submit weekly information on new issues of CDs to the Ministry of Finance. But it was common knowledge that some banks were continuing to market CDs through the "banker," and the authorities could neither monitor nor intervene until the system collapsed. After the collapse the authorities had to intervene in a total of five banks, remove their management, and declare them bankrupt. More important, as of the beginning of 1983 the deposit interest rates were reregulated, the Central Bank being authorized to set the rates.

The period of free interest-rate determination thus lasted for 2.5 years. Perhaps the most remarkable aspect of the crisis was that growth was maintained in 1981 and 1982, although there was some slowing down during the latter year (Table 10.1). In fact, all macroeconomic indicators continued to improve during the period. One explanation is that the manufacturing sector was increasing capacity utilization, which had fallen sharply due to import shortages in the 1978 to 1980 period. The drive for exports played a double role in this respect. On the one hand, it was instrumental, together with massive external aid that was made available as mentioned in the introduction, in alleviating import shortages. On the other hand, it replaced domestic demand, which was contracting due to the stabilization measures. Meanwhile, the agricultural sector remained mostly immune from the financial turmoil, and output was maintained.

The essential regulation was finally initiated in 1985, when the new Banking Law was enacted. The new law introduced a provision for a minimum capital base as well as a capital adequacy ratio, to reach 8 percent in 1992, according to BIS guidelines. Credit extended to a single customer was limited to 10 percent of bank equity capital. The ownership structure of banks was also regulated, bringing limitations to cross-share-holding among banks and corporations. The law also introduced a definition together with guidelines for reporting and provisioning of nonperforming loans. Furthermore, uniform accounting and reporting principles for the banks were introduced and became effective in 1986. A Bank Supervision unit at the Central Bank became operational in 1986. Thus, five years after the initial deregulation of domestic interest rates, an adequate regulatory and institutional framework was defined and became operational.

Interest rates were partially deregulated again in 1987, when the banks were allowed to fix their rates subject to ceilings determined by the Central Bank. In October 1988, banks were allowed to determine their rates on all maturities for periods of one month. As a result of the sudden jump in the interest rates and signs of an intensifying price war among banks that followed, the Central Bank had to intervene within a few weeks and set temporary ceilings again. Later the ceilings were removed, but the banks were required to report their intended rate changes two days in advance. This meant effective deregulation of deposit interest rates. In other words, an orderly deregulation was implemented, and there has been no comparable upheaval since then. The reasons are twofold. First, the Central Bank had gained supervisory and regulatory powers as well as institutional means of intervention (such as interbank markets) that came as a result of a series of institutional arrangements that are described below. Second, starting from 1989, new opportunities were opened for the banks in the form of unrestricted access to external borrowing so that a fierce competition for domestic funds based solely on offering even higher rates on deposits have been largely unnecessary, except perhaps for temporary periods.

The somewhat bitter experience of the initial period did in no way reduce the enthusiasm of the reformers. After the general elections in November 1983, Turgut Özal, architect of the January 24 package, returned to office as the elected prime minister.[7] On December 29, 1983, an important move was introduced in Decree 28[8] by way of simultaneous trade and partial external financial liberalization.[9]

The initial phase of external financial liberalization was partial in the area of lifting capital controls. Only authorized banks, corporations holding investment incentive certificates, and foreign trade companies were allowed to borrow from international markets. Authorized banks were also allowed to maintain foreign-exchange positions abroad and engage in forward trading in international markets. In other words, the restrictions on inflow and outflow of capital were maintained, except for a limited set of agents that could be subjected to control. The measures were essentially directed to easing the regulations on current account transactions and had elements that favored the flourishing export sector. As far as allowing nonresidents to issue liabilities and hold assets in domestic market was concerned, nonresidents were given considerable freedom to acquire real or financial assets within the country and repatriate the earnings or capital invested.

The real impact of the move was in the final area of external financial liberalization, whereby all restrictions on foreign-exchange transactions among residents were lifted and residents were allowed to open foreign-exchange deposits at domestic banks. To understand the significance of this move one has to consider the state of foreign-exchange markets prior to the move. The sizeable Turkish migrant worker population in Europe, especially in West Germany, had made possible a buoyant parallel foreign-exchange market, popularly known as the Tahtakale market. Although direct estimates are not available, the Tahtakale market had always involved substantial sums of transactions. The market was the source of finance for illegal imports, especially gold, foreign cigarettes, and other consumer goods and even intermediate inputs in the crisis years of 1978 to 1980. Following the decree, Tahtakale was legalized, and black marketeers became foreign-exchange dealers overnight. The measures aimed at institutionalization of the foreign-exchange market, for which a scaling down of the Tahtakale was necessary.[10] The freedom to buy, sell, and deposit foreign exchange at banks was instrumental in increasing the role of the banks in receiving and managing the increased foreign-exchange earnings not only from exports but also from the invisibles.

At this point, we note an aspect of externally indebted middle-income countries, of which Turkey is one, that has received insufficient attention in the literature. Such countries usually start the reform process with high levels of external debt, most of which is public-sector liability. The foreign-exchange needs arising out of debt servicing as well as those arising out of fresh funding continue to exist. While part of the need may be met from increased foreign-exchange earnings resulting from export-oriented policies, the balance has to be met by fresh borrowing. In the first case, the question of how to transfer the foreign-exchange flows arising out of increased current-account earnings to the public sector gains importance. In other words, there is the internal financial transfer problem, distinct from the transfer problem proper. The transfer problem proper pertains to the real burden of the domestic tradeable surplus generation that is necessary for increasing exports. The internal financial transfer problem, on the other hand, arises from the simple fact that while it is the private sector that earns foreign exchange, a substantial burden of external debt servicing falls on the public sector. Thus, there is the need to ensure an orderly flow of foreign exchange to the public sector and to raise the domestic currency necessary to purchase the flow of foreign exchange from current-account transactions. As far as external borrowing is concerned, one has to resort to international financial markets, given that official borrowing is no longer available, except perhaps for a limited grace period. If external borrowing is delegated to the private sector, there is again the problem of how to transfer the proceeds of borrowing to the public sector, which is in need of them to service the debt. The logic of liberalization leads inevitably to capital account liberalization so that the domestic financial institutions become the main agents that coordinate the external borrowing of the country, as happened in Turkey in 1989.

The initial system envisaged by the authorities can be summarized as follows. The public sector continued with external borrowing. During the period 1984 to 1988, external borrowing was essentially long-term, and the dominant share belonged to the public sector. External borrowing by domestic financial institutions remained modest until 1990.[11] In other words, the bulk of external borrowing was done directly by the public sector, at least until after 1989, so that the financial transfer in this respect did not pose problems initially. As far as the transfer of increased foreign-exchange earnings of the private sector was concerned, the system was to rely on the banking sector. The banking sector would become the central agent in the foreign-exchange markets, managing the foreign-exchange flows arising from trade flows and the invisibles. The banks, in turn, would be the source of flow of foreign exchange to the Central Bank, which would use these flows in official debt servicing. To ensure an orderly flow of foreign exchange to the Central Bank, two related measures were introduced. First, exporters were required to sell at least 80 percent of their earnings to the commercial banks within three months of the realization of the earning. Second, a 20 percent surrender requirement on the banks was imposed, whereby they were required to sell at least 20 percent of their purchases of foreign exchange to the Central Bank.

The new regime introduced an important policy problem. The exchange-rate policy at the time was one of daily adjusted crawling peg that had started in May 1981. The policy was effective in maintaining a path of real depreciation that lasted until 1989, with the exception of 1985 during which the domestic currency appreciated slightly in real terms (Table 10.1). The fact that the currency moved along a path of real depreciation meant that there were positive real returns to holding foreign exchange—a higher rate of real depreciation implying a higher real rate of return to holding foreign exchange. This obviously resulted in currency substitution. The exporters, for example, had every incentive to repatriate the proceeds as late as possible as they did in late 1987. In fact, had it not been for the tax rebates, the exporters would underinvoice their earnings in order to keep a higher portion of their foreign-exchange earnings. The problem was more marked as far as the earnings from increasingly important invisibles were concerned, as they were neither eligible to tax rebates nor subject to compulsory sale to the banking system. They could be deposited with the banking sector, sold at the Tahtakale market, or simply hoarded, and the flow of foreign exchange to the Central Bank would be curtailed.[12] The related problem was how to secure the convergence of the market, commercial bank, and official rates of exchange. Initially, the banks were allowed to fix their rates within a 6 percent band around the official rates, provided that the spread between their buying and selling rates did not exceed 2 percent. While this was sufficient for aligning the commercial bank and the official rate, the problem of the spread between the market and the official rate remained an acute one, considering the fact that the Bank at the time had no means to intervene in the market. So long as the market rates exceeded official rates by a substantial margin, the sale of earnings from invisibles would be directed to the market rather than to the banking system to the detriment of the orderly flows of foreign exchange to the Central Bank. The basic point here is that while the policy of continuous real depreciation is instrumental in increasing foreign exchange earnings, it is detrimental for the internal financial transfer problem. In other words, it is one thing to earn more foreign exchange and quite another to surrender the proceeds to authorities, the latter being a portfolio decision.

The main policy tool to reverse currency substitution and contain the prolonged divergences of the market and official exchange rates in the hands of the authorities was the deposit rate of interest. Interest rates on deposits of different maturities were subjected to many changes throughout the period. While the interest-rate realignments were effective in reversing currency substitution during certain periods and containing the spread between the market and the official rates, the overall effect of the reform has been to increase currency substitution as measured by the increase in foreign-exchange deposits and the measures of monetization as reported in Table 10.2. It is readily seen that the remonetization of the economy after the 1980 package, as measured by increased M1/GNP and M2/GNP ratios, was either reversed or stagnated after 1984. The M2/GNP ratio was maintained until 1988, after which date there were marked reductions. By contrast, the ratio of M2Y to GNP (M2Y = M2 + foreign-exchange deposits of residents) kept on increasing throughout the period. The other important observation is the fall in the ratio of Central Bank Money (CBM) to GNP, CBM being total TL liabilities of the Central Bank.[13]

There were no large-scale capital inflows following Decree 28. This is attributable to the fact that Turkey was just emerging from a major debt crisis with substantial arrears ahead, and the world debt crisis had reduced the willingness as well as capacity of international creditors to lend. Authorized domestic banks on the other hand were also reluctant to borrow internationally to lend in a domestic market that was recovering from the financial turmoil of 1982. In any event, large-scale capital inflows became a

Table 10.2. Financial indicators (percent of GNP).

	M1/Y	*M2/Y*	*M2Y/Y*	*TD/Y*	*FXD/Y*	*CBM/Y*	*1*	2
1980	13.9	17.4	n.a.	3.5	n.a.	10.6	0.2	n.a.
1981	12.7	21.3	n.a.	8.6	n.a.	13.2	10.7	n.a.
1982	13.3	25.2	n.a.	12.0	n.a.	11.4	12.6	n.a.
1983	15.0	25.0	n.a.	10.0	n.a.	12.7	8.4	n.a.
1984	11.0	24.8	26.0	13.7	1.3	10.8	39.5	636
1985	9.7	24.2	26.3	14.5	2.2	8.9	39.8	1,337
1986	10.3	23.8	28.5	13.5	4.8	8.4	40.0	2,187
1987	11.5	23.5	30.7	12.0	7.1	8.6	28.2	3,995
1988	8.8	21.1	28.4	12.3	7.4	9.2	22.5	4,139
1989	8.5	20.5	26.6	12.0	6.1	8.0	34.4	4,690
1990	7.9	18.0	23.5	10.1	5.5	6.0	36.3	6,021
1991	7.4	18.5	26.5	11.1	8.0	6.9	52.4	9,077
1992	7.1	17.3	26.6	10.2	9.4	8.0	54.0	12,400
1993	6.5	14.1	23.7	7.7	9.5	6.4	50.9	16,674
1994	5.9	16.2	30.7	10.3	14.5	5.0	51.7	16,200

Source: Central Bank.

Notes: First six columns show the ratios of M1 = narrow money, M2 = M1 + time deposits, M2Y = M2 + resident foreign-exchange deposits, TD = total time deposits, FXD = resident foreign-exchange deposits, and CBM = Central Bank Money to GNP, respectively. In the memorandum item (1) is the ratio of three-month time deposits to TD, while (2) is FXD in millions of U.S. $. n.a. means "not applicable."

problem only after 1989, and the policy of real depreciation was maintained until then. There was, however, a relative abundance of foreign exchange, and the amount of foreign exchange sold to the Central Bank in excess of surrender requirements increased sharply. The source of this relative abundance was, in all likelihood, the private hoards of foreign exchange that were held domestically or abroad. The reform increased the confidence and the feeling of security of the private sector with the system, and there was a flux of foreign exchange.[14] As a result, and contrary to expectations that there would have to be a new round of negotiations for debt rescheduling, Turkey was able to meet all of its external liabilities that were due in 1985, the end of the grace period that was extended in 1979 to 1980. This helped Turkey resume creditworthiness in international markets, a fact that Mr. Özal never failed to mention. Encouraged by the initial abundance, the 20 percent surrender requirement was relaxed in July 1984. Later, in June 1985, the band on the commercial bank exchange rate was lifted, and banks were set free to determine their own rates. This was the first attempt at floating the currency.

However, by the end of 1985, the flow of foreign exchange to the Central Bank was seriously curtailed. The situation is aptly described in a Bank paper: "Some banks were using foreign exchange as a means of investment rather than a means of international payments. Moreover, the volume of credit obtained from international markets was above acceptable levels from the point of view of the general macroeconomic targets of the country. On the other hand, the regular flow of foreign exchange to the Central Bank, necessary in order for it to undertake its foreign obligations in an orderly manner, was not always possible because of these reasons. The tendency of banks to hold foreign exchange was also detrimental to the development of interbank markets that were expected to strengthen" (Altay 1987, p. 55). In other words, the banks that had become the central agents in the foreign-exchange market were holding foreign exchange as an asset to the detriment of the internal financial transfer. The response of the authorities was to reintroduce the 20 percent surrender requirement at the beginning of 1986. In addition, a 20 percent reserve requirement against foreign-exchange deposits was introduced. A foreign-exchange risk ratio was also introduced, whereby the banks had to maintain the ratio of foreign-exchange assets to direct foreign-exchange liabilities (foreign-exchange deposits + foreign credits) between 90 and 110 percent. Moreover, in March of the same year, bank rates were constrained within a band of 1 percent around the official rate, thereby ending the first attempt at floating.

Despite these measures, the tension between the authorities and the rest of the economy concerning internal financial transfer continued. After the general elections of November 1987, there was a burst of inflation fueled by public-sector price hikes, which were held constant over the year. The expectations of an imminent devaluation intensified the speculation against the TL, and the spread between official and the market rates came to exceed 10 percent. The internal financial transfer could not be effected. These developments culminated in the February 4 policy package. All measures were aimed at reversing currency substitution and increasing the flow of foreign exchange to the Central Bank. Thus, interest-rate ceilings on TL deposits were increased with the effect of rates increasing approximately 15 percent on all maturities. Higher reserve and liquidity ratios as well as higher surrender requirements were introduced. Furthermore, a 5 percent withholding tax on foreign-exchange deposits was introduced. Exporters would not receive any tax rebates if it took them more than three months to bring in the proceeds, while they would receive an extra premium in the first month. As a result, the amount of foreign exchange surrendered to the Central Bank increased substantially, and the Bank started accumulating liquid foreign-exchange reserves.[15]

An important development in 1988 was the establishment of the Foreign Exchange Interbank Market under the auspices of the Central Bank, which became fully operational by October. The Bank had already started open market operations at the beginning of 1987. The TL Interbank market was established within the auspices of the Central Bank back in April 1986. The Bank first acted as a blind broker in the market until April 1987, when it started lending and borrowing operations within the market. The volume of transactions in the TL Interbank and grown rapidly, and it was an essential part of the financial markets by 1988.[16] In other words, a full set of markets had become operational so that the Central Bank had all the institutions and the means of effective intervention in the markets. Against this background, a speculation led by banks against the TL started in September. In mid-October the Central Bank, which had been reducing TL liquidity using the TL Interbank and open-market operations, intervened in the newly operational foreign-exchange interbank. The banks, which were short in liquidity, were forced to sell foreign exchange, and the TL appreciated, for the first time, in nominal terms by 10 percent in one day. A parallel move was to lift the ceilings on deposit interest rates as we have described above. The shocking realization that it was possible to lose money from holding foreign exchange and the increase in deposit rates resulted in a dramatic reversal of currency substitution.[17] This was the turning point at which the policy of real devaluations were reversed, and the TL settled on a path of real appreciation.[18]

The final move in the liberalization process was introduced with Decree 32 of August 1989 and some amendments that followed within the next few months, whereby all restrictions on capital movements were lifted. Later in April 1990, Turkey notified the IMF that it accepted the obligations of the Fund's Articles of Agreement relating to the convertibility of a currency—namely, Article VIII, sections 2 to 4. Thus, from mid-1989 Turkey became a fully financially open economy,[19] and some months later the TL was to become a convertible currency. After 1990, the problems of maintaining macroeconomic stability became the major issue, overshadowing any possible positive impact of the reforms. These problems are the subject of the next section.

Post-1989 Development

Anti-inflationary policy became the focus of new policy setting following the reversal of policy of real devaluations at the end of 1988. High fiscal deficits financed from Central Bank sources was seen as the main cause of persistent inflation. The Bank had acquired new powers in containing foreign-exchange market fluctuations, as demonstrated in October 1988, and could impose a slower rate of nominal depreciation. The understanding was that if the volume of Central Bank credit to the government could be contained, a slower rate of nominal depreciation would eventually be reflected in a slower rate of price inflation and lower interest rates—that is, the economy would settle on a path of gradual deflation. At the time, the public-sector deficits was not particularly high, but there were pressures on the public-sector resources that resulted in rapidly deteriorating fiscal balances after 1990 (Table 10.1). The increase in PSBR in 1989 to 1990 was largely due to public-sector wage and agricultural support price increases of 1989. These increases came as a result of popular unrest following a long period of falling real wages, and the public-sector real wages were more or less restored to pre-1980 levels. The main sources of deteriorating public-sector balances, especially after 1991, were twofold. First, the military operations against the armed insurgency in the Kurdish provinces intensified, especially during 1992 to 1994. The unofficial figures suggested for the costs of these operations are no less than U.S. $6 to $7 billion per year over the period. Second, interest payments on debt stock become a sizeable[20] and a fixed expenditure item (Table 10.3). The latter was the direct result of the new policy setting as will be described below.

At the beginning of 1989 the Treasury and the Central Bank agree to limit the Central Bank credit to the Treasury to 15 percent of total budgetary appropriations.[21] The Bank was already following a policy of restricting credit to commercial banks: the share of claims on commercial banks in total assets of the Bank had fallen from around 19 percent at the beginning of the decade to 7.5 percent in 1988. The meaning of this was that the Bank would create liquidity essentially against foreign assets. The financing of fiscal deficits, on the other hand, would rely essentially on domestic borrowing, as share of the public sector in short-term external borrowing was substantially reduced.[22] In other words, the internal financial transfer mechanism (in addition to usual financing needs of the government) was to be effected through domestic borrowing,[23] and external borrowing was delegated to private financial institutions. Note, however, that since foreign-exchange purchases by the Central Bank became the main source of money creation, this mean that the ultimate source of financing of the fiscal deficits would be short-term capital inflows.

Having reduced the pressure from the Treasury, and after accumulating reserves of around U.S. $3 billion in 1989, the Central Bank, for the first time in its history, publicly announced a monetary program for 1990. The program was somewhat unconventional, in that it did not involve any targets for the monetary aggregates such as M2. It was part of a medium-term program with the aim of restructuring the balance sheet of the bank.[24] The program set target bands for growth rates, given in brackets, for the Central Bank Money (CBM) (35 to 48 percent), total assets (12 to 22 percent), total domestic assets (6 to 16 percent), and total domestic liabilities (15 to 25 percent) of the Central Bank. From these targets, it is clear that the program envisaged an increase in the share of CBM in total domestic liabilities, as the target growth for the CBM was set higher than the other two. In particular, this would mean a reduction in the share of foreign-exchange liabilities to residents, which in turn required a reversal of currency substitution. Also, as the target growth rate for total assets exceeded that for total domestic assets on average, the Bank was in effect making it public that its preferred source of money creation would be accumulating foreign assets.

In the end, the realization for the CBM was only 27 percent, while it was 24 percent for total assets, 12 percent for total domestic assets, and 21.5 percent for domestic liabilities. The implied target band for foreign assets of the Bank was 22 to 32 percent, while the realization was 45 percent. The meaning of this is that the Bank was unable to contain the growth of total assets, and as it was successful in limiting the growth of domestic credit, the source of the growth in total assets had to be accumulation of foreign assets. The Bank could not create as much of CBM as it desired, but the CBM was nevertheless the fastest growing item. There was also some success in reducing the inflation rate, as shown seen in Table 10.1. Note, however, that despite a lower inflation rate, there was a dramatic fall in total central bank assets per GNP ratio in 1990, and all financial indicators of monetization deteriorated (Table 10.2). In 1990, external debt increased by U.S. $7.2 billion, 3.8 billion being short term. Of this $3.8 billion, $2.3 billion was in commercial bank short-term foreign liabilities. In short, the fate of the new policy regime was (or should have been) revealed from the start. It was clear that the policy of reducing inflation relied on external funding. The reason for a relatively better inflation performance was the external funding implicit in the strategy of domestic borrowing, which reduced the claim of the public sector on domestic resources.

After a relative setback in 1991, as a result of a short-lived financial panic during the Gulf War, the Bank continued with its monetary programming with decreasing success. The reason for this was twofold. First, the Bank, having left no other way of money creation, was obliged to purchase the proceeds of the massive inflows of short-term capital. Otherwise, the problem of real appreciation of the currency would become even more acute,[25] and also without the money so created the government could not borrow. Second, the pressure from the Treasury for more cash credits was increasing. The Treasury, on its part, was attempting to escape the increasing burden of debt servicing and was partially successful in drawing on the Central Bank resources.[26] Despite this, by 1993 the burden of the domestic debt on the public sector had reached such proportions that the situation was decribed as one of a "chain of prosperity," a term coined by the prime minister to refer to the increased intensity and frequency with which capital was flowing in and out of the country to take advantage of the interest parity. In an attempt to "break the chain," the Treasury started borrowing directly from abroad as can be seen from the increased share of external borrowing in deficit financing (Table 10.3). At the same time, the regular Treasury auctions were being cancelled whenever the demanded interest rates exceeded what was thought to be acceptable.[27]

At the beginning of 1994 the Treasury used all the available credit limits from the Central Bank within the first two months, while the persistent attempts of the Treasury to avoid domestic borrowing raised the fears of a shift of policy toward monetization of the deficit.[28] The system finally exploded in the first quarter of 1994. The TL depreciated by more than 100 percent in nominal terms within the first three months of the year, the loss

Table 10.3. Consolidated budget and domestic debt indicators (percent).

							Domestic Debt Stock				
			Financing					*% Composition*			
	PBD/Y	*BD/Y*	*EB*	*BOND*	*TB*	*CBA*	*D/Y*	*Bond*	*TB*	*CBA*	*INT*
1980	–2.6	–3.1	7.4	–8.7	26.8	69.1	7.3	36.6	12.6	50.7	0.4
1981	–0.6	–1.5	80.6	–12.9	125.8	125.8	6.0	33.2	18.3	48.6	0.5
1982	–0.7	–1.4	–7.5	12.5	40.6	20.0	5.7	30.7	25.2	44.0	0.3
1983	–0.7	–2.1	–54.2	99.4	–57.7	42.9	5.4	47.7	7.4	44.8	0.6
1984	–2.4	–4.4	32.5	13.4	27.7	18.5	6.3	37.9	24.3	37.8	0.8
1985	–0.3	–2.2	–25.1	55.0	25.6	29.4	6.6	44.5	21.2	34.3	0.7
1986	–0.1	–2.7	–0.4	29.7	41.6	16.0	6.6	44.7	24.3	31.0	1.3
1987	–0.4	–3.5	–10.4	34.9	35.6	13.8	7.6	42.0	33.5	24.5	1.7
1988	0.9	–3.0	4.5	61.7	9.9	17.1	7.4	51.4	26.7	21.9	2.4
1989	0.3	–3.3	–5.0	73.5	12.2	4.1	7.4	64.1	20.9	15.0	2.2
1990	0.5	–3.0	0.3	64.3	15.6	2.7	6.8	69.3	20.1	10.6	2.4
1991	–1.5	–5.3	5.7	6.8	38.3	32.1	8.9	43.7	32.3	21.0	2.7
1992	–0.6	–4.3	8.3	32.5	50.6	36.7	14.5	54.1	26.5	19.4	2.8
1993	–0.9	–6.7	15.0	22.5	16.6	39.6	16.3	58.4	19.9	21.7	4.6
1994	3.9	–3.8	–46.9	–48.2	167.3	35.5	17.1	35.9	45.7	18.4	6.0

Source: Undersecretariat of Treasury and Foreign Trade.

Notes: PBD/Y = primary budget deficit/GNP, BD/Y = budget deficit/GNP, EB = external borrowing, BOND = government bonds, TB = treasury bills, CBA = Central Bank advances, D/Y = domestic debt stock excluding consolidated debt/GNP, INT = interest payments/GNP.

of reserves of the Central Bank amounted to U.S. $5 billion, and three banks were declared bankrupt because of their inability to meet their foreign-exchange liabilities. An austerity program[29] was introduced in April, and the "chain" was restored in May with spectacularly high interest rates. Moreover, after a ten-year interval a stand-by agreement with the IMF was signed in June. This time, the source of capital flows was from within. That is, in the face of very attractive returns on government debt instruments[30] and the restoration of confidence, partially as a result of the agreement with the Fund, foreign-exchange hoards were converted into domestic currency.[31] The maturity structure of borrowing and domestic debt stock became even shorter (Table 10.3). The current account registered a U.S. $2.6 billion surplus, from U.S. $6.4 billion deficit in 1993. Inflation rate increased to three-digit figures, and the growth rate was –6.1 percent (Table 10.1).

The nature of the post-1989 developments we have surveyed is contained in the observation that domestic borrowing by the government relied implicitly on short-term external borrowing. The short-term nature of external borrowing had to be matched by the maturity of government debt instruments. Thus, the government became obliged to borrow on shorter maturities, thereby increasing the burden of interest payments. Given the other pressures on the public-sector resources mentioned above, government borrowing soon turned into a Ponzi scheme. On the other hand, debt financing was possible only if the government bonds in private portfolios could be converted into foreign exchange at maturity, which in turn required regular debt servicing by the government. But the government had to borrow to honor its obligations—that is, the private sector had to lend more to recover what was lent in a previous round of borrowing. Thus, the private sector had either to roll over its foreign debt, or to borrow more, or both. In other words, domestic Ponzi finance on the part of the government eventually required external speculative or even Ponzi finance on the part of the private sector. Once the amount of speculative and/or Ponzi financing reached a certain magnitude, foreign creditors withdrew from the process, and the 1994 crises ensued.

Following the interest-rate hikes at the beginning of the second quarter of 1994, the TL started appreciating in real terms, the June 1994 to June 1995 rate of real appreciation being 24 percent. Once the external credit facilities became available in 1995, as a result of uninterrupted external debt servicing in 1994 despite the lack of net credit from abroad, the externally financed growth process was resumed. Toward the end of 1995 the cycle seemed to be repeating itself, and the expectation is that there will be a severe stabilization program, including at least some measures in the way of a fiscal reform, after the general elections to be held in late December.

Conclusions

Every financial system, repressed or liberal, has its own ways and rules of creating liquidity, but in all cases the ultimate source of liquidity is the Central Bank. The Central Bank is, thus, the essential part of any financial system, and as such it is an integral participant of the financial markets, where it has a big say in the determination of the terms of liquidity creation. It is precisely these terms that form the basic inputs to financial decision making or give the basic signals to financial decision makers. Without these signals the financial markets cannot function[32] because, unlike commodity money, (fiat) liquidity cannot be priced in financial markets without knowing the intentions and the terms of its ultimate source. For one thing, it is the prerogative of the Central Bank to determine the set of assets against which liquidity can be created. This does not mean that the Central Bank can unilaterally set the terms of liquidity creation at any rate with absolute freedom or without disturbing price stability in the economy. The argument is that financial reform will typically change the way and the terms of liquidity creation, so that unless the new institutional framework of liquidity creation is defined, the markets cannot be expected to function effectively. This is one reason why reform attempts resulted in a financial crash in many countries. In Turkey it took al[illegible] lecade to build up the new institutional framework, after the initial deregulation of interest rates, which ended in a financial debacle. The problem is, of course, that the logic of reform does not admit a long period of institution formation before initiating the necessary measures. An element of trial and error is likely to remain in the future reform attempts elsewhere.[33]

Perhaps the most important lesson that comes out of Turkey's experience is the problem of what we have called the internal financial transfer problem. The problem is the result of the fact that the public sector has to service a sizeable external debt stock. This means that there is a constant flow demand for foreign exchange by the public sector. The mechanism by which the public sector comes to purchase the necessary amounts of foreign exchange assumes a crucial role in maintaining macroeconomic stability. We have seen that after 1985 economic policy was conducted under increasingly tense conditions, the source of difficulty being the internal financial transfer problem. The strategy of domestic borrowing under conditions of fully liberalized capital account transactions resulted in rapidly deteriorating macro balances as explained in Section 3. The Turkish experience is, no doubt, blurred by the increased military expenditures in the post-1990 period. In retrospect, it seems reasonable to conclude that lifting capital controls was an immature move. The newly acquired powers of the monetary authorities could be used more effectively to contain the foreign-exchange market flucturations, had the controls on capital account been maintained. Under such conditions domestic borrowing would be funded essentially by current account earnings,[34] and perhaps some inflow of capital, but the unsustainable path of short-term borrowing would not have been the major problem it has been.

One cannot help concluding this survey of the Turkish experience by the following line from Hegel, quoted in most philosophy books: "The owl of Minerva spreads its wings only with the falling of dusk." A popular, perhaps simplistic, interpretation stated in familiar terms may be that "wisdom is necessarily ex post." While some may find it disputable at least in terms of the meaning of science in general, Hegel's judgment has an undeniable force as far as our knowledge of the effects of financial liberalization is concerned.

Acknowledgments

I am grateful to my colleagues Eyüp Özveren and Cem Somel for helpful comments that have greatly improved the presentation of this chapter. Remaining errors and imperfections are my responsibility.

Notes

1. See, for example, the papers in Collier and Mayer (1989), especially Fry (1989) and McKinnon (1989), Fischer and Reisen (1993), Akyüz (1993), Gibson and Tsakalotos (1994), Grabel (1995).

2. This definition is due to UNCTAD (1991, pt. 2, ch. 3). As explained there, the concepts of external financial and capital account liberalizations are not entirely equivalent concepts. The latter, by definition, would include transactions between residents and nonresidents only, while the former includes, in addition, the liberalization of transactions among residents. The broader concept of external financial liberalization is adopted in this study.

3. The reasons for the 1977 to 1980 crisis and subsequent developments have been studied extensively by a number of researchers (e.g., Celasun and Rodrik, 1989; Ekinci, 1990).

4. There was a 28 percent real devaluation in 1980 alone. Public sector real wages fell by 40 to 45 percent during 1980 to 1988. Over the same period domestic terms of trade deterioration were around 15 percent. The ratio of tax rebates to exporters to GNP ratio was 1 percent by 1982, being as high as 1.9 percent of GNP in 1984. Tax rebates were phased out until they

were completely abolished in 1989. For details see Ekinci (1990) and Celasun and Rodrik (1989).

5. The real interest rate on time deposits was –35 percent in the last quarter of 1980. In the four quarters of 1981 the real rate was –1.8 percent, –0.3 percent, 4 percent, and 13 percent, respectively.

6. For a more detailed examination of bank, depositor, and borrower behavior in this period, see Atiyas (1990). See also Atiyas and Ersel (1994) for an overview of the period 1980 to 1990.

7. He was the minister responsible for economic affairs of the cabinet appointed by the military, but he had resigned in the critical days of the Bankers crisis.

8. Most important changes of the reform process were introduced by decrees of the cabinet. This reflected Mr. Özal's general approach to government, whereby the prolonged parliamentary procedures of law making were effectively bypassed, having been empowered to rule by decrees by the parliament in which he held a majority.

9. Trade liberalization involved abolition of import lists and adopting a negative list approach effectively removing quantitative restrictions. Tariffs were also substantially reduced. However, contributions to extrabudgetary funds, which could be very high and subject to arbitrary changes, replaced reduced tariffs. Another wave of major reductions in tariff and fund contributions came in 1989 and continued since then. It is estimated that, as of the beginning of 1995, Turkey had achieved a 90 to 95 percent conformity with the tariff reductions that were required when the prospective customs union with the European Community materialized as of January 1996. For details of trade liberalization see Baysan and Blitzer (1990).

10. For example, after import liberalization the state monopolies started importing foreign cigarettes, effectively closing this source of lucrative business for the Tahtakale market. However, the most important sources remained. In the post-1980 era the market was the source of finance for "fictitious" exports. The mechanism was to obtain foreign exchange from the Tahtakale market, transfer them to subsidiaries abroad, and repatriate them as proceeds of exports earnings through overinvoicing of exports and to become eligible for the generous tax rebates on exports. This was the result of multiple exchange-rate practice implicit in the tax rebate system. This source of business could be removed only with the removal of the tax rebate system in 1989. The other main source of business, that of gold dealings, was removed with the establishment of foreign-exchange and gold market within the auspices of the Central Bank in 1989. The account given here of the early phases of external financial liberalization in Turkey draws on Altinkemer and Ekinci (1992).

11. From 1984 to 1989 total external debt increased by U.S. $21 billion, 18 billion of which was long-term debt. The increase in the total long-term liabilities of the public sector (including the Central Bank) was approximately $17 billion.

12. These types of currency substitution did no doubt exist prior to the reform. What the reform did was to open the way for the general public, which could now walk into a foreign-exchange dealer, purchase foreign exchange, deposit it with a bank, or simply keep it in private hoards. The demand from the general public for foreign currency notes, ranging from just a few to hundreds of DM or US$, increased the turnover in the market and added to market volatility.

13. The fact that there was the need to define a concept measuring the total TL liabilities of the Central Bank is in itself indicative of the extent of currency substitution. The need arose out of the fact that the Bank kept on accumulating foreign-exchange liabilities to residents largely in the form of required reserves against foreign-exchange deposits of the banking system.

14. The role of money laundering must also be mentioned. The rule was, and still is, that the origins of the foreign exchange sold to the banking system would not be questioned. There is much sense in the argument that Mr. Özal did in fact initiate the reform in order to attract the foreign-exchange hoards, held domestically or abroad, of Turkish citizens, which were known to be sizeable.

15. In January 1988 the amount of foreign exchange surrendered to the Central Bank was U.S. $147 million, compared to a monthly average of U.S. $364 million in the rest of the year.

16. The monthly average volume of transactions in the TL interbank in 1986 was 155.2 billions of TL, which increased to 445.5 billions by 1988. When deflated by the WPI this means a 27 percent increase in real terms. From 1988 to 1994 the increase has been 140 percent in real terms.

17. In one week, interest rates on deposits of all maturities increased on average by 20 percent. In the last quarter of the year total TL deposits of the banking sector increased by 32 percent.

18. The amount of real appreciation was 30 percent over the period 1988 to 1990 (Table 10.1). There was some real depreciation during 1991 and 1992, but it was far from sufficient to reverse the fall in exports to GNP ratio. The real appreciation of the TL was fully removed in 1994 when the index of real exchange rate returned roughly to 1988 level.

19. According to standard measures of financial openness, as explained and calculated in Montiel (1994) for a large number of countries including Turkey, the degree of openness in Turkey ranks as "intermediate" for the period 1980 to 1990. This is in accordance with the partial nature of external financial liberalization as introduced in Decree 28. For the period after 1990, we may use the amount of gross short-term capital flows to the banking system and its relation to the net usage of short-term capital (which are reported by the Central Bank after 1991 as part of the Balance of Payments statistics) as an indicator of financial openness. For the years 1991 to 1994, net inflows of credit into the banking system were, respectively, U.S. $0.7, $2.4, $3.8, and $–6.6 billion. The gross inflows, on the other hand, for the same period were respectively, U.S. $43.2, $64.8, $122.1, and $75.4 billion. Thus, for a net usage of $3.8 billion in 1993, a gross inflow of no less than $122.1 billion, and a gross outflow of $118.3 billion was realized. This is indicative of the ease and the increased frequency with which funds could flow in and out of the country.

20. After 1988 interest payments has not been less than 2 percent of GNP increasing to 4.6 percent in 1993. These figures should be compared with total revenues of the public sector (consolidated budget + state economic enterprises + local administrations + extrabudgetary funds), which were on average 19 to 20 percent of GNP over the same period.

21. The Bank credit to the government has two components: direct credits and the "revaluation account." The latter is essentially the accumulated losses of the Bank resulting from foreign-exchange transactions with or on behalf of the Treasury in the face of ongoing nominal depreciation of the TL. In part, it reflects the losses accumulated on foreign exchange surrendered to the Bank as part of the internal financial transfer mechanism described earlier. In other words, part of the TL equivalent of foreign-exchange needs of the Treasury is financed by "indirect" credit from the Bank. The agreement of limiting Central bank credits to the Treasury pertained to cash credits (or Central Bank Advances). Later in 1992 part of the stock of revaluation account was redeemed in exchange for Treasury Bills and the share in total assets of the Bank of the revaluation account fell to 20 percent from 43 percent in 1990 and 34 percent in 1991. However, as the interest rate on these bonds are low compared to market rates and the Bank uses them in open market operations, it started accumulating losses because of the interest differential. These losses now appear as credit to government in addition to the

revaluation account. In other words, there has always been an "indirect" credit mechanism to the government.

22. During the 1988 to 1993 period total external debt of Turkey increased by U.S. $27 billion, of which U.S. $12 billion was short-term debt. The increase in short-term external debt of the banking sector was around U.S. $9 billion.

23. Regular auctions for government debt instruments had already started in 1985. The new Central Bank Law put into effect in the same year forbid the Bank directly acquiring domestic debt instruments. The main source of demand for the instruments has been the banking sector. Domestic debt instruments have always been exempt from taxation, and banks are required to hold them as part of liquidity requirements imposed on them.

24. In 1981 the share of Central Bank Money (CBM) in total assets of the Bank was 59.6 percent. The share in total assets of foreign-exchange liabilities to residents (FXLR), in the form of import deposits, was only 2.3 percent. By 1989, the share of CBM had fallen to 37.8 percent, while that of FXLR had risen to 20 percent. In other words, the balance sheet of the Bank was in clear need of restructuring. In 1992 the share of CBM increased to 49.2 percent, to fall to an all-time low of 27.9 percent in 1994.

25. "The over-expansion of the balance sheet since August 1990 has been due to the reserve accumulation. The Central Bank could not allow foreign-exchange reserves to dwindle because of the expected upward pressure on exchange rates in a period where the Turkish Lira was already appreciating." This is the conclusion of Ersel and İskenderoğlu (1993) concerning the Monetary Program of 1990. In other words, to prevent overappreciation of the TL the Bank was obliged to accumulate reserves.

26. Domestic debt indicators are reported in Table 10.3. The increased burden of debt financing is not immediately visible from the debt stock to GNP ratios as reported there. For example, the ratio did not change significantly in 1989, and it actually fell in 1990. This is due to the fact that the maturity of debt is short and it is rolled over within the year, which is not reflected at the end-of-period stock figures. A better indication of the increased burden of debt is the ratio of interest payments on domestic debt to GNP, which increased in 1990 despite a 9.4 percent real GNP growth and a falling debt to GNP ratio. On the other hand, while the share of Central Bank Advances (CBA) in financing of the consolidated budget deficit was as low as 2.7 percent in 1990, it increased sharply in 1991 and remained high.

27. This fact is sometimes put forward as the most important reason for the crisis in 1994. Interest rate on domestic debt instruments was an instrument, as far as the Bank was concerned, to be used in maintaining the target path of nominal depreciation of the currency. For the Treasury, on the other hand, it became the target, given the increasing burden of debt servicing. There was, thus, a problem of policy incoordination. But the buildup of the crisis had to do with the unsustainable path of short-term external borrowing. Even if the Treasury maintained the volume of domestic borrowing at increasingly high interest rates, this would only help postpone the crises for some (not very long) time but not prevent it.

28. Perhaps as a reflection of the same fear, the international rating agencies reduced the rating of Turkey in January 1994, the Standard and Poor's rating being reduced to B- from BBB.

29. The program involved an once-for-all income tax surcharge, referred to as the Economic Equilibrium Tax, a wage freeze for public-sector employees, and a freeze on all current and investment expenditures, excepting the military. As a result a primary consolidated budget surplus of 3.9 percent was recorded.

30. The ex post rate of return in terms of foreign exchnage on three-month Treasury bills in the last three quarters of 1994 was 29.1 percent, 11.3 percent, and 6.2 percent, respectively.

31. The net errors and omissions figure in the balance of payments accounts for the first

quarter of 1994 was U.S. $–2.7 billion, while it was U.S. $4.4 billion in the last three quarters. This indicates the scale of currency substitution and the buildup of hoards in the face of increased uncertainty in the first quarter, and the amount of funds that returned to the system in the last three quarters.

32. Arguments along these lines have been forcefully put forward by Hyman Minsky (1982). Within the mainstream school J. Stiglitz has been influential in stressing the essential differences of financial markets and permeating the idea that there is a role for the state to play in financial markets (see Stiglitz, 1993, for an overall review of his arguments).

33. A good example is the lifting of all restrictions on capital movements in Turkey in 1989. Country experiences in this respect from Latin America, such as Chile, were known at this time. Especially the accepted wisdom that capital accounts should be opened only after establishing a sound fiscal balance had almost become a textbook proposition.

34. In other words, interest paid on domestic debt instruments would replace the tax-rebate scheme that would have to be abolished because of international agreements.

References

Akyüz, Y. (1993). "Financial Liberalization: The Key Issues." In Y. Akyüz and G. Held (eds.), *Finance and the Real Economy: Issues and Case Studies in Developing Countries* (pp. 19–68). Santiago: United Nations Conference on Trade and Development.

Altay, Ö. (1987). "Foreign Exchange Position Management of Commercial Banks." *Central Bank Economic Research Bulletin* (June): 53–63 (in Turkish).

Altinkemer, M., and N.K. Ekinci. (1992). "Capital Account Liberalization: The Case of Turkey." *New Perspectives on Turkey* 4: 89–108.

Atiyas, I. (1990). "The Private Sector's Response to Financial Liberalization in Turkey: 1980–82." In T. Arıcanlı and D. Rodrik (eds.), *The Political Economy of Turkey: Debt, Adjustment and Sustainability*. London: Mcmillan Press.

Atiyas, I., and H. Ersel. (1994). "The Impact of Financial Reform: The Turkish Experience." In G. Caprio, I. Atiyas, and A.J. Hanson (eds.), *Financial Reform: Theory and Experience*. London: Cambridge University Press.

Baysan, T., and C. Blitzer. (1990). "Turkey's Trade Liberalization in the 1980's and Prospects for its Sustainability." In T. Arıcanlı and D. Rodrik (eds.), *The Political Economy of Turkey: Debt, Adjustment and Sustainability*. London: Mcmillan Press.

Celasun, M., and D. Rodrik. (1989). "Debt, Adjustment and Growth: Turkey." In J.D. Sachs and S.M. Collins (eds.), *Developing Country Debt and Economic Performance*. NBER Country Studies: Volume 3. Chicago: University of Chicago Press.

Collier, P., and C. Mayer (eds.). (1989). *Finance and Economic Development*. Special issue of *Oxford Review of Economic Policy* 5(4).

Ekinci, N.K. (1990). "Macroeconomic Developments in Turkey: 1980–1988." *METU Studies in Development* 17: 73–115.

Ersel, H., and L. İskenderoğlu. (1993). "Monetary Programming in Turkey." In

Y. Aşıkoğlu and H. Ersel (eds.), *Financial Liberalization in Turkey*. Ankara: Central Bank of The Republic of Turkey.

Fischer, B., and H. Reisen. (1993). *Liberalising Capital Flows in Developing Countries: Pitfalls, Prerequisites and Perspectives*. Paris: OECD.

Fry, M.J. (1989). "Financial Development: Theories and Recent Experience." In P. Collier and C. Mayer (eds.), *Finance and Economic Development*. Special issue of *Oxford Review of Economic Policy* 5(4): 13–28.

Gibson, H.D., and E. Tsakalotos. (1994). "The Scope and Limit of Financial Liberalisation in Developing Countries: A Critical Survey." *Journal of Development Studies* 30: 578–628.

Grabel, I. (1995). "Speculation-led Economic Development: A Post-Keynesian Interpretation of Financial Liberalization Programmes in the Third World." *International Review of Applied Economics* 9(2): 127–149.

McKinnon, R.I. (1989). "Financial Liberalization and Economic Development: A Reassessment of Interest Rate Policies in Asia and Latin America." In P. Collier and C. Mayer (eds.), *Finance and Economic Development*. Special issue of *Oxford Review of Economic Policy* 5(4): 29–53.

Minsky, H. (1982). *Can It Happen Again*? New York: Sharpe.

Montiel, P.J. (1994). "Capital Mobility in Developing Countries: Some Measurement Issues and Empirical Results." *World Bank Economic Review* 8: 311–350.

Stiglitz, J.E. (1993). "The Role of the State in Financial Markets." In *Proceedings of the World Bank Annual Conference on Development Economics 1993*. Supplement to *World Bank Economic Review* and *World Bank Research Observer*.

UNCTAD. (1991). *Trade and Development Report*. New York: United Nations Publications.

Index

MIX
Papier aus verantwortungsvollen Quellen
Paper from responsible sources
FSC® C105338
FSC
www.fsc.org

If you have any concerns about our products,
you can contact us on
ProductSafety@springernature.com

In case Publisher is established outside the EU,
the EU authorized representative is:
Springer Nature Customer Service Center GmbH
Europaplatz 3, 69115 Heidelberg, Germany

Printed by Libri Plureos GmbH
in Hamburg, Germany